How Traumatized Children Impact
Adoptive and Foster Families

Wounded Children, Healing Homes

**JAYNE E. SCHOOLER, MBS, BETSY KEEFER SMALLEY, LSW,
TIMOTHY J. CALLAHAN, PSYD**

Contributing Authors

Elizabeth A. Tracy, MSW, LCSW, LICSW
Debra L. Shrier, MSW, LICSW
Grace Harris

Key Consultant

Hope Haslam Straughan, PhD, MSW, ACSW

NAVPRESS

A NavPress resource published in alliance
with Tyndale House Publishers, Inc.

NAVPRESS ◐

NavPress is the publishing ministry of The Navigators, an international Christian organization and leader in personal spiritual development. NavPress is committed to helping people grow spiritually and enjoy lives of meaning and hope through personal and group resources that are biblically rooted, culturally relevant, and highly practical.

For more information, visit www.NavPress.com.

From Jayne E. Schooler

To the beautiful children we know and love living in an orphanage in Kyrgyzstan:

Victor, Dima, Maksat, Slavic, Anya, Aibek, Nastya, Angelina, Sasha, Vanya, Eelia, Colya, Nazik, Argen, Meesha, Aziz, Kumushai, Aisuluu, Alymbek, Kenat, and to our missions team, who loves them, too — two incredible Canadian families — Lynn and Ruby Johnston and John, Julie, Emma, and Bekah Wright.

You are precious in God's sight.

From Betsy Keefer Smalley

To all families, but especially my own: Guy Smalley; Cory, Steve, and William Matyas; Drew and Jessica Keefer; Russell, Paula, and Emily Smalley; Stuart Smalley; and Lois Smalley.

From Timothy J. Callahan

To the resilient nature of the human body and spirit.

CONTENTS

Parenting Traumatized Children: The Impact on Foster and Adoptive Parents

This book is a gift to adoptive families and children today. Since I entered the field of adoption in 1963, there has been a 180-degree shift: first, in the needs of the children who require permanency; and second, in how services are thought about and delivered. The children being placed for adoption today arrive with multiple traumas, developmental delays, and challenging behaviors that may stretch their new family, sometimes to the breaking point.

Addressing the needs of the traumatized child requires hard work for both professionals and for the families who parent these children. Everyone must dedicate time in their already busy lives to address these needs. The therapists and social workers supporting these families must use many creative tools during the first few years to help them through the rough times, after placement, and after the adoptions are finalized. The parents must adapt rapidly, do all the initial adapting, and commit to a child they don't yet love, and may not even like, for awhile. This is what has become "professional" parenting.

Research and literature from the fields of neurobiology, trauma, and attachment inform our work as professionals, as parents strive for healthy family relationships. Teaching families how to respond to the child's trauma-induced behaviors requires a new set of skills and new language. Parents must recognize that behaviors are the child's way of speaking about the past. The behaviors that once helped him now threaten his placement and healthy development. The child's strong, reactive emotions, based on that early trauma, are "catchy" and can quickly create trauma in the family—not just for the parents but also for the other siblings in the home. Having parented traumatized children myself, I know that the child's feelings of helplessness, avoidance, isolation, and rage are easily triggered in the new family. I remember such a moment when I was enraged with one of our children. I glanced at myself in the hallway mirror and saw the face of a raging shrew staring back at me! I had never met that part of myself before.

Healing begins as parents see their role as external regulators for their children, working to increase pleasure and enhance attachment. They may see powerful results in using the five senses and playing together as much as possible. They can learn nonverbal tools such as art, dance, music, rocking, singing, and "time-in" instead of "time-out" discipline.

These new parenting techniques are different from how most of us were raised. They often trigger negative reactions from grandparents. Siblings may not think it is fair that the traumatized child is treated differently. Many adoptive families find themselves creating new family systems because family-of-origin members leave, fearing that the traumatized child behaviors will impact their children. Friends, especially other adoptive families, become our new family systems. As a parent and professional, I've learned how important it is for families with traumatized children to develop a large, well-trained support network.

Families need to be reminded that healing takes place over time; that change is slow and, at times, barely visible. Parents must pass the many tests their child may devise to see if he can truly trust this new family. The tests lessen over time but may emerge when another trauma, large or small, occurs for the child or family. Trauma leaves vulnerable spirits.

The joy and success grow through the years, making it all worth the effort. Meanwhile, therapeutic parenting must continue. Therapists and agencies owe these families a long commitment. We must become their secure base: knowledgeable touchstones, while the family provides a quality environment for their children. Professionals working in this arena must be highly skilled in the knowledge of trauma, loss, adoption, attachment-based parenting, family therapy, and developmental re-parenting.

This is an exciting time to be in the field of child placement and to parent a traumatized child. As professionals, we are learning from other disciplines, blending their expertise into our social work practice. We must distill this information into a useable body of knowledge, so that families can digest it and create health for the children to whom they are committed. This book takes us a giant step forward on our journey.

SHARON ROSZIA, MS
EMISSARY, KINSHIP CENTER EDUCATION INSTITUTE

ACKNOWLEDGMENTS

From Jayne E. Schooler, MBS

Wounded Children, Healing Homes brings together some of the most remarkable people I have had the privilege of knowing. Each one of them brings to this project his or her own understanding and insight, born out of life experience and extensive professional experience.

Betsy Keefer Smalley, LSW

Betsy is not only a coauthor in this project; she and I also are great friends. We have worked together on many projects for over fourteen years. We think a lot alike but also have the great freedom to challenge each other's thinking and writing. Betsy has worked in the field of child welfare for thirty-seven years. She has been instrumental in writing and developing adoption training curriculum for professionals used in Ohio, across the United States, and overseas. She has been my mentor and tremendous encourager. We coauthored *Telling the Truth to Your Adopted or Foster Child* in 2000. This book received a national award due to its contribution to child welfare.

Betsy's compassion for struggling adoptive parents is obvious in her chapter contributions:

- Chapter Seven: Confronting the Crisis of Adoption Breakdown
- Chapter Eight: Managing the Crisis of Adoption Breakdown
- Chapter Twelve: Taking Care of Yourself: The Parent's Neglected Task
- Appendix Two: Building a Support System and Finding Resources

She has spent incalculable hours counseling adoptive families in crisis, and because of those life experiences, she brings incredible depth to her work. She is the adoption and foster care training manager for the Institute for Human Services, a nonprofit agency that provides competency-based training to child welfare professionals, foster caregivers, and adoptive parents. To contact Betsy for training or consultation, e-mail her at: bkeefer@ihs-trainet.com

Timothy J. Callahan, PsyD

I have had the privilege of knowing Dr. Callahan for only a couple of years. I have deep respect not only for his work but also for who he is—a compassionate and wise person. He has a keen sense of understanding the needs of abused, neglected, and traumatized children and the adults who care for them. He has accumulated a wealth of knowledge about human development and the impact of early experiences on a developing child. He has worked extensively with adopted and foster children and their families, and he is a true advocate for an educated, compassionate, and artful approach to parenting and treatment. Tim's contributions to this book span a range of topics:

- Chapter Four: Attachment, Development, and the Impact of Trauma
- Chapter Nine: The Maltreated Child in School
- Chapter Ten: School Interventions for the Maltreated Child
- Chapter Eleven: Living with Children with Attachment Trauma: Understanding the Terminology, Diagnosis, and Parenting Strategies

Each chapter offers solid information, research, and solutions for families. Dr. Callahan is currently the director of mental health services for the Greene County Educational Service Center. He implements and oversees school-based mental health services and programs aimed at helping children and teens thrive in their school environments. To contact Dr. Callahan for training or consultation, e-mail him at: tcallahan@GreeneESC.org.

Elizabeth A. Tracy, MSW, LCSW, LICSW

Elizabeth brings to this project something no one else does. She grew up in a foster home, as the birth child of foster parents. I have known Elizabeth for a number of years and our friendship began at the NACAC (North American

Council on Adoptable Children) national conference. She has contributed much to the field of foster care and adoption with her life experience, extensive research, and a heart sensitive to the needs of families and children.

In chapter Six: Living with Traumatized Children: The Impact on Birth and Other Adopted Siblings, Elizabeth offers practical strategies for families navigating these uncertain waters.

She is a national trainer and consultant for corporations and agencies, specializing in mental health issues, interagency dynamics, leadership/team development, conflict resolution, and crisis intervention. To contact Elizabeth for training or consultation, email her at: wefindhope@aol.com.

Grace Harris

This coauthor has chosen to write under an assumed name to provide readers with a rich, honest, and complete window into the life of her forever family, while protecting each family member. She contributes two chapters:

- Chapter One: Embracing a Love like No Other: A Story of Hope
- Chapter Thirteen: A Story of Hope: The Rest of the Story

Both accounts capture the real-life experiences of struggling adoptive families. They also share the hope and determination to be a forever family for traumatized, wounded children.

Debra L. Shrier, MSW, LICSW

Debra is a brand-new friend. I met her in the spring of 2008 at a conference where I was speaking. It was, in my opinion, one of those divine encounters. She has much personal and professional experience working in the field of adoption, especially with post-adoption issues. What she brings to this book is a perfect fit:

- Chapter Three: Adoptive Parents and the Impact of Their Own Personal Trauma History

It covers material I have not personally seen in other adoption literature.

Debra has been involved in the field of adoption for over fifteen years and is on the board of directors for Adoption Community of New England. She is a post-adoption counselor at Wide Horizons for Children/Massachusetts, where her work involves all members of the adoption triad (birthparents, adoptive parents, and adopted persons). Her areas of adoption interest include everything from working in pre-adoptive education, post-placement/post-adoption work, and searches/reunions with birth parents and adopted people. She also has an interest in attachment, the impact of trauma on individuals and families, transracial/transcultural adoption, and school advocacy related to adoption. To contract Debra for training or consultation, email her at: deb@debshrier.com.

Hope Haslam Straughan, PhD, MSW, ACSW

Hope has served as a vital consultant on this most important project. She is an adoptive mom and assistant professor of social work at Wheelock College in Boston, Massachusetts. She is a volunteer foster care case reviewer for the Department for Children and Families, and she is engaged in collaborative research on the impact of transracial adoption on forever families. To contact Hope, e-mail her at: hstraughan@wheelock.edu.

Lisa Abbott

The intense job of editing a manuscript is a daunting task, especially when working with six different authors. Lisa has been that editor who has gone above and beyond in doing her very best. As a writing team, we all agree that Lisa is the best editor any one of us has ever had!

My Family

This is my seventh major writing project. My incredible husband, David, continues to be my greatest supporter and encourager, even when writing and research tasks take away from family time. He is my greatest joy. My children, Kristy, Rick, Ray, and grandkids, Micah, Annalise, and Lacey, also share the excitement of each new endeavor.

I believe that God opened the doors over seventeen years ago for me to write in the adoption field. He gave me the passion and desire. It has been through His empowerment, strength, and grace that these projects were begun and the work was accomplished. I thank Him for all He has done.

From Timothy J. Callahan, PsyD

I want to thank Jayne Schooler, most of all, for giving me such a great opportunity. She is one of the most grounded, caring, and committed people I've ever met. She is a rare individual who truly is altruistic and selfless in her aim to improve the lives of the people she touches. I want to thank Jayne's amazing daughter, Kristy Matheson, who is responsible for putting Jayne and me in contact a few years ago. I want to thank Betsy Smalley for her support and guidance through this process. Her focus and perseverance were inspirational. Lastly, I want to thank my wonderful family—my wife, Kelley, and daughter, Lucy, whose bright lights kept me going through the challenging times.

From Betsy Keefer Smalley, LSW
I would like to acknowledge the skills, encouragement, and friendship provided by Jayne Schooler for many years. Tim Callahan has brought remarkable insights, as well as delightful wit, to this writing project. Deb, Hope, and Elizabeth have been a great team to bring this book to fruition, in an effort to support adoptive and foster parents in their commitment to help children.

I would also like to acknowledge the following professionals who added their insight to the depth of the material included here: Juli Alvarado, Heather Forbes, and Nancy Milliken, a very good friend.

Finally, I would like to acknowledge the contributions of my husband, Guy Smalley, who is always my primary supporter. My adult children, Drew Keefer and Corinne Matyas, inspire me to help as many parents as possible to raise children as wonderful as they are. And I am indebted to my many colleagues at the Institute for Human Services, who challenge me to grow and learn after almost four decades in the field.

Facing the Reality of the Need

By Jayne E. Schooler

Adoption is a beautiful way to build a family. However, while adoption is healthy and normal, circumstances may arise that challenge the growing relationship between adoptive parent and child. These circumstances can and do have a great impact on the adoptive family. They cannot be ignored. Families who are aware of the issues they will face, who come realistically to the adoption of an abused, traumatized child, will be successful. They will remain emotionally healthy and able to provide a nurturing family for that child. However, families who come unprepared to the adoption of a wounded child will be broadsided by shattered expectations. The prospect for this family is clouded and uncertain.

During our six months of work in Kyrgyzstan in 2008, I met several American families who were there adopting children—infants, a few toddlers, and older children.

One afternoon, I sat across the table from a family and a six-year-old boy they were adopting. When I looked at him, I took note of his eyes. He is a beautiful boy, but his eyes spoke of immense pain, trauma, and loss. He was found underground in the sewer system just a year earlier. He had lived with older children on the streets and then in an orphanage. He had no family history. In our brief time together, the adoptive parents assured me that all this young boy would need was love. I tactfully tried to share the potential impact of his trauma. But I think in the excitement of adding this child to the family, they didn't want to hear me. They basically said, "He will do fine with the love we will give him, thank you very much." I said no more, but grieved at what may be ahead for these unprepared and unrealistic parents.

For over thirty years as an adoptive parent and adoption educator, I have had the privilege of meeting thousands of adoptive parents and adoption professionals across this country. I have become deeply aware of the struggles many families have faced as they have shared their stories with me. The challenges of parenting traumatized children overwhelmed some families beyond anything they anticipated. Professionals who work with adoptive families talk of the same struggles in varying degrees.

This book opens and closes with the story of one family, Grace and John Harris. In the opening chapter, Grace sets the stage for the following chapters by sharing their emotional journey as brand-new adoptive parents of extremely traumatized young children. Many of you will identify with Grace as she chronicles her family's journey through serious attachment and trauma issues. You'll find hope in this story of healing and connection.

Grace concludes this book with "the rest of the story." She tells of the initial phone call, when they first learned about their two children. She details the long process of bringing them home and working through the very difficult adjustments of those early years. She concludes with short, anecdotal stories about her children and a statement that will give you hope for your own family.

I knew that writing a book for parents who have adopted deeply wounded, traumatized children would be difficult. We may be criticized by those who wish to portray only a warm and fuzzy picture of adopting traumatized children. This is not the type of adoption book that makes for adoptive parent recruitment material. However, it is a book that had to be written to address the needs of so many families. We'll address many specific needs of the adoptive family.

The purposes of writing this book are to:

- Validate the struggles, heartbreak, and disillusionment of some adoptive parents, who with a willing and open heart, adopted a deeply wounded child
- Equip adoptive parents and professionals with understanding and practical tools for a positive, successful journey
- Acquaint prospective adoptive parents with the realities of the potential challenges and needs of all family members when adopting a traumatized child

Four particular chapters contain information that has not yet been addressed significantly in adoption literature:

- Chapter Three: Adoptive Parents and the Impact of Their Own Personal Trauma History by Debra L. Shrier, MSW, LICSW
- Chapter Six: Living with Traumatized Children: The Impact on Birth and Other Adopted Siblings by Elizabeth A. Tracy, MSW, LCSW, LICSW
- Chapter Nine: Maltreated Children and School by Timothy J. Callahan, PsyD
- Chapter Ten: Managing the School Challenges by Timothy J. Callahan, PsyD

We hope that these chapters, as well as the others in the book, will equip parents and professionals to embrace a love like no other.

PART ONE:

The Journey Begins

Loving and living with a traumatized child means embracing a love like no other. It is love lived out every day in a new and unfamiliar way. It is commitment cemented through the challenges and struggles of uncertainty. It is a life journey walked on unknown paths. It is a faith, a hope, and a vision that the future will hold something far better than what you are experiencing now and perhaps ever dreamed possible.

WHAT'S AHEAD?

Chapter One

Embracing a Love like No Other: A Story of Hope

By Grace Harris

I knew that adopting children, who, like our sons, had been abused, neglected, or abandoned, would have its challenges. I knew the kids might have toileting, hoarding, stealing, behavioral, and cognitive issues. I knew that we would not "look" like many other families, especially as we pursued a transracial adoption. I knew that we all entered this situation from a place of loss that would, in many ways, serve as a backdrop to our beginning connections and collective sense of family.

I knew that often in the lives of children who have experienced trauma, what first might appear to be a serious behavior problem really is a series of behaviors motivated by survival and self-protection. Our sons had mastered skills such as manipulating, lying, hiding things, sneaking items in and out of the house, and hoarding both food and what appeared to be random, inconsequential material items.

Josh (age four) and Brent (age three) needed new skills and abilities to replace these innate, survival-oriented skills. The process of acquiring these skills and abilities has been, and in many ways continues to be, very long! It is easy to forget that the motivation for our sons' behaviors lies in the trauma they experienced and that the behaviors simply are not a choice for them. Trying to keep this truth at the forefront of my mind reminds me of our losses as we bravely, and not so bravely, forge ahead in our forever family formation.

I also knew that creating a forever family through adoption is about connection, not just loss. This connection occurs over long periods of time, through shared intimate, daily experiences that build trust, belief, and hope. As we try to lay the groundwork for attachment and meaningful connection in our family, it never seems to happen quickly enough for me. Yet the glimpses of connection every now and then are sweeter than anything else I have experienced in my life.

This miraculous connection develops when people interact in a healthy, safe, generous way. It grows in the thousands of exchanges at home, in the car, or walking to school. It happens in soothing a frightened child in the middle of the night, in making that favorite meal (again), by playing basketball in the back yard, or mourning the death of a beloved pet together. Each exchange is a transparent, fragile strand in a tapestry woven over a lifetime.

But the loss is still very real, raw, and viciously strong. The patterns of uncertainty ingrained in our young children led to great fear, an inconsistent ability to connect or attach, and unpredictable outbursts. The idea of a strong, connected, "forever family" seemed like a crazy and hopeless dream in those first months and years together. But we talked about it as if it already existed. We defined what it was and what it was not.

Miraculously, I found that we *were* weaving a strong tapestry. We wove it in the joy of watching our youngest child work a puzzle; in hearing my oldest son call me "mom" one morning, after he'd been calling me "Grace" or "John" interchangeably for weeks; in seeing John sit near our youngest child, who continued to cry, scream, and thrash.

Our connection is fragile. Yet the depth of our intentions, the love, care, and compassion of these daily exchanges just might replace some of our kids' survival skills with love, openness, generosity, hope, and possibility.

What I Did Not Know

I knew a great deal going into this adoption process. I knew that becoming a mom meant sharing my life with my husband, dog, and two young boys who had lived through more uncertainty, loss, and violence than anyone ever should. What I did *not* know, however, was much greater.

I was not prepared for how much space these children ultimately would take up in my life. It wasn't just the demanding logistical details of a busy family of four with two full-time working parents and a dog. Nor was it the weekly therapy, consistent contact and communication with teachers, inclusion specialists, reading specialists, aides, occupational therapists, and others on our support team. It wasn't the daily time spent together in living—taking baths, playing together, reading, learning prayers, creating predictable routines and schedules. It wasn't even the surprising amount of time a child talks—from the time his feet hit the floor in the morning until he is fully asleep at night. (Who knew? One of our sons even talks while he is sleeping!)

I was stunned by the vast *emotional* space the children required in our lives.

I was only partially prepared for the *cognitive* space all of this interaction, dialogue, communication, and planning took up in our brains. The commitment was enormous, as it is for parents of most children. But the unanticipated emotional challenge of parenting our children brought, on many days, an unfathomable drain.

Supporting Josh and Brent as they struggle, despair, and push against us, is, at times, utterly consuming and often exhausting. Many of Brent's direct verbal and physical attacks on me, as his mom, are common for children with attachment challenges. At times, I've felt deeply hurt and hopeless. At times, the vigilance required to be prepared for his damaging behaviors has nearly done me in. With his extreme violence and propensity to run away, I lost all confidence in my ability to manage an evening alone with the boys, or even to get my kindergartener into school safely by myself.

I was the one who was with Brent most of the time outside of the school day. John did not experience or witness much of his behavior. John believed and loved me, but he could not imagine the severe nature of my experience with Brent. This dynamic intensified the isolation and rejection I felt. Thankfully, several important things emerged and strengthened the fragile strand of our tapestry.

Working with numerous professionals gave us the encouragement, wisdom, and tools we needed to continue. Setting up daily support gave us someone to help diffuse our mounting frustrations and confusion. In the process, Brent gradually began to trust me. He began to develop healthy, appropriate skills to deal with his rage and fear. The intensity of that season lessened, and his development brought more peace to our home and my heart.

The truly ironic and most heart-breaking piece of all was this: Brent was unable to drive me away with his offensive, degrading screaming or with his destructive tantrums that left me bruised and battered. He was learning that people commit to one another forever and stay connected. I wondered how it was possible for experiences so violent and inappropriate to actually show him that he was loved and accepted.

During these long, difficult months, I would wake up in the morning with a sense of panic, anticipating what horrors I would experience with him on this new day. But I would get up uttering this prayer: "May I be present where I am today, until I leave." I implored God's help to be available, to love and accept Brent, no matter what happened. And though I cried a lot and felt deep despair, I was, in fact, present. On good days, I was able to creatively anticipate his rage, or to demonstrate generosity in my response and reaction to him. These moments of acceptance and care further strengthened the tapestry that was becoming our forever family.

Learning the Meaning Behind the Behaviors

Within their first few overnight visits to our home, we noticed a number of Josh and Brent's behaviors that seemed to be connected to their early deprivation, trauma, and abandonment: hoarding, resistance to change, great difficulty with transitions, challenges with attention and organization, rages and violent behaviors, running away, fear of being physically hurt, and an inability to comprehend connectedness and the "forever" part of our "forever family."

One of the most visibly shocking results of the boys' trauma surfaced whenever we moved suddenly, particularly in the perceived direction of either son. They recoiled, cried out, covered their heads with their hands, and cowered. The first time this happened, John was taking his belt off of his pants, after being dressed up for work. As he sort of whipped the belt out of the loopholes, Josh dove across the floor, yelping, whimpering, and crying. He huddled in the corner, as if he were protecting himself from harm. Oh, how our hearts broke. We were stunned and mortified that a sudden movement, especially of our arms, would alert him to danger and violence.

This scenario, in one version or another, happened dozens of times. A visceral fear response threatened to keep our boys from our safe and loving home. This fear immediately transported them to a time and place that was unstable, uncertain, and violent. Over the years, this scenario has happened less and less. The boys are more able to accept our soothing assurances of safety, as we hold them closely and remind them that they will not be hurt in our family.

Living with Their Memories

John and I have learned so much from the team of people that supports us and our children. In the first few months we started to learn about and understand body memories. Both boys were very young when they were abandoned. Only Josh, the oldest, was verbal. Many of the boys' memories of their biological mother, father, and family were stored as body memories. The extreme heat of summer, coupled with the sounds and sights of fireworks, for instance, trigger a time of great anxiety, fear, and uncertainty for both boys. As it turns out, they were abandoned on a very hot seventh of July day, following great, city-wide Independence Day celebrations, which of course included fireworks.

More often, though, we have found it difficult to decipher the boys' memories that are activated by a sight, sound, or smell. Without an obvious clue, we often don't know what they are remembering or feeling, or why. Because the boys lacked verbal abilities as those traumatic memories were developing, they can't explain what is happening inside their heads, and they're simply overcome by their emotions. Sometimes we don't realize when this happens. Their emotions and behavior do not seem to match the current situation. We've learned to try to stay with Josh or Brent and not dismiss their extreme reactions.

These body memories create another issue for the boys as they struggle to be self-aware and connected to their bodies. Our younger son, now nine years old, has made great progress in the past year or two. He is aware of his need to go to the bathroom but still consistently has accidents, especially during periods of transition and change. He will pause (when we make him do so), consider whether or not he needs to go to the bathroom, emphatically say that he does not, and run off to play. Within minutes, he'll fly to the toilet, trying to make it in time. Or he simply continues playing with his shorts wet, still convinced that he could not tell just three to four minutes earlier that he needed to go.

Similarly, he is unable to tell whether or not he is still hungry. He goes for nine to ten hours, refusing to eat snacks and lunch, only to have insatiable hunger later. He eats as quickly as possible. He's unable to tell when his body has had enough food. Therapists work with him and us on these things. Even with a good support system, building skills in this area is a long, slow, and frustrating process.

Living with "Never Enough" and Other Survival Skills

Brent struggles with deciphering the meaning of relationships and material items. He collects the postcard-sized papers or inserts from magazines. He picks them up off the ground in stores, parking lots, and even digs through trash cans for these treasures. In addition, one or two of anything is never enough. He "needs" five crackers if each child is getting one; he "needs" three library books if each child is allowed to check out two; he "needs" four staplers and pencil sharpeners, instead of one of each at home and in his desk at school. He has an unquenchable and driving need for acquiring things and he struggles mightily to keep them in meticulous order. His behavior seems rooted in early years of want, in the loss of things that were dear to him, and the unconscious fear and belief that he won't have what he needs.

Brent's inability to distinguish between the worth of material goods (magazine postcards versus his favorite stuffed animal) also comes out in his relationships with people. Within the first two years of his life with us (ages three through five), he was more likely to tell a complete stranger or peripheral person that he loved them, rather than those of us who shared his daily life. The chaos of moving from place to place in his first two years of life, supervision by various people, and no predictability about whom he might attach to, caused confusion about why one person would be dearer to him than another.

While we struggle to help our children (and ourselves) understand how to live within our means, identify our needs versus our wants, and set limits on material stuff in our home, we have to overlay those desires with Brent's very real and dramatic need for hoarding and collecting things. We try to figure out ways to set limits while reassuring him that his needs are being met and that he has what he needs and more.

His obsession with gathering things is a visceral, innate reaction to the world around him. When Brent took and hid things from children on play dates, or from stores, we struggled with the foundational moral message of not taking things that are not ours in any circumstance. We realized that there are very real reasons for his behavior, but others simply saw a young child stealing.

His survival skill of manipulation produced struggles, as well. He is masterful at charming women, men, and children alike in his playful, darling way of talking and looking at someone. At school, as soon as he got the costume he wanted in the dress-up area from the child who was already wearing it, he ignored that person and moved on with his play. He would not reciprocate when that child wanted to share something he had. By discovering, anticipating, and holding what Brent *really* needs, we have strengthened the interconnectedness and love in our "forever family."

Living with the Motivation for the Behavior

The Department of Social Services provides required parenting classes for all potential foster or adoptive parents. We learned that we should pay attention to the *motivation* for our children's behavior. Whether it's the magazine insert craze or hoarding food, both boys behave in ways that, at first, might be seen as bad or inappropriate. A parent, teacher, or other authority figure might respond with a logical consequence. However, with children who have experienced extreme trauma, loss, and neglect, it is critical to try to find the *reasons* for their behavior, so you can address their actual need and not just their obvious misstep.

I have found only one children's book that illustrates the ongoing complexity of the adopted child's thoughts and feelings about his biological, foster, and adoptive families. *Zachary's New Home: A Story for Foster and Adopted Children*[1] uses the tumultuous life of a little kitten named Zachary to reflect the ongoing fear, worry, potential growth, and eventual transformation of many foster and adopted children.

We began reading this book with the boys within the first weeks of our lives together, then proceeded to give it to all of our immediate family, close friends, and all teachers involved in the boys' lives for years. We tried to honor the reality that Josh and Brent were adopted into a safe and loving "forever family" *and* that they had early years which were unpredictable, unsafe, and that left them with many challenges. *Both* realities were true.

We didn't expect Josh and Brent to forget the other homes they had lived in, or to cease caring about their biological mom, or to appear to be thrilled about being adopted all the time.

Expecting those things would have dismissed their complex life experience, denied their memories and areas of strength and growth, further fractured their own identities, and stunted the integration of their experiences.

In order to help us understand these profound truths, the social workers showed us a video about a preteen foster child who continually stole and hid things from her foster family. After describing the natural consequence that any child might receive, the foster mother in the video showed a surprising, alternative response. She sat with the child on the couch. She talked with her about the stealing, acknowledging that she knew about it and that it was not acceptable behavior in that family. Then, she reached into her pocket and extended her hand with her most prized necklace and locket. She asked the foster child to hold onto it for her, keep it safe, and treasure it.

The foster mother knew that the preteen had moved from one home to the next many times as a young child, surrounded by uncertainty. Often, her belongings were left behind and she frequently did not have enough food to eat. The foster mom was able to connect the girl's impulsive "stealing" with her much deeper need for security, connection, and permanency—to both material items and important people.

We have found that when we respond to the deeper hurt and need that is causing the behavior, the boys have been able to open up, cry, and, in some cases, take responsibility for their actions. We have felt a much deeper connection as we trudge through the grief and dark places together. In this seemingly endless life of loss, we are finding our way to connection over and over again.

Our lives have been forever changed by Josh and Brent's presence. Even though the violence, deep pain, and uncertainty that accompanied them into our home is exhausting and sometimes overwhelming, it is the sweetness, the transformation and depth of connection we share, that sustains us.

John and Grace's journey with Josh and Brent reflects the experiences of families adopting traumatized children. It offers hope. It is for these families that this book has been written. The following chapters contain essential information and tools that we hope will strengthen the fragile strands of tapestry for other adoptive families.

Jayne Schooler

Chapter Two

The Power of Unmet Expectations

By Jayne E. Schooler, MBS

"I expected my new child to appreciate all that I do for her. After all, look where she came from."

"I expected my birth children to sacrifice for this new child in our home."

"I expected my extended family to take to this new child as they would a birth child."

"I expected the agency to be readily available to me with answers and support."

"I expected that I would feel happy and fulfilled because we've helped this child."

"I didn't expect to get so angry."

"It wasn't supposed to be this way!" That statement could be the title of a book written by almost anyone who has confronted unmet expectations.

Every parent has expectations, hopes, and dreams, whether the child joins the family by birth or adoption. It is a normal and natural part of parenthood. We expect our child to walk and talk at the right time. We expect our child to be more than ready for kindergarten and beyond. We dream of a child who excels in school, in sports, or the arts.

Occasionally, based on their child's pictures or their own imagination, adoptive parents create an image of the child they hope to adopt. They enter the relationship with high expectations of performance and behavior for themselves and the child. When those expectations go unmet, parents may find it difficult to invest in the child.

"As adoptive parents, we have the same dreams that all parents have, although we usually embark on our trip with less information about the biological road map of our children," says Ellen Singer, LCSW-C. "Although many of our friends find that their children by birth are surprisingly different than they expected them to be, it is true that we take a fork in the road when it comes to perceived certainty about the future. Whether we adopt because of infertility or not, we are told we must set aside our 'fantasy child' in order to be emotionally prepared to love and attach to one who brings her own set of genes, family history, and talents. Logic tells us that she may look and be different from what we hoped our biological child would be like."[1]

However, what happens when the surprises are viewed as negative or undesirable? What if the child's temperament and characteristics are a mismatch for the family? What if the child's behavior or accomplishments don't measure up? What if the child's needs are exceptional? What happens then? Why is it important to raise the subject of unmet expectations?

Unmatched or unmet expectations about the child often create unyielding tension on the newly formed family system. The ground underneath the adoption commitment begins to shift.

Numerous studies have examined predictors of adoption disruption. It is estimated that adoption disruption rates are highest among children with special needs and older children, with rates ranging from 10 to 20 percent.[2] The greatest predictors for disruption among special-needs adoptions relate most to the adoptive family: unrealistic expectations, rigidity, insufficient social support for the adoptive family, and the adoption by new or "matched" families (as opposed to foster families adopting a child they already know). Other predictors relate to the child: a history of physical and sexual abuse, prenatal exposure to drugs and alcohol, and acting out behaviors.[3] It is significant that adoptive parents' unrealistic expectations top the list as a predictor for risk of adoption disruption.

Parents who don't adjust their expectations of themselves, the child, their birth children, extended family, and the adoption agency, will find themselves cornered in a maze of frustration without resources to find their way out. They may find themselves broadsided by shattered assumptions.[4]

We don't want to blame the parents for struggling with their unmet expectations. Rather, our goal is to create awareness of potential pitfalls, even land mines, related to unmet expectations. We will look at ten expectations often found, consciously or unconsciously, in the new adoptive family. We will talk about myths and how they impact our expectations, and, finally, we will offer proactive strategies to manage disappointment or disillusionment.

Ten Expectations About Adoption

1. Our love will be enough.

Tony and Krista walked out of the adoptive parents' orientation meeting with excitement. During the session, the pictures of children available for adoption were shared. One particular little girl, Autumn, age three, caught their eye. They read the brief description about her with great interest and fell in love with her on the spot. All the way home, they both said to each other, "I know all Autumn will need is our love, and we can do that." They called their caseworker in the morning, eager to begin their home study right away. Their caseworker, Jackie, responded with equal enthusiasm but with a note of caution in her voice as well. "Let me come over and share more of Autumn's story," she said. "There is much more for you to hear and understand. Yes, Autumn needs love, but she needs much more than that."

With wisdom and sensitivity, Jackie told them that when Autumn was thirteen months old, she had been found left alone in her crib in a very dirty apartment. It was evident that she had been alone for an extended period of time, perhaps as long as a day, maybe two. Empty, spoiled milk bottles were scattered on the floor.

Autumn entered her first of four foster homes. Her disruptive and erratic behavior as a toddler prevented any sense of attachment with her foster parents. She lasted just three or four months in each of her first three foster placements. Her most recent foster parents struggled with her behavior, but they refused to give up on her.

"You see," Jackie explained, "there is no question that Autumn needs love—and much of it. She will also need parents who truly understand what happened to her and how that will impact the relationship."

Many adoptive parents who fall in love with a picture of a child begin a fantasy journey of what life will be like. They believe that love will heal all wounds. With that belief, they fail to hear the child's story and aren't open to the potential of how it might affect their family.

2. We will feel love and connection to this child quickly.

"When we planned to adopt, I never questioned whether I would feel love for this child. There wasn't a child who couldn't be loved," said Katie. "However, what I felt totally surprised me. It was something I couldn't tell anyone, I felt so guilty about it. There were days that I dreaded getting up in the morning. I felt absolutely no connection to this child we brought home from Russia. I felt anger and remorse over bringing her into the family. I beat myself up daily and told no one. Something had to be very wrong with me that I didn't feel any love for or connection to Sarah. I wish someone had told me that it might be that way."

Katie's experience is similar to a number of adoptive parents who have been broadsided by how they feel about their child. They are caught by surprise at the lack of connection with their child and the negative emotions they feel. They wonder what is wrong with them.

Some of Jason and Bekah's friends told them they should feel the same way about their new daughter as they did their biological child. "Natalia had only been home for three months, and we didn't feel the same way," says Bekah. "We were concerned about mentioning that to anyone, so we didn't. It has been a full year now since our daughter came home from Kyrgyzstan. We can say now that the love and connection are there, but it didn't happen as we envisioned it. It took much more time."

3. This child will step into our family system and easily learn how to function within our rules, goals, and ambitions.

When a family adopts an older child, expectations for the child to fit right into the family system and adapt to their goals and ambitions may be unrealistic. Parents forget about barriers to a child's adjustment into the family.

According to Miriam Reitz and Kenneth W. Watson, vulnerabilities within the family system should be explored during the home study process.[5] Adoption professionals can identify a lack of healthy communication skills, inability to cope with stress, or limited or impaired ability to build attachment.

They write, "Any family, regardless of type or level of functioning, can be struck by events (developmental or some other kind) that overwhelm its ability to operate by its usual [family] rules. At such times of anxiety, the operations of the family system often fluctuate, intensify, and/or reach a crisis state."[6]

As members of that family system attempt to solve the problems that emerge, they may work their way through the crisis in a number of ways:

- The family demonstrates resiliency and becomes more flexible.

- The family insists on maintaining or returning to the old family system and becomes rigid.
- The family fails hopelessly in all directions and loses all sense of a functional family system.[7]

"I really appreciated our caseworker, Robert, who did an excellent job of keeping us focused," said James, the adoptive father of nine-year-old Micah. "On his regular visits, he would remind us that it wasn't the child who needed to make all the adjustments. We needed to be incredibly flexible in our expectations of just how Micah would fit into the family. And if adjustments needed to be made, we, as the parents, were the ones that needed to do that. He would regularly ask us how things were going, related to being more flexible with how our family ran in the past."

4. This child's needs will be just like those of our biological children.

When David arrived home at six years old, he became the youngest child in the Wittenbach family, which included three kids, two dogs, mom, and dad. Rachel and Robert felt competent as successful parents of their older children, who ranged in age from nine to seventeen. "When we decided on the adoption of an older child, we felt this would be a breeze . . . we knew how to parent," they explained. "However, we were perplexed that the parenting techniques we used with our other children had no effect on David. There didn't seem to be any consequence that mattered to him. We began to feel incompetent as parents and really questioned ourselves and our ability to parent this child."

The Wittenbachs expected that parenting David, whose traumatic history involved severe neglect and sexual abuse, would be just like parenting their other children, who had no traumatic history. It was through the guidance and support of other adoptive parents that Rachel and Robert learned more about parenting a traumatized child. For them, it was a relief to understand that their competency wasn't at stake. Closing their knowledge gap eased the crisis. They both took the challenge to learn as much as they could about the unique parenting needs of their spirited new son.

When familiar, tried-and-true parenting techniques fail to work with a newly adopted child, parents may plunge into deep frustration. They may question themselves, wondering if they're competent enough for the task ahead. Often, they fail to share their concerns with those who could help them the most.

5. *Our biological children will embrace this new child as a sibling.*

"Both Carrie and Josh were in favor of this adoption from the very start," sighed Carolyn at a support group meeting. "I have seen a side of my children that I didn't know even existed. They have been irritable, selfish, and uncaring with Jacob and Emma since they arrived four months ago. They are angry because we have to have different rules for Jacob and Emma than we do for them. I don't know where the children I thought I knew went."

Whenever a new child joins the family, whether by birth or adoption, the existing children in the home will be affected by the changing family system. Biological children are asked during the home study process how they feel about adoption, and they usually answer, "excited," "happy," and so on. However, as in the case of Carrie and Josh, these children have not experienced what it is like to have a new child or children enter the home. In chapter 6, we will take a look at the impact of adding adopted children with a background of trauma to the family and how that addition affects the children already in the home.

6. *Our child will fit well into our extended family and be welcomed by them.*

"When we first decided to adopt, our extended family was excited for us. They were warm and welcoming to Alexander when he came home. They viewed him as an adorable, normal three-year-old," Rick said. "However, over time, it was obvious that his behavior was anything but normal, and our family's response to him changed. My parents invited us over less and less and developed a whole list of excuses why they couldn't come over. Christy's family did almost the same thing. We began to feel so isolated from them."

Many adoptive families experience incredible family support. However, when that support disappears as a result of the child's difficult behaviors, it becomes a crisis.

Debbie Riley, executive director of The Center for Adoption Support and Education (C.A.S.E.) in Burtonsville, Maryland, has observed this family dynamic. "Perhaps from the beginning, the prospective adoptive family received ambivalent messages about adoption from their extended family members," she explains. "Some of those messages included subtle questions like 'Why would you take on those problems? Why don't you wait and get a baby?' Once the older child arrives home, and the extended family members see the family struggling, they become angry at the child and begin to withdraw what little support and encouragement they offered in the beginning. They also become angry at the adoptive parents because they are determined to maintain their relationship with the child. Extended family members may be particularly concerned about the impact of the adoption on other children in the family, causing them to feel protective of those children and resentful of the 'intruder.' As the family continues to embrace the child, the extended family withdraws their support, leaving them alienated and cut off from key support system."[8]

For some adoptive parents, the withdrawal of support and help from their extended family sends them into uncertainty and grave disappointment. The child-grandparent relationship they dreamed of is threatened by the difficulties of managing not only the child's behavior, but family members' as well.

7. Our friends and acquaintances will validate our role as parent in our child's life and support us through the adoption process and beyond.

- "Why don't you just send him back? You didn't expect this and shouldn't have to deal with it."
- "You are more than welcome to come over, but if you are bringing your children . . . well, maybe you won't want to stay too long."
- "You aren't the real parent anyway. Just call the agency and tell them to come and get her."

Fantasy statements? No, these are real-life experiences for some adoptive parents dealing with the complex issues of parenting a traumatized child. Most adoptive parents expected understanding and support from their friends. What they actually received were the invalidating messages that adoption doesn't make them real parents, that they are parenting a child who can be "thrown away."

Ruth, an adoptive mother, says, "I can't share many of Joe's behaviors because they aren't the same as those of other children. If I chose to share them, I would expose and isolate him even further. To tell others your child bites, scratches, and throws snot at you would label him as odd, a trouble maker.

The isolation at times is overwhelming. No more so than when people try to reassure you, but you know your child is different. My neighbor is very kind. One day, she was trying to reassure me by telling me about her little boy's nightmares. Night terrors, as she called them, were a perfectly normal stage in a child's development. She completely missed the point. My child's nightmares are not a product of his childish imagination; they are caused by real events in his past life. The frustration I feel is overwhelming and adds to my pain and isolation. I can't share his real life events—his trauma."[9]

At support group meetings and training sessions, parents often report losing relationships with friends due to the complex parenting issues confronting them. One adoptive mom mentioned that since her two children, ages three and four, joined the family, no one ever calls to let her know when the next mothers' group meets. Another mom mentioned that she had been asked not to come back to her adoptive parent support group because of her child's issues. What an ultimate rejection—to be kicked out of a support group! These families were broadsided by rejection and isolation—something they never expected.

8. Our child will see us as his family and forget about his birth family and his past.

Moving into an adoptive family does not erase a child's past relationships and trauma. Some adoptive parents believe that once a child is home, all the people and events in his past will be forgotten. They fail to recognize a very important truth: simply, they won't be forgotten. Adoptive parents will benefit if they understand and respond to the impact of psychological presence—the reality that their child may carry thoughts of a family member in his heart or mind. Psychological presence is *the symbolic existence of an individual in the perception of other family members in a way that influences thoughts, emotions, behavior, identity, or unity of remaining family members.*[10]

If parents want to create an environment of open communication, it's crucial that they embrace a foundational reality of adoption: birthparents, primarily birthmothers, often are on the hearts and minds of most adopted children. The child may or may not speak of this reality, but it holds true, even in cases of abuse, neglect, abandonment, domestic or international adoption—whether or not the child has conscious memory of the parent.

How adoptive parents face this issue may dictate how openly they will deal with all aspects of the adoption relationship. Researchers describe two ways parents can choose to manage the reality of the psychological presence of the birthparents:

a. Adoptive parents can deny the psychological presence of the birth family.

For example, a child approaches his mother on his birthday and asks, "Mom, do you think my birthmother thinks about me on my birthday?" An adoptive mother in denial might respond, "John, I am your mother now and I think about you. That is really all that matters." John learns early in his life that his questions and feelings about important things don't matter and it is best to remain quiet about them. He learns to shut down his emotions.

A second response, although not always easy for adoptive parents, is healthier for the youngster.

b. Adoptive parents can acknowledge the psychological presence of the birth family.

The same child approaches his mother on his birthday and asks, "Mom, do you think my birthmother thinks about me on my birthday?" An adoptive mother in a family that communicates openly about adoption might respond, "John, I don't really know for sure. I would think so, because this is an important day. But you know what is also important? I think about your birthmother and I bet you do, too. Do you want to talk about it? Do you want to send a letter or picture to the agency to give to her?" Now the child learns that he can be open about his feelings and questions without worrying about parental response.

Sometimes, adoptive parents believe that people from the child's past are gone from his memory, or perhaps they wish they were. Adoptive parents benefit when they recognize the value of "inviting" those people into their family by talking about them, allowing children to express feelings about them, and acknowledging their psychological presence.

9. We can do for this child what was not done for us, or we will not do to this child what was done to us.

There are two types of wounds. The first type of wound is things that were *withheld from* us, when we don't receive the family blessing or acceptance from our parents. Sometimes, love or acceptance withheld by parents is so drastic that it constitutes emotional neglect or abandonment. The second type of wound involves things that are *done to* us, including various abuses: physical, emotional, or sexual.

In either case, parenting a traumatized child can trigger a parent's own painful memories of victimization or abandonment. Some parents are motivated to adopt out of a desire to rescue a child from a difficult family situation, perhaps one surprisingly similar to their own. Because this is such an important area for discussion, the next chapter will examine this expectation in more depth.

Choosing to adopt a wounded, traumatized child to compensate for one's own wounded childhood may present challenges, feelings, and unexpected emotional reactions in an adoptive parent whose own past mirrors that of his child.

10. We will never feel any regrets or ambivalence in adopting this child with a traumatic past.

In the 1995 spring issue of *Roots and Wings* magazine, June Bond first coined the term "post-adoption depression syndrome" that is still applicable for some families today.[11] Symptoms are very similar to post-partum depression and the causes can be many, from unmet expectations to a sense of loss of control of one's life.[12]

> I dreaded getting up in the morning and facing the tasks of the day. The honeymoon period with Katie and Callie had dimmed. I was exhausted and overwhelmed, and I gradually grew resentful of them. But I kept my fatigue, depression, and anxieties hidden. I kept asking myself, "What have we done?" Of course, it wasn't the girls. I had neglected to communicate my own needs. That was the wrong approach. I just didn't want to appear to be a failure.

"It is important for adoptive parents to know that these feelings are normal and common," explains adoption expert Karen Foli. "Experts agree that stress, depression, ambivalence, and anger are emotions they frequently see, and part of the assistance they offer to parents is to help them realize these feelings are normal."[13]

Expected and unexpected feelings, as well as the many joys and satisfactions of parenting, can occur in healthy adoptive families, just as they can occur in healthy biological families.

Now that we have examined ten expectations commonly found—consciously or unconsciously—in adoptive families, let's examine how those expectations develop and why we get broadsided by them.

The Model of the Myth

Why do we get broadsided by unmet expectations? If we understand the Model of the Myth,[14] we can learn to pay attention to and manage our expectations before they manage us. The Model of the Myth is the process of moving from something we are taught and believe to an expectation, to failure of that expectation, to disappointment.

Model of the Myth

- Something is learned.
- Something is believed.
- Expectations develop.
- Expectations fail.
- Disappointment and despair.

Let's apply the Model of the Myth to a prospective adoptive family:

(1) **Parents are taught**. Prospective adoptive parents go to required classes that help prepare them for the journey ahead. They learn about all the wonderful joys of adoption and the challenges and tasks that will be required of them.

(2) **Parents develop a belief about what they are taught**, using their own filters of interpretation, which may or may not be accurate. They hear about the challenges of adopting a traumatized child, but their own filter of interpretation blocks out what they don't want to hear.

(3) **Parents create expectations based on their filtered understanding**. They believe many of the ten expectations about adoption we've discussed.

(4) **Those expectations encounter reality**. The child doesn't respond to their love and affection as expected. The parents' own negative feelings about their experience or of themselves overwhelm them. Reality hits.

(5) **This new reality in the parents' lives creates conflicts, which lead to disappointments, discouragement, and even despair.** Parents find themselves facing thoughts and emotions they never expected to encounter as adoptive parents. They begin to question their decisions, even their own competency as parents.

Readjusting Shattered Assumptions

The question is not "*If* parents experience shattered assumptions, what will they do?" but rather "*When* parents experience shattered assumptions, what will they do?" Of course, the experience of unmet expectations will fall on a continuum from mild disappointments to severely shattered dreams. So when expectations encounter reality, what can parents do?

1. Examine your own Model of the Myth.

Ask yourselves the hard question, "What did we choose to believe that did not turn out as expected?" Listen to the answer. Open, honest communication about what you thought the adoption experience would be like can begin to replace the Model of the Myth. Use each of the ten expectations to discuss which of them apply and where you fall on the continuum of unmet expectations.

2. Reexamine your motivation for adoption and reframe your expectations.

It is helpful to return to your original motivation to adopt, but also examine why you're still committed to the adoption today. How has your commitment changed? Now that your experience with adoption is not a fantasy, but a reality, how can you reframe your expectations for the future with this child so that your expectations are more grounded in reality?

3. Recognize that feeling ambivalent is a part of the attachment process.

No one feels warm, fuzzy feelings for anyone, even themselves, twenty-four/ seven. The process of living with another person and being responsible for nurturing a wounded child can be both draining and rewarding, depending on the day, the situation, or the parent's or the child's state of mind. Give yourself permission to feel ambivalent.

4. Adjust your expectations of each other and other family members.

One adoptive mom said, "I expected my husband to plan regular activities with our new son. When he didn't, I became frustrated with him. Expecting him to jump right in when he didn't know where he stood with Jimmy was unfair." As you adjust your expectations of yourself, it is also healthy to adjust your expectations of others.

5. Keep communication open and honest as the responsibilities increase.

Successful adoptive parents of traumatized children demonstrate stability and quality in their interpersonal relationships.[15] What qualities characterize these internal and external relationships?

Family members demonstrate the ability to resolve conflicts and problems.

Perhaps the most important function of a healthy home is the family's ability to resolve conflicts. When they face the potential emotional landmines of adopting a seriously wounded child, healthy adoptive families (like all healthy families) have the ability to disagree and negotiate differences without feeling personally threatened.[16]

To the extent that parents rely on the process of negotiation, families confront and resolve problems in a positive way. Children who join an adoptive family at an older age probably have not seen or experienced a healthy approach to solving family problems. A healthy home environment may be foreign or even strange to them.

Family members show the ability to deal with feelings. Adoptive parents who allow each other to express a range of feelings and respond empathically will create an atmosphere where a child can do likewise. Families who block feelings or deny their existence will block the healing of the wounds deeply rooted in a child.

6. Work at keeping the family system open and flexible in responding to unmet expectations.

What do openness and flexibility in the adoptive family system look like?

Family members show the ability to accept and deal with change. When a new child enters the family, whether as an infant or as an older child, the entire family system shifts. New patterns of interaction and everyday living evolve. New relationships form. Stresses unique to this experience arise. Occasionally, the adopted child bears the brunt of blame.

A healthy adoptive family understands that this kind of change is temporary. The shifting eventually will lessen and give way to a new normalcy. The family members persevere through the unsettled environment and everyone takes responsibility for working through the change.

Family members manage flexible boundaries—they allow people in and out of their lives. When a family chooses to adopt, by the very nature of the process, people will come in and out of the family system. It starts with the home study process. Once a child is identified for the family, social workers will interact with the family from placement to, in some international situations, up to two to three years beyond the adoption.

Family members value differences. We often hear biological parents say, "All of my children are different." The same is true with adopted children, only they have genetic differences that can manifest themselves on a larger scale. Each adopted child arrives with a bushel full of differences from his adoptive family. The most obvious difference, of course, may be physical appearance. As the child grows, differences will emerge in mannerisms, interests, talents, habits, and performance ability. Successful adoptive families value these differences and readjust their own expectations rather than rejecting the differences because they were unexpected. They highlight the positive distinctions that create the child's individuality. They put dissimilarities that set the child apart from his adoptive family in respectful focus. They understand that as one human race, all people are far more similar than dissimilar.

Unmet expectations are nothing new for parents. Sometimes managing shattered dreams requires a mourning process, so that the old dreams disappear and new ones emerge in their place. Sometimes it requires that parents recognize the potential for unmet expectations, be open and willing to examine their feelings and thoughts toward those disappointments, and finally, to be proactive in reframing a new picture of the family.

Quick Reference

Key Point 1: Recognize Expectations

Parents who don't understand their expectations of themselves, the child, their birth children, extended family, and adoption agency, will find themselves cornered in a maze of frustration without resources to find their way out. They find themselves broadsided by shattered assumptions. Ten common expectations about adoption are:

1. Our love will be enough.

2. We will feel love for and connection with this child quickly.

3. This child will step into our family system and easily learn how to function within our rules, goals, and ambitions.

4. This child's needs will be just like those of our biological children.

5. Our biological children will embrace this new child as a sibling.

6. Our child will fit well into our extended family and be welcomed by them.

7. Our friends and acquaintances will validate our role as parents and support us through the adoption process and beyond.

8. Our child will see us as his family and forget about his birth family and his past.

9. We can do for this child what was not done for us, or we will not do to this child what was done to us.

10. We will never feel any regrets or ambivalence in adopting this child with a traumatic past.

Key Point 2: Readjust Shattered Assumptions

The experience of unmet expectations will fall on a continuum from mild disappointments to severely shattered dreams. So when expectations encounter reality, what can parents do? The following are six ways to manage expectations:

1. Examine your Model of the Myth.

2. Reexamine your motivation for adoption and reframe your expectations.

3. Recognize that feeling ambivalent is a part of the attachment process.

4. Adjust your expectations of each other and other family members.

5. Keep communication open and honest as the responsibilities increase.

6. Work at keeping the family system open and flexible in responding to unmet expectations.

DISCUSSION QUESTIONS

1. Describe what you envisioned your adoption process to be like. How has that expectation been met? How has it not been met?

2. Describe what you envisioned your parenting experience to be like. How has that expectation been met? How has it not been met?

3. Of the ten expectations discussed in this chapter, which applies most directly to you?

4. Identify and list additional unmet expectations you have experienced.

5. What strategies have you used to manage disappointments and unmet expectations?

Chapter Three

Adoptive Parents and the Impact of Their Own Personal Trauma History

By Debra L. Shrier, MSW, LICSW

"Fire can warm or consume, water can quench or drown, wind can caress or cut. And so it is with human relationships: we can both create and destroy, nurture and terrorize, traumatize and heal each other."

—Bruce D. Perry, MD, PhD and Maia Szalavitz,
The Boy Who Was Raised As a Dog[1]

Traumatic experiences influence relationships, especially those between a parent and child. We know that children who have experienced trauma bring a set of wounds to the family, but what about the adult or prospective parent who also has a history of trauma? Is there a way to determine how that trauma will affect his ability to engage in healthy parenting?

The word "trauma" evokes strong images of scarring abuse or horrific maltreatment. Most people who have experienced the neglect of an absentee parent, a chaotic family life, or witnessed domestic violence may not necessarily describe it as traumatic per se, but more as a sad episode in their life history. Regardless of the severity of the event, however, all of these descriptions constitute trauma, and they leave a significant psychological impact. The inability to recognize these events as trauma often leads to surprise "triggers" later on, as well as a lack of resolution from the difficult experience.

In her book, *Nurturing Adoptions*, Deborah Gray states that "a traumatic stress reaction is a normal reaction to an abnormal event."[2] This simple statement normalizes the traumatic response. It is a very necessary follow-up to a harmful situation. It is also important to note that Gray's statement does not categorize the depth of the traumatic event. It involves anything outside of the "normal" experience.

An individual's own traumatic experience shapes relationships later in life. Those issues will affect a parent's relationship with a child.

Understanding Your Own Trauma

Elizabeth and her husband, Ted, were thrilled when they received a call from their social worker. She offered them an opportunity to become foster parents to two young children, Cameron and Shayla. They "fell in love" with the photos of the two children, ages four and two, with their big brown eyes and dimpled chins. The couple felt great sadness as the social worker reviewed the children's history of physical abuse, neglect, and two different foster care situations, but they were confident that they could provide a loving and stable environment.

Several months after the children arrived, Cameron became physically aggressive and somewhat violent toward his sister. He also became very angry with Elizabeth.

Often, her normal requests or limit-setting triggered his rage. His yelling and screaming upset Elizabeth the most. She questioned whether she was causing this new behavior. In response to Cameron's anger and behavior, Elizabeth shut down and began to cut herself off from the family. Her interactions with her husband and children suffered, and she questioned her personal competence, ability, and overall sense of self.

Although Ted listened to his wife's reports, he never witnessed the behaviors Elizabeth described. Ted maintained that Cameron was just "being a boy" and felt that in time, his son would outgrow these tantrums.

After sharing her concerns with their social worker, Elizabeth and Ted sought counseling for both Cameron and Shayla. Elizabeth was concerned that the children suffered from complex trauma. She wanted to find ways to help the children, especially since they were taking steps toward adoption. However, she didn't realize that she needed help herself.

At one of the therapy sessions, the clinician asked the couple about their own childhoods. Ted, whose father was in the military, described a very predictable, stable family environment. With prompting, Elizabeth shared that her family life was chaotic. Her father was diagnosed with bipolar disorder, and he often had episodes of rage. During those times, she recalled feeling powerless and frightened. She often wondered what she had done to trigger her father's anger. Elizabeth shared a vivid memory of hiding in a closet, waiting quietly until her father's shouting ceased, or the front door closed. She found ways to remove herself from his rage. Although her recollections were clear, she had not thought about these episodes in decades.

Over time, through therapy, Elizabeth saw a deep connection between Cameron's rage and her feelings of powerlessness as a child.

Elizabeth initially didn't see her own childhood experience as traumatic. She protected her father's memory by minimizing times when his actions left her feeling alone and scared. Elizabeth was unable to disclose her fears, even to her husband. It took a while for Elizabeth to talk with the therapist about her fears and her father's behavior, verbal tones, and actions. When Elizabeth explored her feelings about those experiences, she was able to connect them with her response to her son's explosive and violent episodes. Her son's outbursts tapped into her own deep, hidden emotional trauma.

Once a person is able to acknowledge his traumatic experience, he may wonder why and how this experience has finally surfaced. "This question raises issues about memory retrieval and the unique configuration of unresolved traumatic memory," explain authors Daniel J. Siegel and Mary Hartzell in their book *Parenting from the Inside Out: How a Deeper Self-Understanding Can Help You Raise Children Who Thrive.* "Several factors make the retrieval of a certain memory more likely. These include the associations linked to the memory, the theme or gist of the experience, the phase of life of the person who is remembering, and the interpersonal context and the individual's state of mind at the time of encoding and at recall."[3]

To gain greater insight into how these protected memories are kept, let's look at the complex ways the brain develops and functions.

The brain stores memories in various categories, which are often connected to sensory experiences (more information on this in the next chapter). Those memories may be retrieved and released when they are triggered. Sometimes, the triggers are sounds, tastes, smells, or visual stimuli. The brain reads the sensory experience as dangerous or traumatic.

People who understand their trauma history have some sense of resolution. For others, it may be very difficult to work through the trauma. They may not even recognize it as trauma. This is considered unresolved or "buried" trauma. Understanding one's own history of trauma takes a certain amount of insight, patience, and support. Quite often, the process requires a support group or skilled therapist to do individual therapy.

The challenge for someone who has not resolved the trauma experience is to face the reality that a traumatic past will influence their relationships with others. The parent must understand his own trauma history, or it may easily be triggered by something that occurs with his child.

Personal Trauma's Impact on Parenting

When problems arise, a parent who doesn't understand his own trauma may feel like his child is deliberately trying to manipulate him.

"The traumatized child becomes the associational connection to the parent's unresolved trauma and loss issues, shifting the parent into a deep fear state," reports Heather T. Forbes and Bryan B. Post in *Beyond Consequences, Logic and Control: A Love-Based Approach to Helping Children with Severe Behaviors*.[4] This dynamic adds yet another level of stress to parenting, which eventually can hinder the parent/child relationship.

Parenting is a challenging and rewarding experience, but it often brings an individual back to his own history. Consider the case of Robert:

Robert spent most of his middle childhood trying to keep his secret of sexual abuse to himself. He did not know how to explain it to anyone and felt guilty that he may have been responsible in some way for what occurred. He did not believe his family would understand how anything so tragic could have happened during his life, especially at such a young age. Fortunately, when the offender moved to another state, the abusive episodes stopped, but Robert was left trying to make sense of what had happened to him between the ages of six and twelve.

As an adult, Robert shared his tragic history of sexual abuse with his wife, Anne. She supported Robert when he began therapy to deal with anxiety that he believed was caused by a stressful work environment. At the time, he did not realize that therapy would help him decipher the details of his traumatic childhood experiences.

When Anne and Robert began to explore building their family through adoption, their social worker talked to them about some of the experiences of children who needed families. Since Robert was able to disclose his history of abuse, the social worker was able to further assist the couple in considering how the experience might be triggered again as they parented.

Robert and Anne successfully adopted two children. When his children were young, Robert sought additional counseling. He further explored his abuse and began to foster a healthy attitude toward his children's normal sexual development.

An adoptive parent may also bear personal trauma from how he was parented. His own parents' actions may have left emotional scars that surface later in his life. Individuals often parent in a way similar to the way they were parented.

Sophia brought her eight-year-old daughter, Sandra, to a therapist because she "never listens." The therapist requested that Sandra's father, Jim, join the sessions. It was several weeks before he showed up. Jim felt that Sandra was disrespectful and that their current methods of discipline (discussion, withholding privileges) were not effective. Jim appeared agitated and angry about his daughter's behavior.

The therapist explored what it meant to Jim when he said that Sandra was disrespectful. She also asked Sophia and Jim about how discipline was handled during their childhoods, and what their relationships were like with their parents. Sophia had never experienced real consequences for behaviors outside the family rules. Jim's parents yelled a lot and sometimes used physical discipline with the children.

The therapist explored this further, asking Jim to try to remember how he felt when he was punished, especially by his father, who was "very strict." Jim became sullen and stated that he was afraid of his parents. As a child, he often changed his behavior out of fear that his father would become involved.

The fear state can bring about additional memories. David Wallin, noted author and clinical psychologist, explains that "intrusive memories of unresolved trauma as well as the defenses against such memories produce a sense of helplessness. Naming the feelings associated with trauma confers a growing sense of mastery."[5] Understanding the traumatic history is how healing can begin.

The desire to parent does not necessarily help someone understand themselves or their past experiences. Many people parent with all the best of intentions. However, many misunderstand how earlier life experiences may surface as they parent.

Jamie, a six-year-old who recently had been adopted from an eastern European country, began to tell the story of her chaotic and neglected life with her birth family. She often referred to her birth mother as the "bad mother," in comparison to her foster mother, whom she referred to as her "good mother."

Her adoptive parents, Robin and Kyle, listened to her stories, recognizing that some of them might not be completely accurate. Yet, they felt it was important to hear her story the way Jamie understood it. They could see that she needed to be cared for by a different set of parents.

Kyle, a soft-spoken and calm person, was especially saddened when Jamie talked about her experience with her dying grandmother. Her vivid stories reminded him of his own experience with his mother, who died from a chronic illness when he was thirteen years old. Due to her pain and debilitating health, his mother was emotionally unavailable for several years leading up to her death. During his mother's illness, Kyle felt he was somehow responsible for her pain. He often tried to wish his mother's illness away. He never shared his sadness. Instead of talking through his feelings, Kyle withdrew and put his energy into his schoolwork.

Listening to his daughter's story about her biological family increased Kyle's own feelings about his mother. Until that time, he was not fully aware of his unresolved loss and trauma.

Kyle had not considered the significance of the loss of his mother. He didn't connect his daughter's history with his own sadness. According to Siegel and Hartzell, "If we have leftover or unresolved issues, it is crucial that we take the time to pause and reflect on our emotional responses to our children. By understanding ourselves, we give our children the chance to develop their own sense of vitality and the freedom to experience their own emotional worlds without restrictions and fear."[6]

Adoption Preparation as a Mutual Assessment

It is important for clinicians to look at the prospective adoptive or foster parents' experiences. What were their childhoods like? What are their motivations for adopting or fostering a child with a traumatic history? What resources do they have in place, not only for the child, but also for themselves, should challenges develop?

Within the home study process, prospective parents are asked to explore, evaluate, and consider their own experiences. The social worker guides the process, helping the prospective parents examine their past and assessing their ability to parent effectively. However, the evaluation should not begin and end with the social worker's exploration. Prospective parents should also consider their perspectives and experiences.

For individuals with a trauma history, it is critical to consider the impact of the trauma, how that experience has shaped or affected them, and whether they have been able to resolve the experience. The ultimate question lies in how they are able to relay their life story.

Dan Hughes, family therapist and noted attachment author, also describes the relevance of trauma in the parent/child relationship. In his book, *Attachment-Focused Family Therapy*, he explains that "The therapist is likely to have been able to successfully help the parents to understand and begin to address how their own histories are having an impact on their relationships with each other and with their children," says Hughes.[7] With this approach, he adds, "the need for joint family therapy is greatly reduced."[8]

However, he says, "it is often still helpful to include the child in joint treatment with the parents after the initial sessions with the parents alone. The initial sessions with the parents make the joint sessions more beneficial and efficient."[9]

The Adult Attachment Inventory (AAI), developed by researchers Mary Main, N. Kaplan, and Carol George, provides a useful, often used assessment tool in the adoptive preparation process. It provides insight for close relationships in a person's life. The AAI questions ask parents to:

- Recall the family in which they grew up, starting with earliest memories.
- Provide adjectives to describe the family in which they grew up and associated memories to support each adjective.
- Describe memories of rejection by parents, reaction to rejection, and opinions as to whether the rejection was recognized by the parent.
- Describe which parent they felt closest to and why.
- Recall whether parents threatened or frightened them.
- Reflect on how their childhood has affected their adult personality.
- Discuss any childhood or adult loss of parents or loved ones, including how that affected them.
- Contrast how family relationships and perceptions of those relationships changed between childhood and adulthood.
- Summarize their current relationship with their parents.[10]

According to adoption authority Deborah Gray, "The AAI does not attempt to capture factors such as parenting skills, support, or financial resources. Yet, it can predict the style of attachment that parents will form with their children about eighty percent of the time. This prediction provides important information when making initial placement decisions or when assessing the support and therapy needs for a family."[11] A critical aspect of the AAI is its ability to highlight what an individual has learned through the experience of being parented, because this primary relationship sets the foundation for each relationship that follows. The AAI can be used as a tool within the home study process to complement, but not replace, the social worker's interviews and clinical work.

Additionally, the AAI can help a prospective parent identify the type of attachment he had as a child and how that relates to his own style of parenting.

The quality of relationships between parent and child stem from early experiences with parents or caregivers and is greatly influenced at various points in time by other significant people in a person's life, such as relatives, teachers, childcare providers or counselors.[12] Since early attachment history forms the foundation for all relationships that follow, it makes sense to explore what type of attachment style an individual will bring into the parent/child relationship.

Parent Attachment Styles

Children are born with a drive to survive. Infants stay close to caregivers for safety and comfort when they are distressed. When parents are protective, attuned, and responsive, children feel secure and develop a secure "attachment style." The parents become a secure base from which children can explore their environment and learn to handle separation without serious distress. "Children cannot develop patterns of attachment that are of the secure base styles unless the parents themselves are capable of this type of attachment," says adoption expert Deborah Gray.[13]

Children develop working models for relationships from these early experiences that influence how they think about themselves and about other people. For example, children whose parents are protective and responsive learn that they are worthy (positive self) and that other people can be counted on (positive other).

Sometimes children's experiences lead them to develop an insecure attachment style. Behavioral researchers John Bowlby, Mary Ainsworth, and Mary Main have categorized various attachment styles. Let's look at three of them:[14]

Dismissive or Unresponsive Attachment Style

Some children experience their parents' absence, harsh communication, and a lack of sensitivity. According to Gray, "It is interesting to note that often these parents cannot remember their own childhoods, or present an idealized view of their own parents even when the facts do not support that."[15]

Ambivalent and Inconsistent Attachment Styles

Other children experience their parents' presence inconsistently. "Often, these parents are distracted by their own past attachment experiences," explains Gray. "They invest their energies in the past, are still brooding, resignedly passive, or angry over their own childhoods. They may be present for their children in body, but not there emotionally for them."[16]

Disorganized, Abusive, Unpredictable Styles

Children experience their parents as frightening and dangerous, as well as sometimes a source of comfort. It is likely that parents with this attachment style were parented by disorganized, unpredictable parents themselves.

Attachment Styles Are Not Permanent

Fortunately, attachment styles can change in time. Although a child may come into a family with a history of difficult attachment, therapy with the foster or adoptive family can help the child develop a different attachment style. According to Siegel and Hartzell, "Some people worry that the findings of attachment research indicated that our early years create our destiny. In fact, the research shows that relationships with parents can change and as they do, the child's attachment changes. This means it is never too late to create positive change in a child's life. Studies also demonstrate that a nurturing relationship with someone other than with a parent, in which the child feels understood and safe, provides an important source of resilience; a seed in the child's mind that can be developed later on as the child grows. Relationships with relatives, teachers, childcare providers, and counselors can provide an important source of connection for the growing child. These relationships don't replace a secure attachment with a primary caregiver, but they are a source of strength for the child's developing mind."[17]

The Role of the Home Study

As mentioned earlier, the home study process is critical to identify strengths and weaknesses an individual or couple will bring to parenting. The Consortium for Children (CFC) has developed a concise questionnaire known as the Structured Analysis Family Evaluation (SAFE) to assist social workers in their evaluation process. Adoption professionals throughout the United States currently use this tool to identify and deal with issues before a child is placed with a family.

According to Kate Cleary, executive director of the CFC, the questionnaire helps to produce a more focused interview, so that the clinician can get to the "root of the issue" within the first or second client interview.[18] Cleary notes that "whether or not you parent a child by birth, foster care, or adoption, your trauma will come up. It may be at different stages for the child, depending upon when he or she came to your family. When parenting a child with a history that is equal to or worse than your own trauma, it will certainly trigger some issues for you." The social worker may advise the individual or couple to pursue supportive therapy before moving ahead with foster care or adoption.

According to Cleary, SAFE has helped many individuals and couples become better prepared to parent. It has also identified people who need to do some additional work before taking the steps toward foster care or adoption. Parents are not expected to be Super Mom or Dad. Social workers and adoption agencies simply look for stable, caring, and compassionate individuals with a strong desire to parent. They seek people who understand the challenges faced by adoptive families, and who recognize the strengths and weaknesses they bring to parenting. These parents need to offer love, hope, patience, support, and the ability to place their child's needs ahead of their own.

A person with a trauma history is not necessarily disqualified as a potential parent, especially if his history doesn't affect his current functioning. The social worker looks at how the individual has resolved his trauma. Says Cleary, "if it [the trauma] is not resolved, what do you need to do [to work through it] so that you can parent?"[19]

Linda T. Sanford, LICSW, author of *Strong at the Broken Places: Building Resiliency in Survivors of Trauma,* explains that "this [trauma/experience] is something that happened *to* you—it is not *who* you are."[20] Sanford echoes Cleary's sentiment that having a history of trauma should not necessarily deter a person from becoming a parent by birth, adoption, or foster care.

By understanding his own childhood trauma, a parent can nurture a child who may share a similar traumatic history, while allowing himself an opportunity to heal. The individual can parent his child and find healing himself, through one of the most important relationships in his life.

A Success Story

At age twenty-eight, Rose gained a greater understanding of the dysfunction within her family. She grew up as the eldest of four children in a middle-income family. With her father's alcoholism and mood swings and her mother's passive nature, Rose remembers getting through each day by survival.

She also recalled a prolonged separation when her mother was hospitalized to recover from a life-threatening illness. Rose learned over time that the basics she needed in life could not be found in her family. She spent time with friends and got a job as soon as she could drive. She was able to find positive role models (teachers, neighbors, and managers) who gave her great support while she lived at home.

As an adult, Rose relocated out of state, away from her family. The move gave her time to process her full childhood history. Extensive reading and support groups eventually led her to seek therapy, where she began to understand the depth of her childhood experiences with absentee and neglectful parents. She later married and became an adoptive mother at age thirty-six. Her concerns about her ability to parent pushed to the forefront.

When Rose and her husband prepared to adopt, the home study process gave them opportunities to discuss their childhood experiences. When they adopted a nine-month-old child from Guatemala, Rose looked for other healthy relationships—through friends and adoptive parenting support groups—to provide positive parenting models. Her ability to parent differently than she was parented allowed her to heal and to see herself as a healthy, strong, competent parent to her child.

Rose began to understand her own childhood emotional deprivation. She saw that others suffered similar experiences in alcoholic and "chaotic" families. When she became a mother, she needed a deeper understanding about how her childhood would affect her own actions as a parent. As her husband participated and began to understand Rose's history, he saw how much she wanted to alter the dysfunctional pattern for her own daughter. Together, they began a new, successful pattern for their family.

Quick Reference

Experiences of trauma influence relationships, especially those between a parent and child. We know that children who have experienced trauma bring a set of wounds to the family, but so do prospective parents with a history of trauma. It's important to determine how the parent's trauma will affect his ability to engage in healthy parenting.

Key Point 1

A parent's traumatic past can influence his response to a child with a trauma history and impact the parent-child relationship.

Key Point 2
Therapy is an important part of the parent's growth and healing.

Key Point 3
Mutual assessment of attachment styles and exploratory work in the home study process help both parents and adoption professionals to develop effective parenting strategies.

DISCUSSION QUESTIONS

1. Think back on your relationships with your parent(s) during childhood. What do you remember most about how your parents interacted with you?

2. Who were other important adults in your life (relatives, teachers, clergy, and so on)? What was your relationship like with them, and how did they influence you?

3. How were disagreements handled in your family? How were you disciplined? Which parent handled your discipline?

4. What aspects of your childhood would you like to carry into your role as a parent? In what ways do you hope to parent as you were parented? In what ways do you hope to parent differently than you were parented?

5. Have you discussed ways you were parented either with your spouse or another important person in your life? If not, share some examples of difficult experiences or challenges during your childhood and how they were resolved within your family.

6. What aspect of parenting do you feel will be most challenging to you? Why? In what ways can your spouse or support person encourage you as you parent your child or children?

7. What is one childhood memory of your family that you would like to share with your children?

PART TWO:

Understanding Trauma and Its Impact on the Family

Denial. What a powerful and protective emotion—but only for a season. Over time, denial never works. When we deny what has happened in the life of our wounded, traumatized child, we literally block the doors our child can walk through toward healing. When we deny what is happening to us, we also turn our backs on our own opportunity for growth. A powerful principle in life is this: Facing the truth will set you free.

WHAT'S AHEAD?

Chapter Four

Attachment, Development, and the Impact of Trauma

By Timothy J. Callahan, PsyD

The central purpose for developing attachment for young children is to ensure their safety. Once safety is guaranteed, other aspects of childhood can proceed.

—Daniel A. Hughes[1]

Every child has a story, and that story will have an impact on those who love him.

Tommy was born healthy and chubby with a bright looping cry that alarmed his young mother, Brandy. She thought at first an agitated donkey had wandered into the delivery room. Other than the hospital staff, Brandy was alone in the delivery room and alone when she took the baby to her small apartment. Brandy was neglected throughout her life, and she was determined to give her baby what she did not get: namely love, love, and more love.

Love was hard to find at 3:00 a.m. when Tommy's screams jolted her from slumber. He seemed to cry more than he slept. Tommy appeared to Brandy to be a writhing ball of need. His cries were relentless and undeniable. She prided herself in not being like her old group-home peers, who naively believed that having babies would fill the gaps in their lives. She knew babies were hard work. She was also determined that no matter how tempted she might be to repeat her mother's mistakes, she would, by sheer willpower, be a good mother. But, sitting dazed, confused, and edgy from sleep deprivation, Brandy held her fretful baby and wondered whether she was capable of surviving the next few moments. Brandy wished she were dead.

She felt an instinct bubbling up from deep inside, something she had felt all her life—the instinct to escape, to hide under the covers. She fought it off for a while. But after a month, she found herself leaving Tommy alone when she went to see friends, when she went drinking, when she found love from uncaring lovers, and when she just couldn't get out of bed.

Tommy's little body needed food, water, and comfort, and the way he experienced these needs was whole-body distress. The only way to relieve the distress was to reach out to someone, via his incredibly effective cry. But Brandy's absence meant Tommy's body remained in a state of distress. His developing nervous system never settled down, never trusted that the distress would be relieved. Brandy was not there to gaze into his sparkling eyes, to anchor him to the blurry and undifferentiated world around him. He was alone in a strange, unpredictable, and unresponsive place. Tommy could not develop properly because he could not do it alone.

He was removed from Brandy's custody by the child protective services following several incidents where he was left alone and neglected. By the age of five, Tommy was adopted. He displayed a variety of delays, along with terrible tantrums, and a profound lack of trust in others. He rarely talked, gorged food, set his new parents' basement on fire, and threw the kitten down the steps.

His parents committed themselves to learning as much as they could about the effects of maltreatment. They devoted themselves to helping Tommy's brain and body get back on track. They spent lots of time with him. Rather than reacting to his efforts to push them away, they patiently empathized with him, validated his feelings, and relieved his distress. They understood why he acted the way he did. They understood that his behaviors were survival techniques. For the first time in Tommy's life, someone valued and understood him. Over time, he felt connected, supported, and safe. He could finally relax and let others take care of him. He was no longer alone in the world.

Attachment is our first act and the key to our development and survival. Minutes after our formation, we move down the fallopian tube and attach to our mothers. The attachment nourishes and anchors us. After birth, the anchor transfers from the world of the womb to the realm of the interpersonal. Over the next three years of development, attachment to our caregivers provides the necessary base to grow and thrive. From the security of this primary anchor, we learn about the world around us, and ourselves in relation to that world. The brain, as our grand regulator, requires activation and definition through close interaction with our parents.

Attachment, though, is not simply an interpersonal phenomenon. It also is a biological one. It is the foundation for our neurological, emotional, behavioral, cognitive, social, and physical well-being. Early and chronic maltreatment disrupts attachment and affects an infant's ability to establish the necessary foundation. It shapes the way he develops. Many children like Tommy, who enter adoptive homes as older children, experience disrupted attachment.

Trauma affects how the child interacts and reacts to others, how he experiences emotions, how he regulates himself and adapts. It affects how he remembers, meets his needs, navigates through the stages of development, and comprehends himself in the context of the world around him. Understanding the impact of attachment and attachment trauma on a child's development frees us to be more attuned and to respond more effectively to his emotional needs.

Once we comprehend the pervasive impact of chronic early maltreatment, we find ourselves impressed and humbled by human resiliency and the drive to survive and adapt. We are forced to reevaluate our own theories about why our children do what they do. Behaviors begin to take on more meaning and make more sense. Behaviors that seem to us like performances designed to drive us over the brink of madness may, in fact, be attempts to impact a world the child expects to be unresponsive and unpredictable.

When we understand the survival function behind the behavior of maltreated children, we can respond more patiently and more effectively. Parents of children who have suffered attachment trauma face special challenges in helping their young adapt, survive, and thrive. Knowledge and perspective give these parents hope, by helping them see things clearly, in a larger, more meaningful context.

It's crucial for adoptive parents to understand this concept, whether they are adopting children domestically or internationally. This chapter will explore how attachment influences development and what impact complex trauma has on attachment.

Understanding the Attachment Process

The process of attachment appears to be similar across cultures.[2] Human development is rooted in the attachment experiences of the first years of life. Here are some specific aspects of our development that are impacted by early attachment experiences:

Genes and Experience

We come into existence with a prepackaged set of potentials, collected over multitudes of generations. We inherit our basic set of potentials from our parents. Genes carry the codes and blueprints that direct how we develop.[3] Our brains and nervous systems are the command centers that implement the genetic directives. It is estimated that 50 percent of who we are is inherited. The other half is formed through experience.[4] We start our lives with brains that are whole but undefined. Experience carves and differentiates the brain, forming pathways and fresh connections. Early attachment experiences have the most impact, because the infant brain is malleable and impressionable.

Pruning

Human infant brains contain over a hundred billion neurons,[5] more than we actually need. "Pruning" is one of the key mechanisms behind brain development.[6] Early interactions with parents not only activate our brain cells, but also prune away potentials that are not crucial for survival. If we were not able to prune, our brain pathways would be overwhelmingly cluttered and unable to function properly. If the parent does not mirror a trait or process with the infant, the trait or process may be pruned away or remain inactive. Remorse, for example, is a complex, brain-based system that may remain dormant if not activated by parents' loving, empathic responses. If we judge the actions of those who have not been cared for properly, based on their apparent absence of remorse, we overlook the role brain development plays in empathy.

The Brain and the Gaze

The brain essentially regulates everything in our bodies. Along with the inter-related nervous systems, it controls, modulates, and monitors everything from breathing to reading the words on this page. Our basic regulatory processes, including the ability to regulate body temperature, intuitively seem hard-wired. However, they actually depend on the early interactions with parents.[7] The infant brain is unable to adequately regulate on its own. So, the caregiver serves as the infant's regulator through healthy bonding and attachment, primarily in face-to-face interaction. This attachment process is referred to as *coregulation*.[8]

A parent who holds her baby is compelled to gaze into his eyes. Neuropsychoanalyst Allan Schore refers to this as the "mutual gaze."[9] Eye-to-eye contact is a critical link that sets the brain toward balanced regulation. The mutual gaze leads to emotional attunement; a deeply satisfying experience of feeling harmonious oneness and completeness, not unlike the peace experienced in the womb. Without the attentive, loving gaze and emotional responsiveness of the parent, the infant brain struggles on its own to develop and mature.[10]

Emotional Regulation

Interaction between the infant and parents activates and refines many complex regulatory processes, including critical functions such as emotional regulation and distress tolerance.[11] The capacity to tolerate and control distress depends on a parent consistently satisfying a pressing need—be it hunger, thirst, discomfort, sleep, or touch—during the critical first months.[12]

When parents recognize and soothe distress, the infant feels acknowledged and gratified, and returns to a state of equilibrium and comfort. Over time, the infant's brain develops the ability to internally tolerate distress and tension. The infant learns to trust that the world is predictable, responsive, and manageable.[13]

Beyond satisfying a need, parents help by putting words to needs, helping to form the foundation for language development. Children deprived of the opportunity to attach words to emotional experiences struggle to communicate adequately their needs and desires.[14] Without a coregulating attachment, the infant is left alone and helpless to manage his impulses, needs, and distress.[15]

Survival

Survival requires effective reaction to threat. Structures designed to help us survive threat through fight (defend), flight (escape), or fright (play dead) lie deep within the brain. When faced with a threat, our brain signals a cascade of chemical reactions that increase our chance of survival. Our ability to modulate and control these primitive survival strategies depends on attachment experiences that create deep sensations of safety and security. Without good attachment, the child's brain operates from the perspective of threat and responds in kind.[16]

Socialization and Shame

Attachment affects socialization and behavioral control in many ways. Healthy attachment activates the brain to override instinctual reactions to threat. It also serves as the theater in which the baby learns appropriate ways of behaving.

Healthy shame is a painful but naturally occurring emotion that results when we behave outside of acceptable boundaries. A child experiences shame when he transgresses and the parent responds with limits. The painful shame leads to a temporary break in the attachment relationship as the child withdraws from the parent.[17]

The key to resolving the shame in a healthy way is the "interactive repair" experience, when the parent repairs the relationship by reuniting and ensuring that the bond remains intact.[18] The feeling of shame is isolated to the *behavior* and not to the sense of *self*. This shame becomes the experience of guilt, a healthy and necessary driving force behind socialization and behavior control. Shame is a powerful influence in developing behavior controls. But shame can be detrimental if it's left unresolved. If there is no "interactive repair," the child attributes the shame to his whole self, not to the behavior. It becomes pervasive and overwhelming.

A parent who chronically allows unresolved shame to grow out of control by shunning or ignoring the child during the critical window of opportunity for repair sets into course a lifetime of toxic humiliation and self-loathing.[19]

Self

Healthy attachment helps build an autonomous sense of self, which is the unifying core of our personalities. In terms of a core sense of self, the infant during the first year is not fully differentiated from his parent.[20] It's necessary for the infant to experience oneness through attunement and coregulation so that he is anchored to the world. But this experience must give way to the formation of a separate sense of self.

A child who feels safely anchored can begin to define himself as independent and take risks to explore his world. The word "no" during the "terrible twos" is a word that outwardly reflects the necessary process of trying out the autonomous self.

Without oneness, we have no individual sense of self; without a separate self, we cannot function autonomously; without self-reliance, we are at the mercy of forces beyond our control; once we lose control, we lose the capacity to adapt. We all need a coherent, meaningful view of ourselves to experience the external world. Without an intact sense of self, our life story is like a book missing chapters and in no particular order.

Language and Expressiveness

We are compelled to make baby talk, coos, and exaggerated facial expressions when interacting with babies. Babies elicit parent response and vice versa. Mirroring facial expressions is crucial to activate the subtle facial muscles responsible for nonverbal expressiveness.[21] Babies and parents are prewired for baby talk and primitive utterances that elicit responses from each other.[22] Language forms out of these early infant-parent dialogues. Attachment experiences set the stage to develop social awareness, including the capacity to read cues and understand humor.

Plasticity and Resilience

Our amazingly adaptive brains are able to reorganize and form new connections even after processes have been pruned away or damaged. Our brains have the capacity to compensate, a process known as "plasticity."[23] Infant brain processes that weren't activated during critical periods may develop later but through different pathways.

Hope remains for those whose development was delayed or halted by maltreatment, because the brain's association cortex can make up for lost functions. Without plasticity, treatment and parenting would not help the brain get back on the track of balanced regulation and adaptability.

Humans are resilient by nature. We are, for the most part, capable of tolerating enormous stress and strain and can adapt to trauma more than we think possible. Incredibly, children who have suffered severe maltreatment often do not develop impairments in functioning, particularly when in stable, loving care.[24] But some children struggle severely and may cause suffering to those closest to them.

Complex Trauma and Its Impact on Attachment

Alexei cried and no one came. The orphanage staff members were kind, but there were too few of them to respond to all the cries. Alexei eventually stopped crying, not because she was satisfied, but because crying did not work as it was intended. She had no one who was her very own, no one she could tether to, no one she could depend on, no one to make her feel real. Alexei turned inward, because the outside world made no sense. The outside world seemed more like a dream to her than her actual dreams. She entertained herself by watching the images on the back of her eyelids. She fondled herself because it felt good; it was about the only thing that did.

Prospective adoptive parents came to visit the orphanage when Alexei was three years old. They immediately noticed her beautiful face, so perfect and sweet, yet blank and distant. Alexei was the calmest child in the toddler group, sitting by herself, pretending that her hands were animals. They adopted Alexei and took her home. Alexei was not sure what any of this meant but was glad someone thought she was worth having.

After a year of adjusting to her new home, Alexei still did not talk much. She played by herself exclusively and showed no response to her parents' love and attention. Her beautiful face had no expression as if she were more a doll than a person. She refused to eat her food in front of others. She soiled herself daily and did not seem to mind being in dirty diapers. Alexei showed little emotion but had explosive fits for no apparent reason, ripping the heads off toys and throwing blocks across the room. Her concerned parents sought advice. Their family physician suggested the possibility of autism; a psychologist suggested the possibility of a neurological impairment or reactive attachment disorder. Her parents were overwhelmed with labels, diagnoses, and recommendations for specialized treatment facilities. Somehow they knew everyone was missing something, and that something was Alexei.

The first day of preschool resulted in her parents being investigated by child protective authorities because Alexei masturbated in class. The well-intentioned but uninformed teacher assumed someone "taught her to do that." Alexei just looked blankly and shrugged her shoulders when leadingly asked, "Who touched you? Was it someone at home?" The investigation resulted in the parents being cleared but also contributed to their decision to give Alexei up for adoption.

Alexei went into one foster home after another. After two more failed adoptions, she was placed in a group home. Alexei watched everything going on around her as if it were a movie; unreal, random, and poorly directed. The world inside was so much more responsive and meaningful, so she turned away from the craziness around her. Alexei was alone, and she preferred it that way.

The *American Psychiatric Association's Diagnostic Statistical Manual* (DSM-IV-TR), the diagnostic handbook for mental health professionals, describes post-traumatic stress disorder (PTSD) as a constellation of symptoms that stem from exposure to threatening and frightening experiences. A person suffering from PTSD persistently reexperiences the traumatic event(s), develops impairments in functioning, avoids and numbs to cope, and experiences persistent arousal, including irritability, insomnia, and/or hypervigilance.[25]

The concept of PTSD was developed out of literature on the effects of war. Previously, it was referred to as "shell shock" or "battle fatigue." PTSD appeared in the 1980 edition of the DSM to respond to traumatized soldiers returning from Vietnam. The concept of PTSD comes from traumatic events, such as combat, disaster, and rape. Exposure to prolonged trauma over time or early in life, however, can have a more pervasive impact on development than PTSD describes.

According to Van der Kolk and Courtois (2005), PTSD as a diagnosis is not broad enough to capture the experiences of many victims of prolonged trauma, including profound changes in feelings of safety, trust, and self-worth.[26] Judith Herman developed and popularized the concept of complex trauma in her book, *Trauma and Recovery,* as a way to describe experiences of those who have been prisoners of war, hostages, members of cults, and victims of early chronic child maltreatment.[27]

According to Herman, complex trauma involves totalitarian control over a prolonged period of time that has long-term effects on affect, consciousness, self-perception, perception of the perpetrator, relation to others, and ability to make meaning and sense out of one's life. Totalitarian control refers to complete authoritarian dominance over another, which includes dictators, captors, and hostage-takers. In the case of dependent maltreated children, the abusive or neglectful caregiver serves as the totalitarian controller. The key feature of PTSD is unpredictable and uncontrollable danger, and nothing is more dangerous to a developing infant than the absence of a parent who reliably and responsively protects and nurtures.[28] Infants and toddlers who have been abused, neglected, or exposed to violence may experience deep, broad, and lasting effects.[29]

A U.S. Department of Health and Human Services report states that there were 3.6 million referrals to child protective agencies in 2005, of which 900, 000 children were determined to be victims of abuse or neglect.[30] Early, chronic maltreatment takes the form of emotional, physical, and sexual abuse; neglect and deprivation; exposure to domestic violence; and an array of experiences that disrupt the primary attachment. Babies left to cry unattended in orphanages, witnesses and victims of terrible violence, the used and abused, babies left hungry and cold by uncaring parents—all constitute maltreatment.

Early, chronic maltreatment is a deep source of injury because the trauma is to the attachment anchor. Considering the role attachment experiences play in our development, any significant disruption to the link may have many lasting effects.[31] The chart on the next page outlines areas of impairment in children exposed to complex trauma:[32]

I. Attachment	II. Biology	III. Affect Regulation
• Problems with Boundaries • Distrust • Suspiciousness • Social isolation • Difficulty attuning to other people's emotional states • Difficulty in perspective-taking	• Sensorimotor development • Analgesia • Problems with coordination, balance, body tone • Somatization • Increased medical problems across a wide span (pelvic pain, asthma, skin problems, autoimmune disorders, pseudoseizures)	• Difficulty with emotional self-regulation • Difficulty labeling and expressing feelings • Problems knowing and describing internal states • Difficulty communicating wishes and needs
IV. Dissociation	V. Behavioral Control	VI. Cognition
• Distinct alterations in states of consciousness • Amnesia • Depersonalization and derealization • Two or more distinct states of consciousness • Impaired memory for state-based events	• Poor modulation of impulses • Self-destructive behavior • Aggression toward others • Pathological self-soothing • Sleep disturbances • Eating disorders • Substance abuse • Excessive compliance • Oppositional behavior • Difficulty understanding and complying with rules • Reenactment of trauma in behavior or play	• Difficulties in attention regulation and executive function • Lack of sustained curiosity • Problems with processing novel information • Problems with object constancy • Difficulty planning and anticipating • Problems understanding responsibility • Learning difficulties • Problems with language development • Problems with orientation in time and space • Two or more distinct states of consciousness • Impaired memory for state-based events

VII. Self-Concept
• Lack of a continuous, predictable sense of self • Poor sense of separateness • Disturbances of body image • Low self-esteem • Shame and guilt

- **Attachment**—Tommy and Alexei, from the stories in this chapter, distrusted people because no one met their needs when they most needed it. Their early attachment experiences created a view of others as untrustworthy and unreliable. The lack of attachment, stimulation, and attention early in both children's lives affected their brains so that they struggled to read social and emotional cues. They lacked awareness of personal boundaries. Alexei appeared to others to be unpredictable, but in fact the world around her was random, arbitrary, and confusing. Alexei adapted to being alone during critical periods of her life by withdrawing.

- **Biology**—Alexei had difficulty reading and managing her sensory and physical cues, such as knowing when her bladder or bowels were full. She scratched herself bloody, not out of a desire to harm herself, but because she did not seem to feel the sensation of pain. Complex trauma affects the very fabric of children's biological being and makes them prone to health problems.

- **Affect Regulation**—Both Tommy and Alexei had difficulty regulating their rage and feelings in general. Both children had difficulty describing feelings and internal states, and they struggled to communicate wishes and desires.

- **Dissociation**—Dissociation refers to altered states of consciousness, including amnesia, impaired memory, and feeling unreal. Alexei felt as if she floated away, and she often felt as if she was not real, "kind of like I'm dreaming but awake."

- **Behavioral Control**—Tommy and Alexei struggled to modulate impulses, control their aggression, and understand the impact of their behavior on others. Unlike Alexei, Tommy understood rules but did not feel they applied to him. He acted before he thought and felt little control over his impulses.

- **Cognition**—Complex trauma affects the child's ability to focus on and process information. Tommy and Alexei had difficulty with executive functions, such as logic, reasoning, insight, and judgment. Both children struggled with planning, anticipating, and completing tasks. Complex trauma affects language development and may lead to learning problems.

- **Self-Concept**—Maltreated children may have difficulty seeing themselves as continuous and fluid. Instead, they view themselves as fragmented and unpredictable. Alexei had a disturbed image of her body and self, and once described herself in a self-portrait as "pieces of stuff floating in a pool of gooey goop."

The effects of maltreatment correlate with the very same aspects of development that are linked to healthy attachment. Other influential factors can affect development, including in-utero toxin exposure (nicotine, drugs), malnutrition, developmental disabilities, and environmental stressors.[33] However, attachment trauma stands out as one of the most significant risks to the health and well-being of a child.

Early and prolonged trauma impacts the developing child and reorganizes his adaptive systems toward survival. What eventually appear as problems in functioning are, in fact, the child's resilient solutions to a world he expects to be unpredictable, unreliable, and ultimately dangerous.

When a maltreated child behaves in ways that seem maladaptive, it is tempting to attribute the behavior to the child's personality. As Herman observed, the concept of complex trauma prevents "blaming the victim." The victim's problems in functioning are a response to trauma and not from underlying psychopathology.[34]

Understanding the impact of trauma helps us unveil the true function behind a problematic behavior. For example, oppositional and defiant behavior for traumatized children may serve to protect them against a perceived threat by "freezing" them in their tracks—a primitive but effective survival strategy. Freezing allows for keener senses to scan for threat and can act as a "camouflage" to reduce attracting predators.[35]

Severely maltreated children may eventually display many symptoms and problems that cluster into an attachment disorder. For example, Tommy displayed several disturbing behaviors, including fire-setting, inconsolable violent rages, and sadistic behavior toward animals. Alexei withdrew into her internal world where she felt secure and successful. In doing so, she became uninterested in and unresponsive to the world around her.

Chapter 11 will follow up on the concepts presented in this chapter and concentrate on what it is like to live with a child with symptoms of an attachment disorder, specifically focusing on assessment, diagnosis, treatment, and parenting strategies.

Quick Reference

Attachment is the key to our development and our life-sustaining anchor to the world. Our lives literally depend on it. Attachment nourishes and activates us, defines and refines us. Fundamental features of our lives, such as how we feel, how we view ourselves, how we think and remember, how we relate to others, how we regulate ourselves, and how we find meaning, are founded in the early parent-child attachment experiences.

Key Point 1

When attachment is disrupted by early chronic maltreatment, the course of the child's development is significantly affected.

Key Point 2

Attachment trauma affects the neurological, physical, emotional, behavioral, social, and cognitive well-being of the child. Attachment trauma impacts everything in a child's world from family relationships, to school performance, peer relationships, and beyond.

Key Point 3

Children who have experienced early and chronic maltreatment need to be understood as survivors, resiliently attempting to adapt to an unresponsive, threatening, and unpredictable world.

Key Point 4

Knowledge about what is truly happening to a developing child's brain and body provides us the necessary perspective and appreciation to interact effectively with him. Perspective gives us hope because we can see the child's behavior in a meaningful context. Once we begin to fathom the complexities of human development, we can begin to appreciate our adaptability and drive to survive.

Key Point 5

Parenting children who have experienced such trauma is very challenging as well as deeply rewarding.

DISCUSSION QUESTIONS

1. What do you think and feel when you read this statement: "Every child has a story, and that story will have an impact on those who love him?" How much of your child's story do you know?

2. What do you know about the early attachment experiences of your child? In what ways have you noticed that those experiences have affected him?

3. Think about the children in the foster care system in this country or in orphanages overseas. What life events have they possibly experienced that put them in survival mode? Now think about your child. Does he appear to live in the "fight or flight, flight or fright" mode? How do his responses affect you as his parent?

4. What do you understand about the differences between Post-Traumatic Stress Disorder (PTSD) and complex trauma?

5. Think about your child again. Review the domains of impairment with complex trauma and behavioral signs related to those domains (refer to chart). In what ways do you see your child reflected there? How have you been affected by these behaviors?

Chapter Five

Living with Traumatized Children: The Impact on Parents

By Jayne E. Schooler, MBS

Because a parent has compassion for a child, he feels with him. He enters his pain from his point of view. Entering into a child's pain comes at great emotional cost to the foster or adoptive parent.

—The Traumatized Child[1]

Author's Note: This chapter paints a difficult picture of the adoption experience for some families. It is meant to validate the experiences of those parents who are seriously struggling with family life as it is. It is also meant to remove the "rose-colored glasses" from parents preparing to adopt traumatized children. We are not blaming the children or blaming "adoption." However, these issues and struggles have long been ignored. Parents have been blamed instead of supported, criticized instead of encouraged, and judged instead of validated. This chapter does not answer the issues raised within it. However, throughout the rest of this book, we will present suggestions and strategies to manage these painful issues and problems.

Every Child Who Enters Foster Care Has a Story—That Story Will Impact Those Who Love Them

Katie was only four years old when she was placed into her first foster home on a hot August afternoon. In her short life, she had experienced more trauma and horror than most adults. What brought her to foster care was a story almost beyond belief. Just days earlier, a neighbor found her wandering outside her mother's apartment. Slashes to her neck were nearly hidden by dried blood.

When that neighbor entered Katie's apartment, she found her murdered mother's body on the floor. It was apparent she had been dead for well over a day.

Once the horror of the story emerged, it was apparent that this tragic event was not the first trauma for Katie. She also encountered domestic violence while still in the womb. Going from boyfriend to boyfriend, Katie's pregnant mom often landed in abuse shelters. After Katie was born, stories of severe neglect surfaced but went unreported. The cycle of domestic violence and severe neglect continued. Her mother's involvement in the chaotic, devastating world of drugs ended in her death by a deal gone bad. It almost ended Katie's life as well.

Now this precious child is alone. Everything about her is changed by the traumas that stole her childhood from her. The way she behaves, the way she thinks, the way she sees the world around her are etched with the memories of abuse and violence. She will carry those emotional, traumatic memories into every relationship. Her story will deeply impact those who love her.[2] It will change them. Some of those changes will be good changes, growth changes.

However, unless her new parents are attuned to the impact this little life will have on them, some of those changes will not be healthy and good.

Frog in the Kettle

The story of the frog and the kettle, probably more a fable than truth, may provide a wake-up call for parents caring for traumatized children:

> It's been said that if you put a frog into a pot of boiling water, it will leap out right away to escape the danger.
>
> But, if you put a frog in a kettle filled with cool, pleasant water and *gradually* heat the kettle until it starts boiling, the frog will not become aware of the threat until it is too late. The frog's survival instincts are geared toward detecting sudden changes.

This story is often used to illustrate how humans have to be careful to watch slowly changing trends in the environment, not just the sudden changes. It's a warning to keep us paying attention not just to obvious threats, but to more slowly developing ones.[3]

What does this story have to do with adoptive or foster parents and traumatized children? Here's the recipe:

1. One loving, excited, potentially unprepared adoptive family

2. One new child, who has had significant trauma and has developed strategies of survival

3. One "cool and pleasant" home

4. An emotional thermostat to which no one is paying attention

Let's look more closely at what happens when ingredients in this recipe come together.

Child Meets Family

When a child experiences trauma that disrupts the budding attachment process, he invents strategies for survival. (Refer to the previous chapter for a more extensive discussion.) These strategies serve several purposes for the child: retention of control, hypervigilance to any threat or dangers, and dissociation from a potential threat, including his own feelings of sadness or fear.[4]

When this child moves into his new adoptive home, he moves in with his survival skills, but they don't work for the new parents. Megan Hirst, in *Loving and Living with the Traumatised Child*, writes, "The child finds her own solutions to the problem of protecting herself from her dangerous environment. The resulting behaviors become a problem when the child is placed in a loving, open, and trusting family. The messages being transmitted between the child and his new adoptive parent become confused and misinterpreted. It is as though they are each speaking different languages."[5]

The following are examples of some of these confusions:

- The child may believe himself to be bad, but his adoptive parents (or school staff) want to encourage him with praise. The result is that the child believes the new parents (or teachers) are lying and therefore not to be trusted.

- Because the child has learned that he cannot trust adults, he tells his new parents what he thinks they want to hear. The parents interpret these as deliberate lies and conclude that the child cannot be trusted.

- The child believes that adults are not safe (including his new parents) and that he needs to protect himself from their approaches, but the parents interpret this behavior as rejecting their love, and they increasingly feel incompetent and inadequate.

• The child believes that he needs to keep himself safe, so he gives his attention a wide focus, but his parents and teachers believe that he cannot concentrate on his work (narrow focus), and he gets labeled with attention deficit disorder (ADHD). The result for some families is chaos and strong emotions that make normal parenting practically impossible.

The Thermostat Rises

As parents and child experience ricocheting emotions, the emotional thermostat (just like the boiling pot for the frog) begins to rise. Everyone knows things are not working well, but everyone steps into denial about what is happening. No one is watching the emotional thermostat. Before long, the entire family is sucked into a negative cycle of relating to one another, and the thermostat begins to overheat.[6]

Three Parental Responses

A tremendous challenge stands before foster and adoptive parents while caring for a traumatized child. There are three main elements in parents' responses to their child's trauma and behavior:

1. Believing and validating their child's experiences

2. Tolerating their child's affect (emotions)

3. Managing their own emotional responses[7]

Believing and Validating Their Child's Experiences

"Dillon's caseworker told us about the extreme sexual abuse he experienced as a toddler. I knew it was truth, but believing such horror could be done to a child is another thing. Can you know something is true but still not believe it? I know that doesn't make sense. I know it is true. I just have to believe it."

—Christa, adoptive mom of four-year-old Dillon

For many adoptive parents, believing and validating their child's abuse experiences is a tremendous challenge. No one wants to accept the fact that the innocence of the beautiful child who is now part of the family was stolen by physical, emotional, psychological, or sexual abuse. To believe it means to feel it as well.

Tolerating Their Child's Affect (Behaviors)

"If you had told me a year ago that I would be tolerating certain behaviors in my home, I would have said, 'You are crazy!' But now, here we are, navigating through these behavioral challenges that were so unexpected."

—Carolyn and Rick, parents of nine-year-old Jacob

One of the most important character traits for adoptive parents of traumatized children is flexibility—extreme flexibility. Juli Alvarado, an adoptive mother, treatment foster parent, and adoption therapist, uses the expression, "expanding your window of tolerance." Old ways of managing difficult behaviors may not work. Parents find themselves dealing with behaviors that are totally out of the sphere of their previous parenting experiences.

Managing Their Own Emotional Responses

"I had no idea that I could get so incredibly angry," David stated. "I have always been able to manage my own emotions, but this seven-year-old triggers such frustration and anger in me, I feel out of control."

—David, adoptive dad of seven-year-old Bekah

Hundreds of foster and adoptive parents were surveyed in workshops across the country. They were asked, "Of the three elements above, which is most difficult for you?" They responded overwhelmingly: "managing our own emotional responses." Why would this be true for so many?

Many adoptive parents find themselves in an unfamiliar place. They perhaps have had parenting experience, but only parenting nontraumatized children. They have not cared for children who lack extreme impulse control and who have problems with boundaries, oppositional behavior, difficulty expressing emotions, and so on. They are at a time and place in their lives they have never been. It has stopped feeling good, and they do not like what they are becoming. What are some of the early signs that negative transformation is taking place?

Early Awareness of Negative Family Transformation

In their book *Troubled Transplants,* Dr. Richard Delaney and Dr. Frank Kunstal talk about a number of identifiable issues for families as the emotional thermostat begins to rise and they begin to experience negative transformation.

Splitting

Delaney and Kunstal define splitting as "the psychological phenomenon—an inner defense—which explains why troubled foster and adoptive children think in all-or-nothing terms." This type of black-and-white thinking paints some people as all good and others as all bad. Examples include:

- The child idealizes the foster or adoptive father and devalues the mother.
- The child perceives the birth parents as sainted and the foster or adoptive parents as evil.
- The child views himself as alternately all-wonderful or as totally worthless.

Pathological splitting occurs when a child fails to integrate his good and bad feelings toward his first caregivers. This may occur because the child experienced maltreatment at the hands of his birth parents and is forced to suppress any angry feelings toward them. These feelings can only emerge safely and be expressed toward foster or adoptive parents who have not hurt the child.[8]

Often the splitting happens in the adoptive home as the child hurls his anger at only one parent, usually the mother. He often does this when the father is not around, so dad rarely sees the outbursts or other negative behavior. The parents then see and experience the child in two different ways. They are "split" in their perception of the child, their feelings toward the child, and their discipline of the child. And, the child knows!

A second sign of negative transformation is called "reenactment."

Reenactment

Reenactment is the "child's stubborn tendency to relive old, destructive parent-child relationships in the foster or adoptive home."[9] Essentially, the child replays old scripts repeatedly because they are familiar and understood. These old patterns feel comfortable and safe to the child, even though they definitely are not. According to Delaney and Kunstal "Over time, the disturbed child's impact on the foster or adoptive family often results in the 'new family' resembling the past, maltreating family. That is, the foster and adoptive family may find itself negotiating less and becoming more dictatorial; they may find themselves feeling abusive impulses; they may discover that the child has attempted to place them in a child's role, while clutching to his habitual role as 'pseudo-adult'; they may find themselves increasingly estranged and distant from each other; communication between spouses may grow more strained and less clear; and blaming others (agencies, the school system, or one's mate) becomes the family norm."[10]

A third sign of negative transformation is called "reverse effect."

Reverse Effect

When the child negatively influences the family, a "reverse effect" has occurred. The direction of the influence is not from the top down—from the parents to the child. Rather, it is from the bottom up—child to parent.[11] The child, not the parents, has control of the emotional thermostat in the home. Foster and adoptive parents may look very dysfunctional to professionals who see the family after months or years of coping with the challenging behaviors of a traumatized child. They may appear to be creating the difficulties in the family rather than displaying symptoms of and reactions to the child's emotional and behavioral problems. The foster or adoptive family begins to transform into the child's picture of family.[12]

If these signs are ignored, the family is at risk for continued negative transformation. They are at risk of experiencing vicarious, secondary trauma.

Vicarious Trauma: What Is It? Who Is at Risk? What Does It Look Like?

Over the last several years, there has been an increased look at what is called "vicarious trauma" or secondary trauma. Margaret Blaustein, PhD and contributor to *The Traumatised Child*, defines vicarious trauma as:

> . . . the cumulative impact of a child's trauma stories, behaviors, and reenactments on the foster/adoptive parents. Vicarious

traumatization is a transformation of a parent's inner self resulting from an empathic, compassionate connection to a child who has experienced trauma.[13]

Who is at Risk for Vicarious Trauma?

This important question deserves serious examination. According to the Child Trauma Academy, those who work or live with traumatized children or adults are at risk for vicarious trauma.

- **Anyone who, by nature, is empathetic.** Social workers, by nature, are empathetic. That is why many chose the profession. Adoptive parents are also empathetic by nature. An adoptive family is a healing place, and children get better because their parents are there for them emotionally. However, by empathizing with a child or "feeling their pain" [a parent] becomes vulnerable to internalize some of the child's trauma-related pain.[14]

- **Any adoptive parent who does not allow himself/herself sufficient recovery time.** Parents often find themselves listening over and over again to their children's horrific stories and also living with the behavioral aftermath. Because it's difficult to find restorative respite care, adoptive parents don't have any time to "fall back and regroup." There just isn't any break in managing their child's serious emotional and behavioral needs.[15]

- **Any adoptive parent who has experienced his/her own personal trauma and has not had the opportunity for personal healing.** See chapter three for an in-depth look at this most crucial aspect of parenting traumatized children and how this scenario can trigger one's historical emotional and psychological wounds.[16]

- **Any adoptive parent who finds himself/herself isolated from family, friends, and professional supports.** In discussing the issue of vicarious trauma with many adoptive parents across the country, one common problem stands out for many of them. The extreme nature of their child's behavioral or emotional needs causes family and friends to disengage from them and withdraw from consistent, regular contact. Other parents report that the professionals who were with them in the beginning now blame *them* for the chaos and challenges in their homes, rather than understanding the impact on the family of parenting their new son or daughter.[17]

- **Any adoptive parent who struggles due to a lack of systemic resources.** Social and economic reasons make post-adoption services and funding hard to find. Families fend for themselves through the complicated world of educational and psychological resources for their children, and for themselves.

What Does Vicarious Trauma Look Like?

A number of studies have examined the effects of *secondary* trauma on professionals. They provide insight into the potential effects for parents. Distressing emotions felt by professionals working with traumatized children and adults included:

- Anger
- Sadness
- Rage
- Depression or anxiety
- Physical complaints (headaches, stomach aches, lethargy, and so on), nightmares
- Avoidance of certain situations or people
- Impaired work habits (tardiness or missed appointments)
- Disconnection from loved ones
- Social withdrawal
- Cynicism, negativity, and irritability
- No time or energy for self
- Diminished self-capacities
- Unclear thoughts

If professionals who work with traumatized children and adults experience these symptoms, we must ask, "What about parents who live with these children? Are they being impacted as well?"

A ground-breaking research study, which was conducted in 2004 with adoptive parents, lends additional insight. The goal of the study was to look at what was happening in the adoptive home when a parent loved and lived with a traumatized child. The results identified challenging effects as well as positive outcomes.

Top Effects of Caring for Traumatized Children

This group of adoptive parents identified challenging effects they have experienced as they parent traumatized children. Frustration, which was the major effect named by many adoptive parents, comes because of three major deficits: (1) lack of validation as being the parent of their child, (2) lack of understanding about the difficulties they are living with, and (3) lack of support.[18]

Frustration appears to be a universal issue for adoptive parents. My own work with adoptive parents across the United States supports these findings. Parents consistently share the following frustrations:

Frustration Due to Lack of Validation

"I guess I really shouldn't expect my family and friends to understand what we are living with. They aren't here twenty-four/seven," said Rebecca, a single adoptive mom of Cassie, age eleven. "If I share anything with my family, they tell me I can always send her back. I don't need that type of comment. I am her mom and will always be her mom. I wish they would see our relationship, even with its challenges, is as 'real' as the relationship with the biological kids in the family. Sometimes I feel so invalidated."

Frustration Due to Lack of Understanding

"I rarely share my frustrations and concerns with anyone, because I know they don't understand," commented Betsy, a mom of three children adopted from an orphanage in central Asia. "Prior to living at the orphanage, these children survived by begging and scouring the city dump for food or items to sell. They were five, six, and seven years old when they went to the orphanage. If I shared anything with others about their behaviors at home, it would isolate them and us even more."

Frustration Due to Lack of Support

Many adoptive parents find few resources to help them with their children's challenging issues. They experience a lack of support from the mental health field, and the child welfare and educational systems.

"We often feel blamed for the problems of our children and the difficulties we face," Kevin, an adoptive dad of four-year-old Jacob, said. "Some of it is subtle; other times, people give us advice with an underlying message that leaves us feeling incompetent and at fault. Frustration with those who should be in a place to help us sometimes feels overwhelming and defeating."

Other Effects Include the Following:

Living with Uncertainty

One adoptive mom stated, "It is like living with a walking time bomb. I don't know who might be getting up in the morning. Will quiet, calm Jackie be getting up, or will it be angry, aggressive Jackie? Even if quiet Jackie gets up, I still feel like I am walking on eggshells all because I don't know just how long her good mood will last. As a result of this uncertainty, I don't know sometimes how to plan my day. Should I meet with my other adoptive mom friends in the park for a play day? Or will it collapse into what happened last time? What about going to the mall? I think that sounds like a good idea, until I remembered what happened last time we all tried to go together. It just isn't worth the effort."

One's Own Extreme Emotions and Mood Swings

Living with chronic emotional tension in the household can be, and often is, emotionally draining. One parent described her experience this way: "I never knew I could get so angry over little, unimportant things. It never used to be that way for me."

Another parent shared, "I always considered myself a pretty stable person, but all that is out the door now. When I wake up in the morning, I wonder if I will have any positive, happy, or even neutral moments with our son. Jonathan is an angry seven-year-old, and his depth of rage has spilled over onto me. It happened slowly. I didn't even notice it until one afternoon I totally lost it with him. That was one wake-up call."

Drained Emotional and Social Energy

Parenting and caring for a traumatized child ramps up the meaning of hard work. If subtle emotional changes are taking place and no one is paying attention, parents find themselves with no emotional energy to care for themselves. They get lost in the emotional chaos of managing their child's issues. Even the thought of going out for a social event takes too much energy.

"We are 'lectured' by well meaning friends all the time to stop and take time out for ourselves. I know they are right, but they also have no concept of what it would mean to arrange for an evening out. We have burned up every responsible babysitter within a reasonable driving distance and family members are usually busy. Planning an evening feels more like a massive chore than a pleasant, relaxing thought," Betsy shared. [Note: see chapter 12 on parental self-care strategies for ideas to refill a drained emotional reserve.]

Relationship Strains and Loss

During a recent adoptive parent support group meeting, Kevin and April quietly shared their deep feelings of isolation and loneliness. They adopted Claire and Bekah from the foster care system in the United States. The girls are seven and eight, and their traumatic history is lived out almost every day in their new adoptive home.

"We anticipated difficulties with the girls; we understand their background and have taken a lot of training to prepare for their coming. What we didn't anticipate is that their behavioral issues would drive a wedge between us and our friends," Kevin said. "Our friends, especially those with children around the ages of our girls, have stopped inviting us over. I know why and can somewhat understand, but it still hurts. Our girls have no idea how to have quality friendships, and when they are with other children, there is always a pretty significant issue. This has been a major loss for April and me."

Impact on Physical Health

- "I've gained fifty pounds since we adopted Kamie."
- "I live with chronic headaches . . . and Kevin is only five."
- "I am thirty-seven and have been diagnosed with serious high blood pressure."
- "My doctor calls it fibromyalgia. All I know is that I have chronic muscle aches and pains. This came on gradually . . . but started about a year after we began parenting Nastya."

Stress is one of the major causes of health problems. In their book, *Healing Parent: Helping Wounded Children to Trust and Heal,* Michael Orlans and Teri Levy list early physical signs of parenting stress: headaches, body tensions, muscle aches, stomach problems, sleep problems, rapid heartbeat, weight gain or loss, dizziness, and nausea.[19]

Personal Growth Opportunities

We've identified a number of the personal effects that impact parents caring for traumatized children. It has been a difficult picture to paint, but one that is realistic and necessary. However, something else must be added. The adoptive families who participated in the 2004 study did not walk away with a totally pessimistic view of their adoption experience. Many of the experiences were heartbreaking, but these parents also experienced incredible personal growth in three areas:[20]

Insight and Understanding

"I have had to stretch and grow as a person and as a parent. I have new understanding about myself and tremendous insight into why our son is the way he is. I no longer play the blame game with myself, because I always lost. I have learned how to reframe what is happening with our family and within me. I am a far more emotionally healthy person because of what we lived through."

—Katie, adoptive mom of nine-year-old William

Perseverance

"Our biggest challenge for our son was managing his educational needs. If you had told me that one day I would be a child advocate dealing with schools, I would have probably said that isn't my thing. Well, now it is. I have persevered for Lissi's educational needs with teachers, principals, school superintendents, anyone who had some level of responsibility. I have grown tremendously because I have learned not to take 'no' for an answer."

—Paul, adoptive father of eleven-year-old Alise

Openness and Improved Family Communication

"We went through the most difficult time in our family about three years after Jonathan joined our family. While we were in it, it was the darkest of times. Now that we are on the other side, and Jonathan is doing extremely well, we can say that perhaps it was the best of times. Our entire family is different. We are far more open and honest about thoughts and feelings in the household. We are all better people because of the valley of discouragement we lived through."

—David and Debbie, adoptive parents of Jonathan, now fourteen

Quick Reference

Key Point 1: The Frog and the Kettle: The Recipe

- One loving, excited, potentially unprepared adoptive family
- One new child, who has had significant trauma and has developed survival strategies
- One "cool and pleasant" home
- An emotional thermostat to which no one is paying attention

Key Point 2: The Challenge to Foster and Adoptive Parents
A tremendous challenge stands before foster and adoptive parents while caring for a traumatized child. Three main elements drive a parent's response to their children's trauma and behavior:

- Believing and validating their child's experiences
- Tolerating their child's affect (emotions and behavior)
- Managing their own emotional responses

Key Point 3: Early Awareness of Negative Family Transformation

- The frog in the kettle provides a picture of what can happen to families who are not paying attention to the issues, challenges, and situations discussed in this chapter.
- Parents in extremely difficult circumstances can find hope, help, and ultimately, experience personal growth.

DISCUSSION QUESTIONS

1. Explain the frog in the kettle illustration. Do you feel it relates to you or your family? In what way?

2. Discuss the three main elements in a parent's response to their children's trauma and behavior: believing and validating their child's experiences, tolerating their child's emotions, and managing their own emotional responses. How have you experienced those challenging responses?

3. Discuss splitting, reenactment, and reverse effect. Do any of these three early signs of family transformation describe what might be happening in your home?

4. Review the challenging effects of parenting traumatized children. Which ones have impacted your life? How are you managing those challenges?

5. How have you grown personally and emotionally as an adoptive parent?

Chapter Six

Living with Traumatized Children: The Impact on Birth and Other Adopted Siblings

By Elizabeth A. Tracy, MSW, LICSW

"Another thing that has really been affected is the amount of time that we spent with our first child, our birth daughter . . . we did not realize how much time has been taken away from her until she said, 'Hey, you don't see me anymore!' And now I make specific time each week that she and I go out."

—Adoptive mother

All families struggle to find equilibrium when they integrate a new member, whether through birth, adoption, or marriage. In time, all families fall into a "rhythm" once they get to know their child (baby sleeps, wakes, eats, and so on). The adoption of an older child may cause the initial adjustment phase to take longer, because the child also needs to learn the household rules; for example, what do we do when we want to borrow something from a family member? What happens when rules are broken? Eventually, though, the family develops some sort of rhythmic pattern.

When a child with special needs joins a family, the rhythmic flow often changes. This predictable unpredictability becomes the rhythm of the house and is usually challenging for the biological children in the family. Their orderly and predictable world no longer exists. Unlike a traumatized child, who is used to an ever-changing environment or mood, biological children have little or no coping skills for such a chaotic home life.

This chapter will focus on four potential areas that a special-needs adoption affects biological children. Research and years of interviews with foster families have shown that most parents have limited attunement to their child's actual feelings and experiences.[2] *Attunement* means that parents have a true understanding of what their child thinks and feels about a particular issue.

Hope is a driving factor for parents who adopt children with special needs—hope that they will create a better life for this child; hope that they will make a difference in this child's life; hope that they will, in some way, heal this child.

For this chapter, my hope is that parents, agencies, and key family supporters will develop sensitivity to and an awareness of the unique situation of biological children. The ultimate goal is that with this new awareness, pre- and post-adoptive strategies will make the entire adoptive family more stable and permanent.

Potential Impact on Siblings After Adopting a Traumatized Child

- Children may witness grief, sadness, and anger when the parents and other family members struggle.[3]
- The family may implement new behavior management (discipline) techniques, and/or house rules may be changed.
- Children may believe their opinions and feelings don't matter.
- Children may become invisible to their parents after a special-needs adoption.

Children May Witness Grief, Sadness, and Anger When the Family Struggles

In an ideal world when the "system" is working well, adoptive parents will attend meetings, receive training, and review detailed records of their newest child. Armed with all this information, they enter into an adoption prepared for the task they are undertaking.

In contrast, biological children have limited information about their newest sibling and typically are told about all the special and wonderful things that are going to happen within their family. Sometimes, they are told that their sibling will have trouble sharing or have tantrums. But for the most part, biological children report that they are told about all the happy times the family will have.

While it is essential that biological children be shielded from their sibling's full history, doing so can set up a negative dynamic. Finding the right balance will be unique for each family. Several factors will influence the disclosure of information: the age of the biological children, the severity of their new sibling's behaviors, and the changes to be made within the family.

Unfortunately, there are times when adoptive parents are not well prepared for the reality their new child brings. This may happen for multiple reasons: an international adoption where the child's medical or trauma history is not fully known; a foster care adoption where full disclosure is not provided to the parents; or, as with any biological child, an unforeseen and unpreventable issue develops, such as a psychiatric or medical illness.

Whether well prepared or not, as soon as the new family addition comes home, parents begin trying to regain their equilibrium and cope with the daily challenges now presented to them. It is during this critical time that biological children are unintentionally forgotten.

Janette's Story
Janette Peterson, now twenty-three years old, shares her story. She was eight when her parents adopted an eleven-year-old girl. She also has a younger sister, Kylie, who was five at the time of the adoption.

> Before we adopted Anita, I would say that my family was typical. My dad worked during the week, and my mother worked part-time so she could be home with my sister and me after school. My parents had minor disagreements, but they always worked them out. I am pretty sure we took family vacations twice a year. It was a nice life. Kylie and I argued, but it was normal kid stuff. It was the happiest time I can remember.

> At first, when Anita came, it was kind of fun. She was older than me and could read better, so we could play more board games, and I had someone I could race on my bike. After a few months, Anita became more demanding and had huge tantrums. I remember the first time I saw her have one. It was as if she was possessed. The look on my mother's face scared me the most. She was ghostly white with eyes wide open. The only thing I remember about that day was feeling fear deep inside me.

To be fair, I think my parents just didn't know what they were getting into. I overheard many arguments between my parents and remember hearing my mother yell at my dad, "How was I supposed to know this was going to happen?" When my dad would come home from work, Anita would become sweet and act like a little angel. Then my dad would look at my mom and say something snippy.

Suddenly, the house felt so out of control. I would try really hard to be good all the time and watch my little sister so Anita wouldn't hurt her or blame her for stuff she didn't do. That was exhausting! My parents were constantly bickering about everything. It was as if a black cloud had settled over our house.

Eventually, Anita started going in and out of the psychiatric hospitals for medication adjustments. Anita would be home for about six months and then back in the hospital for a couple of weeks and then home for six months. After a medication adjustment, she was able to do better and things were okay. My parents got much better at having her put in the hospital as soon as they saw it was time—and that was great. We all really enjoyed the break from the chaos. Later, my parents began scheduling times for Anita to go away for respite. Everyone, including Anita, really enjoyed the time.

I would have to say that the hardest thing for me was watching my mother cry and my parents argue. I lived in daily fear that they were going to separate. I had no idea why Anita would scream and throw things.

Whenever I would ask my parents why Anita behaved that way and why they put up with it, they would tell me to be grateful that they were my parents and that Anita had "some problems." When I was sixteen, my mother finally said, "I guess you are old enough to understand," and then she told me that Anita had been sexually abused by one of her uncles and had

Post Traumatic Stress Disorder (PTSD). Until then, I thought that she was just being a spoiled brat and trying to get her own way.

Most adoptive parents who knew in advance that their child had special needs will tell you they felt fully prepared prior to the adoption. However, these same parents will often say, "I really had no idea what I was getting into." Depending on the medical, physical, psychiatric, or intellectual needs of their child, parents typically state that they underestimated the number of appointments, the number of specialists, and the amount of time and energy needed to get through each day. Parents will often speak of the anguish, grief, frustration, and sheer exhaustion during the initial adjustment phase.

Typically, adoptive parents have a good support network, including the adoption agency, social workers, extended family, friends, spouse, and other adoptive parents. The biological children, however, usually lack an adequate network to provide them with positive support and help them develop effective coping skills.

Sixteen-year-old Crystal stated, "Yes, my parents told me that Rebecca had problems. They said she had tantrums and had learning disabilities. They also said that they could handle it and that as soon as Rebecca felt part of the family, it would stop. But it hasn't. I am not saying they lied. I don't think they really knew how bad it was going to be."

Crystal's parents had been informed that six-year-old Rebecca had been diagnosed with Fetal Alcohol Syndrome (FAS). They knew about her tantrums and school difficulties. Crystal's parents did an excellent job preparing their daughter with the information they had. When Crystal began to express her anger and frustration to her parents, they were understandably confused. "We told Crystal it would be chaotic for a while, until Rebecca learned our family and routines. We explained about the tantrums, so Crystal's anger took us by surprise," said her mother, Judith.

Crystal's parents found a therapist who had experience working with siblings of special-needs children. After Crystal had developed a relationship with her therapist, she was able to express the problem. "Day after day, I watch my parents try so hard to control Rebecca. I watch this little kid hit my mother, and my mom is so sad and stressed out. I hear my mother beg Rebecca to stop screaming, swearing, and to please give her a break. Now, my parents are mad at each other all the time, I think they are getting a divorce."

Although Crystal was prepared for Rebecca's behaviors, she was pained by having to watch her parents struggle. Crystal felt completely powerless and out of control. Her mother was surprised that her daughter was so distressed. "I never thought that Crystal would be affected," she said. "I knew I was having a hard time, but I was handling it. It never occurred to me to let Crystal know that I was okay or to ask her how she felt about the added stress that her father and I were under. I just kept asking Crystal how she felt about Rebecca. I was worried that she might not accept her little sister."

Crystal's parents made several accommodations to help alleviate her distress. First, they helped Crystal develop a positive support network, including her therapist, grandparents, and godmother. During the first year, Crystal visited her grandparents and godmother during chaotic times. Neither child viewed Crystal's time away as a punishment. "I really like being with my Grammy and Gramps. They live in the same town, so I can still hang out with my friends and I don't have to be part of the whole Rebecca scene," said Crystal.

Second, they let Crystal express her feelings. When she did, her parents offered her reassurance that they were in control and were both physically and emotionally safe.

Third, Crystal's parents were more mindful of their behavior (marital disagreements) in the presence of their daughter.

Adults who are confident and convey to their children that they are in control of the household allow biological children to stay out of the caretaking role for their parents. When parents become visibly overwhelmed, their biological children feel the need to step in and make things easier. The results may cause both physical and emotional harm to the biological children, as well as the newest member of the family.

Parents can initiate a simple conversation to alleviate some of the stress on their biological children. For example, they could say, "I want you to know that everything is okay and I can take care of you and the family, even though Mary is yelling at me and having tantrums. I am okay." Parents shouldn't make these types of statements to their children if, in fact, it is clear that the parent is out of control and not handling the situation.

Potential Strategies for Children Who Experience Grief, Sadness, and Anger When the Family Struggles

- *Don't disclose intimate details of abuse or trauma.* It's not
  necessary and may be harmful to disclose everything.

However, explain to biological children that the reason their brother Johnny doesn't share is because he never had his own things before and needs to learn. Explain that in Susie's birth home, she wasn't always safe. Doing so will give biological children something to work with. The age of biological children will guide the amount and type of disclosure. Remember: children do not understand confidentiality and should never be given information that, if shared, could damage, hurt, or embarrass their new sibling.

- *Assure biological children that although it may look like their out-of-control sibling is hurting the parents, they are safe.* (If this is not a true statement, an immediate intervention is needed.) Children need to know that their parents are in control of the home and that everyone is safe. Establish an open dialogue with biological children about the sadness, anger, or frustration they may be witnessing. Create an atmosphere where they can discuss negative emotions to help relieve the guilt and fear they may be experiencing. Biological children have reported this type of communication as one of the most effective interventions.

- *Provide children with a positive support network.* Include adults with whom siblings can share their worries and concerns. A therapist or sibling support group is an ideal place. Peer activities, which allow them to continue living as a "typical child," are important for stress relief and self-esteem.

The Family May Implement New Behavior Management (Discipline) Techniques and/or House Rules or Rituals

Parenting a child who has been traumatized requires creativity, commitment, humor, consistency, perseverance, and a hopeful spirit. A child with special needs may require frequent changes in behavior-management techniques. Some parents find that what worked last month may not be as effective this month, or that they need a blend of several techniques to manage their family successfully.

In an effort to be fair and to treat everyone in the family equally, many adoptive families decide to develop one set of rules. New rules that regulate safety, hygiene, and health should not be negotiable because they are designed for the protection of the entire family.

For example, if a child with a medical issue joins the family, some house rules may need to be adjusted. Visitors may need to be restricted during times when the child is actively ill, or guests may have to wear a face mask to prevent the spread of germs.

Typically, younger children do not have an issue with these types of changes and take them as a normal part of the family routine. Older children, particularly teens, may feel imposed upon or embarrassed by the things they have to ask their friends to do when they visit.

Children with psychiatric, intellectual, or behavioral issues generally have the largest impact on family functioning. Sometimes children who have been sexually abused might be sexually inappropriate. For example, they may touch their own genitals or those of another person. They may try to be sexually provocative with adult visitors or other children in the home. Some traumatized children feel unsafe if they are in an environment where people are not fully dressed or whenever anyone enters their bedroom.

Families may have to adjust their house rules to support their newest member as they develop and maintain control over their feelings and behaviors. For some families, this may mean a significant adjustment in personal freedom.

The Chesterfield Family

The Chesterfield family has two biological children and one adopted child, Danielle. They are in the process of adopting Danielle's eight-year-old biological brother, Nathaniel. The siblings have maintained a close relationship, even though Danielle was removed from their birth home five years ago.

As the Chesterfields finalize Nathaniel's adoption, he has begun spending every weekend with the family. Nathaniel has Post Traumatic Stress Disorder (PTSD) from witnessing violence during his birth parents' drug deals. He was sexually abused from the time he was three until age seven. Nathaniel has been in and out of different foster homes and residential treatment centers for the past two years. His sexualized behaviors include masturbation and provocative conduct with men.

The family's favorite activity is watching Saturday morning cartoons in their parents' bed. "It's a game to see how many of us can get under the covers without pulling them off my dad. Friday night, we all make bets on who is going to get up the earliest," reported ten-year-old Danielle.

Mr. and Mrs. Chesterfield decided that the Saturday morning cartoon activity should be modified to accommodate Nathaniel's special needs. Without warning the other children, they declared that Saturday morning cartoons would now happen in the living room. The Chesterfield children were extremely upset, disappointed, and angry. They demanded that their parents tell them why the ritual had been changed. Mr. and Mrs. Chesterfield initially told their children, "Because we said so."

After relentless badgering, they explained that Nathaniel could not participate because he was not adopted yet. Mr. Chesterfield approached Nathaniel's therapist for guidance. "I don't want the other children to know about Nathaniel's issues," he explained, "but we have to tell them something. Once the adoption is finalized, they are going to wonder why we haven't changed it back. My wife and I are hoping that someday we can go back to the way it was."

Nathaniel's therapist recommended that the Chesterfields develop a list of ways they could modify the current Saturday morning ritual. He also encouraged them to ask their children for their input. Mr. and Mrs. Chesterfield approached their children at a family meeting and told them that since they were expanding the family, they wanted to add something new and different to the Saturday morning cartoon fest.

After much discussion and negotiation, the Chesterfield children developed the following list of options for Saturday mornings:

- Keep it the way it is in mom and dad's room—no changes.
- Put a plasma television in every bedroom and everyone stays in his or her own bed.
- Move to a different bedroom every weekend so everyone gets a chance to have cartoons in his or her room.
- Move to the living room with sleeping bags and eat sugary cereal while watching television.
- Keep the routine in mom and dad's room, use sleeping bags, and eat sugary cereal while watching television.

The Chesterfields and Nathaniel's therapist decided to try the last option. The sleeping bags would provide protection for all and the sugary cereal was definitely a bonus as far as the children were concerned.

Some parents are tempted to apply the same rules to everyone in an effort to help the newest child feel a part of the family. But children with behavioral issues may require more structure and direction than other children in the home.

The Robertson Family

Rachel Robertson is a thirty-two-year-old, single mother who tried this strategy without success. "I had an eight-year-old and a twelve-year-old daughter at the time I adopted five-year-old Katie. Katie's behaviors, at that time, required lots of discipline, sticker charts, and logical consequences with very limited decision-making opportunities. I didn't want Katie to feel like she was not part of the family, and since I am the only parent I told all the girls that the rules applied to everyone."

Both of Ms. Robertson's biological children immediately rebelled. Eight-year-old Hannah stated, "I am not a baby! It's not fair that I can't do stuff just because Katie makes bad choices. I live across the street from my grandma and I used to be able to visit her anytime I wanted. Now my mom says I can't cross the street without her, because those are the new rules so Katie doesn't get hit by a car."

Hannah was so angry about the new limits that she became aggressive toward Katie. "Hannah is such a sweet girl and I was shocked to see her being so mean to Katie by not sharing and being unfriendly," said Ms. Robertson.

Ms. Robertson and Hannah began to argue and their relationship deteriorated. "I was at my wit's end," said her mother. "Then at a conference for the North American Council on Adoptable Children (NACAC), I learned how to provide the structure and discipline that each of my girls needed without making me crazy. I learned to allow each girl freedom and flexibility as they became ready. Initially, I thought this would make it harder for me, but actually it's more natural and easier. For instance, my oldest daughter can make a basic breakfast for herself, and I let her do that.

We live on a little side street and Hannah has been crossing it alone since she was five. She calls my mother when she wants to go over and then crosses. Of course, my mother has always watched Hannah cross from her living room window. I've already told Katie that as soon as she is able to make better choices, she too will earn privileges to do things independently. This new system is working much better."

In contrast, biological children may require more explanation about discrepancies in consequences and/or behavior management strategies when adopting a child with psychiatric issues.

Cassandra's Dilemma

Twelve-year-old Cassandra was in her counselor's office at school crying uncontrollably, "It's not fair, it's not fair! My brother gets suspended from school because he threw a desk at the principal and swore at his teacher and hardly gets any punishment. I don't turn in my homework, get a warning letter, and I get grounded for two weeks. It's not fair! My parents keep telling me that I know better and that my brother has problems. Maybe I should say that I'm depressed and start throwing things at teachers, and then I can get away with anything, just like he does."

Cassandra's reaction is common for a sibling of a child with special needs. Often, parents unwittingly create a discrepancy by placing higher expectations on the sibling *without* special needs. From Cassandra's point of view, she sees that her brother, who is diagnosed with a mental illness, can violently break rules with hardly any consequences, while she, who makes rare and minor infractions, reaps multiple and severe repercussions.

Once they entered family therapy, Cassandra's parents were quick to point out that their son was not totally responsible for his actions because he suffered trauma prior to his adoption and has a mental illness. When given consequences, his behavior escalates. On the other hand, they believe that Cassandra is one hundred percent responsible and in control of all her choices, and they are determined she will live up to her potential.

Initially, Cassandra's parents couldn't see their daughter's point of view. But gradually, they understood that she was being overcorrected. They made significant adjustments, which decreased her resentment toward her parents and brother. Her parents stated, "In our defense, our son has been so out of control that we wanted to make sure Cassandra got the message that *any* type of behavior from her would be unacceptable." Through family counseling, Cassandra's parents also learned that mental illness or trauma does not excuse someone from the consequences of his actions. Eventually, with guidance from a therapist, Cassandra's parents began to impose logical and appropriate consequences for their son's behaviors.

Potential Strategies When New Behavior Management (Discipline) Techniques and/or House Rules or Rituals Are Changed

- *Develop family behavioral guidelines.* Give guidelines to each individual child, giving less structure and more choices to those who can appropriately and safely handle it.
- *Work with the child's support team.* Develop appropriate behavior management and problem-solving plans. The child's

support team can be a great resource when blending various behavior techniques or evaluating their effectiveness.

- *Include biological children as much as possible.* When creating or changing family rituals or house rules, include the other children. Kids enjoy opportunities to create household rules and usually develop consequences that are more creative than their parents'. Many families report that since their children developed the rules and consequences, they accept them without much grumbling.

Children May Believe Their Opinions and Feelings Don't Matter or They May Trivialize Their Own Needs and Struggles

Most parents try to include their biological children in the adoption excitement. When parents ask for their children's opinions, it is with the expectation and hope that they will invest in adding a member to the family.

> Guilty, shameful, and unworthy—that's what I felt, said Marianne, a thirty-two-year-old, married mother of four. My mother and father were pillars of the community, they were servers at church, and they adopted three kids. My brother and I were twelve and thirteen at the time of the first adoption. They adopted my brother and first sister when she was eleven and he was twelve, which made my two brothers the same age. That created conflicts right from the beginning.
>
> I was shocked when my parents said they wanted to adopt again. I was already feeling that my parents were so busy with the church and community work and with my brothers and sister that I wasn't getting the attention I needed.
>
> So when they asked what I thought about adopting another child, I told them how I felt. They basically told me how disappointed and ashamed they were by my attitude.
>
> When I was fourteen, they adopted another girl, Karen, who was a year older than me. We had problems from day one. Looking back on it, I guess it wasn't Karen's fault. I think my parents set us up to be enemies, because they asked me how I

felt about another adoption, and I thought they really cared. I thought they would listen to us kids and not go through with it.

I would get so angry at Karen whenever my parents paid attention to her or had to go to an appointment because of her "disability." She was in special education at school, so they had to go to meetings for her a lot. I'll give you one guess at who got left home to watch over the rest of them. I grew up secretly wishing that my older sister would disappear, and that made me feel even guiltier.

Often, parents point out their biological child's lack of disability in an effort to give perspective and to comfort their child. Unfortunately, this strategy may have the opposite effect. With limited life experience, children are developmentally incapable of accurately interpreting their parents' intent. The result may be that they trivialize their own needs and struggles.

I love my little sister, says nineteen-year-old Joy. She is amazing! My parents adopted her when she was three years old. We have always known that she would never be able to live on her own and eventually would have to be in a group home. Leila has Cerebral Palsy (CP) and is a bit slow to learn things. She's not mentally retarded, but learning new things is really hard for her. She has a great sense of humor and a can-do attitude.

I always felt bad that things were so hard for her. I have always learned things easily and am good at most things I try. When we were growing up, I never felt that I had any right to be upset when I had problems with my friends or my homework was hard. When I compared my problems to Leila's, they seemed trivial. .

I did try to talk to my parents about little problems, but they always seemed to compare mine to Leila's and said, "You think you have problems, look at Leila." When they said things like that, I felt guilty and angry. I know my problems were not as big as Leila's and she had to try really hard, but I still wish that my parents would have realized that even though it was easier for me to be a teenager than for my sister, the least they could have done was let me talk about my problems.

I was reluctant to push any issues because my parents always seemed to be so busy or sometimes overwhelmed by the care that Leila required. I really didn't think my feelings mattered to them because nothing in my life would ever be as serious as the struggles Leila faced every day.

Potential Strategies When Biological Children Feel Their Opinions Don't Matter

- *Develop relationships with all of the children.* Encourage open communication and freedom to express negative feelings or thoughts without fear of retribution or judgment. A parent's ability to tolerate their child's honest expressions of fear, guilt, anger, and disappointment is critical in helping a biological child process and adapt, not only to their newest sibling but also to the changes that have occurred.
- *Inform other children in the family about the decision to adopt.* Ask about their thoughts, feelings, and concerns. They need to know that their fears and concerns are a priority and will be addressed.
- *Realize that a biological child's problems or struggles are just as significant as the challenges faced by the child with special needs.* This recognition is critical to emotional wellness and the healthy development of self-esteem.[4]

Children May Become Invisible to Their Parents After a Special-Needs Adoption.
This potential impact is the easiest to miss and yet has some of the most severe consequences. Take a moment and consider family life without a special-needs child. Make a quick list of services, community supports or service providers that might be involved:

Church
Pediatrician
Dentist
Eye doctor
Classroom teacher
Music instructor
Sports coach

_____

_____

Now consider all the providers that become involved with a family when they have a child with special needs:

Church
Pediatrician
Dentist
Eye doctor
Classroom teacher
Bus driver
Neurologist
Podiatrist
Speech therapist
Occupational therapist
Developmental therapist
Physical therapist
Special Education teacher
Classroom aid
Social worker
Counselor
Birth parents
Birth siblings
Adoption worker
Lawyer
Probation officer
Geneticist
Tutors
Guidance counselor
Principal

Psychiatrist

Parent advocate

Depending on the needs of the child, it is easy to see that this list can quickly grow to include fifty or more professionals. All of these people will require appointments (don't forget drive time) and there still are only 168 hours in a week. Biological children often are the ones who "lose" their time so that their parents can accommodate the scheduling demands for the newest family member. For some families, the consequences can be very serious.

Brian is a fourteen-year-old, morbidly obese child, lying on the gurney in the emergency room. He makes no eye contact, is pale, and shows no emotions on his face. His biological parents look haggard, frightened, and anxious as they speak to the psychiatric evaluator. They explain that he had never done anything like this before. Brian had attempted suicide.

During a private interview, Brian revealed that ten years ago his family adopted Davie, a child with multiple learning disabilities and behavioral problems. Brian is the only biological child of his parents and, in his opinion, "The day my little brother moved in was the day I ceased to exist." Brian talked about all the "providers" who came to the house to "play" with his younger brother (speech, physical, and occupational therapists and social workers). These people, he recalls, brought all kinds of fun toys for his brother and spent hours of one-on-one time with him. His mother joined them for the sessions, too. Brian was left to play in his room or eat a snack at the table.

As his brother grew older, his school behavioral needs became the focus of the family—fights, suspensions, special education meetings, and so on. Davie also began behaving so badly in public that Brian's parents were unable to transport Brian to his school activities. Consequently, Brian dropped out of all activities and began staying home, playing computer games.

Brian was admitted to a psychiatric hospital for adolescents. During the family meeting, this information was revealed to his parents for the first time. They understandably were distraught and filled with guilt.

"I had no idea you felt this way," said his mother. "Davie had so many problems, and you didn't. I had to attend all the meetings and appointments. I never thought you had any problems. You were never abused or neglected, and you are so smart."

Brian was able to tell his parents how lonely he felt and how he was being teased at school for being overweight. He said that many times he approached his parents to tell them how he felt. They told him, "You should be thankful that you are normal and don't have problems like Davie" or "Can you give me a break here? I am exhausted, and your brother has sucked all my energy from me." Finally, Brian said that he didn't know what else to do, so he decided to end it all. "I figured that if I survived, I might finally get special attention from my parents and if I died . . . well, at least I didn't have to live like this anymore."

Four years later, at the family's last counseling session, Brian said, "I am excited that I am leaving for college next week, but I will really miss my parents. After I was in the hospital, things really changed at home. They both began spending time with my brother and me. It has never been equal. He still gets more, and that doesn't matter. I just needed to feel that I was part of the family and important too. It feels good that my parents notice me and are proud of my accomplishments."

Potential Parenting Strategies When a Child Feels Invisible

- *Attend school events, go shopping, or pursue a hobby with each child.* All children need undivided attention with each of their parents. Take advantage of respite services for the child with special needs. This enables you to focus completely on your other children, while providing the newest family member with a positive experience. If respite services are unavailable, some families exchange babysitting and provide childcare for each other when they have important events to attend. This type of community parenting reduces stress on families, both financially and socially.
- *Create an atmosphere where children feel free to communicate.* Initiate conversations. Routine communication often solves problems before they become a crisis.
- *Ensure that biological children's activities or abilities are not restricted.* Some children internalize their sibling's difficulties or challenges and inhibit their own success or involvement as a way to display their solidarity or empathy.[5] Sometimes the time and energy required to keep up with their child's special needs interferes with parents' ability to focus on their biological children.[6]

Quick Reference:

Key Point 1:
In an "ideal world," parents would have adequate training, support, and information regarding their newest family member. Permanent children also need their own support network.

Key Point 2:
Biological children need their parents to be open to hearing the "the good, the bad, and the ugly" when trying to resolve adoption difficulties.

Key Point 3:
Creating a home atmosphere that allows all children to express the joys — as well as trials and tribulations — is in itself a powerful preventative intervention.

Key Point 4:
Adults who are confident and convey to their children that they are in control of the household allow biological children to stay out of the caretaking role. When parents become visibly overwhelmed, their biological children feel the need to step in and make things easier.

Key Point 5:
Seeking your biological child's input is especially important when implementing new household rules or changing family traditions to accommodate a new sibling's needs.

Key Point 6:
Biological children need to feel that they have not been forgotten, replaced, or become unimportant in their parents' eyes.

DISCUSSION QUESTIONS

1. How can I best prepare my biological children for adoption?

2. What behaviors might my biological children struggle with? What behaviors might cause my child to be embarrassed? Angry? Withdraw?

3. How can I convey my openness to listen to my child's "negative" thoughts or emotions?

4. What resources are available in my area to support my children before and after the adoption?

5. How will I address the issues of added appointments, exhaustion, and frustration? How will I address the issue of conflicting appointments/activities?

6. What are my expectations for my biological children? Are they role models? Extra helpers? Disciplinarians?

7. Review each biological child's story from this chapter and discuss the following questions:

   a. What preventative steps could the parents have taken?
   b. What positive action steps did the parents take to resolve the issue?

PART THREE:

Inside the Crisis of Adoption Breakdown

There is perhaps nothing as painful as the crumbling of a dream. Happiness and joy become foreign words. Hope becomes elusive. Any resemblance to the family we dreamed of feels like sand slipping through our fingers. Our attempts to give the pain meaning seem futile. We experience ourselves as different people, and sometimes we don't like what we have become.

A powerful biblical message speaks to those moments of utter confusion and despair:

"I'll show up and take care of you as I promised . . . I know what I'm doing. I have it all planned out—plans to take care of you, not abandon you, plans to give you the future you hope for" (Jeremiah 29:11, MSG).

When all hope is gone, give God time. He can and does make a way.

WHAT'S AHEAD:

Chapter Seven: Confronting the Crisis of Adoption Breakdown
Chapter Eight: Managing the Crisis of Adoption Breakdown

Confronting the Crisis of Adoption Breakdown

By Betsy Keefer Smalley, LSW

"The typical crisis and transition periods (such as adolescence) that all families face can be especially difficult for adoptive families, because they must also address specific adoption-related issues."

—Child Welfare Information Gateway[1]

Jason's birth parents both struggled with depression. Unfortunately, the battle with depression was lost when they each committed suicide. Jason was only eight when his father died, and he was eleven when his mother took her life. Jason was the youngest child in the family, with two young adult sisters. After his mother's suicide, Jason was placed with the oldest sister. She was unable to manage Jason's depression, anger, and feelings of abandonment created by his parents' suicides. Shockingly, his other adult sister also committed suicide.

Jason entered the child welfare system and, at age fourteen, was placed for adoption with a childless couple. These optimistic young parents felt confident in their ability to provide Jason with a nurturing and stable home. They were prepared for problems, but they didn't expect the problems to escalate as time went by.

Following a few relatively quiet months after placement, Jason began to run away, steal from his adoptive parents, and constantly battle for control. His parents felt dismayed that Jason's behavior seemed to get worse instead of better, and they began to wonder what they were doing wrong.

After two years, Jason threatened to kill himself, and his parents were terrified that he would follow the family pattern of suicide. They began to consider terminating the adoption to end the anxiety of managing Jason's behaviors and preventing his suicide "on their watch."

Children entering foster care and adoptive homes in the twenty-first century look very different from the foster and adopted children of a generation earlier. Prior to the seventies, most adopted children were newborns placed voluntarily by birth parents in a confidential or closed adoption.

According to the Adoption and Foster Care Analysis and Reporting System (AFCARS), the number of children entering adoptive homes from the foster care system has been steadily climbing, while infants being placed in voluntary adoptions are declining. The average age of children adopted from foster care in 2003 was 7.0 years, and the median age was 6.1 years. Of the children adopted from the foster care system, 87 percent qualified for an adoption subsidy for children with special needs.[2]

2003/Adoption and Foster Care Analysis and Reporting System

Average age of children adopted from foster care	7.0 years
Median age of children adopted from foster care	6.1 years
Percentage of children adopted from foster care who qualified for adoption subsidy as a child with special needs	87%

Many of the parents accepting these twenty-first century foster and adopted children into their lives have been prepared, like Jason's parents, to expect some adjustment time. They may have expected that the child's attachment issues, ambivalence, unrealistic expectations, and difficulties with trust might be problems that could be "erased" or certainly reduced, with patience and love.

Sometimes, these giving parents are surprised that problems might escalate after placement. The child may be "testing the waters" to see if commitments made by new parents will be honored.

There are two types of family relationship created by commitment rather than biology: marriage and adoption. Statistics seem to tell us adoption is much more stable and "successful" for participants than marriage, which is the more common form of commitment-based family relationship. Relatively few adoptions result in a "disrupted" or terminated placement, while about half of marriages in the United States end in divorce. Only 1 percent of infant placements and about 5–26 percent of children placed for adoption from the foster care system disrupt prior to the adoption finalization.[3] (This percentage varies, depending on factors including age at placement, number and type of special needs, and time since separation from the birth family.) Though adoption tends to be far more stable than marriage, there are certainly challenges to the permanence of the commitments, and some families struggle to maintain the family units they have created through adoption, both before and after the adoption is finalized.

There is increasing concern that disruption rates will rise as more older, traumatized children are adopted from the foster care system. In 1971, the adoption disruption rate in the United States was estimated at 2.8 percent (Kadushin and Seidl). In 1987, almost two decades later, Barth and Berry estimated that the rate had risen to between 7 percent and 47 percent.[4] About 3–6 percent of adoptions from the foster care system dissolve following finalization.[5] It certainly is not easy to accept another person with a different history, culture, and temperament into your intimate life circle. In 2007, Atkinson and Gonet reported that families asking for post-adoption services were facing the following challenges:[6]

Types of Problems	Percentage of Families Reporting Problems (%)
Behavior	60
Diagnosed conditions	54
School-related issues	47
Adoption issues	38
Attachment issues	27
School adjustment	8

Denise Goodman, in her 1993 doctoral dissertation *Here Today, Gone Tomorrow,* states that adoptees were more likely to be placed in substitute care (foster care, group homes, or residential treatment), constituting 10.8 percent of the population in child care facilities in Ohio at that time, while approximately 1–2 percent of the total population is adopted.[7] These studies appear to indicate that adopted children have an increased risk of challenges that can pose problems for the adjustment of the child and the family into which the child has been adopted.

What does it look like when adoptive families are in crisis? Crisis occurs when individuals and families experience an upset in the equilibrium, or state of balance, in their lives. They struggle to return to a state of calm. Three factors determine whether an individual or family system will experience crisis:

1. Exposure to unmanageable stress

2. Lack of resources to cope with the stress

3. An inaccurate perception of the stressful situation[8]

Adoptive parents are vulnerable to all three of these factors, potentially leading families into crisis. First, the stress involved in nurturing a traumatized child is very high, and it is definitely not short-term. The greater the degree of change experienced by an individual or family, the greater the stress. A healthy family system experiences an exceptionally high degree of change when adding a child with a history of complex trauma.

Parents' capacity to cope with this change or stress may be inadequate to restore equilibrium. The preparation many adoptive parents (and the children they adopt) receive is often inadequate to prepare them for the challenges they will face.

Research repeatedly has found that inadequate training and preparation of prospective adoptive parents are predictors of adoption crisis and disruption (McRoy, 1999; Nelson, 1985; Partridge, Hornby, and McDonald, 1986). Further, supportive, post-adoption services for families are noticeably lacking. This is another predictor of adoption crisis and disruption (Goodman, 1993; Barth et al. 1986). See Appendix Two at the back of the book for more information on post-adoption support resources.

Many adoptive parents misunderstand the child's ability to assimilate into a family where they will not be victimized, abandoned, hurt, or rejected. Poorly prepared adoptive parents may assume that love and stability will erase the impact of the child's complex trauma. If this does not happen, they assume their love or parenting skills must somehow be defective or inadequate.

Further, adoptive parents sometimes place pressure on themselves to form an instant bond with the adopted child. While some new adoptive parents find it easy to "claim" the child as their own early in the relationship, many parents of older children are dismayed to find they don't feel attached to the child, as they expected they would.

> Post-adoption depression never crossed my mind. I didn't know that it was quite common among adoptive mothers of older, post-institutionalized children. The reasons vary. But surely it is in part because we are hardwired to attach to wide-eyed, helpless babies. A fit-throwing, non-English speaking, snarling Bulgarian four-year-old does not, at first glimpse, invite adoration. Jesse was not having "attachment" issues, as one would fear might happen in older-child adoption. But I was.[9]

Adoptive families are at high risk for prolonged periods of crisis. If the crisis continues for some time without relief, the adoptive family may conclude that the only way to reestablish equilibrium is to remove the child from the family, either on a temporary or permanent basis. Let's explore in more depth what fuels adoption-related crisis, so we can learn how to prevent or mitigate it. We will look at the feelings experienced by many adoptive parents of traumatized children, the impact of these feelings on their relationships, and common patterns of behavior displayed by families in crisis.

Emotions on the Route to Adoption Breakdown

When an adoptive relationship breaks down, it is devastating for everyone touched by it. It is important to understand that adoption breakdown is a journey through a series of emotions. These emotions are connected to concrete events, but it is the *emotions*, not the events, that demarcate the stages of adoption disruption.[10]

In her book *Our Son, a Stranger*, Dr. Marie Adams writes of her family's own painful journey through adoption breakdown. Dr. Adams and her husband adopted a 2½-year-old boy. For the first years of his life, things were okay in the family. As he grew older, his negative behaviors escalated. By the time he was an adolescent, he had a serious drug problem and was a runaway. At age twenty-one, their son died following an alcohol-related accident.

She describes a significant time, a disruptive/breakdown event, when everything changed and the dream they had for their son died.

It was a moment in time, after years of doing everything they could for their adopted son, when they faced the truth that he would never be the child they had wished for. He would never be an integral part of the family.

Adams describes the emotional journey to that disruptive breakdown event so parents will recognize these emotions, face and deal with them, and remain emotionally healthy.

Denial

Parents ignore early predictions, or unconsciously overlook the severity and duration of the difficulties the child experiences in school, neighborhood, and family. "Denial buys time," says Adams. "It allows the mind to prepare for the challenges and changes that inevitably lie ahead."[11]

Frustration and Anger

These emotions well up when one's efforts are thwarted, when one's presence is resented, when one's opinions and values are ridiculed, when one's energies are exasperated. Adams writes, "Anger [for the adoptive parents] was not a singular emotion, but was embodied in feelings of rejection, helplessness, fear, and confusion, and it was a reaction to the loneliness and isolation they experienced."[12] In her research, Adams found that other adoptive families facing adoption breakdown were angry about many things:

- Their child's self-destructive behavior and wasted potential
- The child's effect on the rest of the family members and their child's insensitivity toward the health and happiness of their siblings
- Negative changes within themselves or their spouse
- Feelings of inadequacy and failure
- Feelings of helplessness and rejection
- Insensitivity and judgmental attitudes of social workers and other professionals
- Deep feelings of betrayal by those professionals who should have been supportive

Shame and Guilt

Shame and guilt arise from a sense that the adoptive parents are failing the mission.

Rick and Sandy enjoyed parenting their three biological daughters. Now that the girls were in their late teens, they both felt they weren't finished with parenting, so they decided to adopt. Cassie entered their home at age ten with a difficult past of severe neglect and multiple foster placements.

The early days of the relationship gave Rick and Sandy a sense of confidence that what they were doing was working well . . . until the honeymoon was over. Sandy commented, "Everything we tried with Cassie didn't work. How we parented our other children just didn't work for her. Each day became more intense than the previous day. I lost all sense of competency as a parent. I felt such guilt, shame, and embarrassment. We were failing the mission."

Many parents are motivated to adopt because:

1. They want to parent and are unable to have children by birth.

2. They have an altruistic desire to help a child in need of a family.

3. They are experienced parents and are not finished parenting.

They see adoption as a way to satisfy certain needs—essentially the very human desire to nurture another vulnerable person, to be needed. Most adoptive parents go to great lengths to become parents (interviews, paperwork, fees, training, research, perhaps even intercontinental travel) and have high hopes for their experience of nurturing a child in need.

When years of effort and nurture are met with anger, rejection, or withdrawal from a traumatized child, many parents assume they have failed at parenting. They may even imagine infertility was a sort of omen that they were not destined to be parents.

Many parents take responsibility for the child's inability to respond to their nurture. They may have moments when they "snap" and are less than patient in relating to the child. They may wonder if they have really loved the child as deeply as a child who was, or might have been, born into the family. The sense of mission failure, shame, and guilt can be overwhelming to adoptive parents who expected their nurture would be welcomed and embraced by a needy child.

Nancy Milliken, MSW, encouraged an adoptive parent who felt a keen sense of failure in her mission to nurture a child. "The disability is in the receiver," she explained, "not in the giver." Yet our culture inappropriately judges the worth of parents by the behavior and adjustment of their children, rather than the behavior and nurturing of the parents.

Many adoptive parents who attempt to nurture a traumatized child may feel guilty when they experience anger and resentment about the child's lack of appreciation for all that they're doing. "In addition to the stress of attempting to control their child's behavior, parents feel enormous guilt and shame," explains attachment specialist, Dr. Gregory Keck. "They intended to adopt a hurt child and nurture him into a whole person. Instead, they are less parents than jailers, less nurturing than controlling, less accepting than rejecting, less loving than hating. What kind of monsters, they wonder, could feel such anger toward a child? Relatives, coworkers, friends, and some professionals often add to these feelings. Into this mix, add a child who can be completely charming and engaging to all outsiders, and it is small wonder these parents feel insane."[13]

If parents have assumed responsibility for the child's difficult adjustment to the family, their guilt intensifies. Unfortunately, adoptive parents often receive a great deal of support in feeling guilty from family therapists who do not understand adoption dynamics, from school personnel, extended family members or community members. Often these professionals or friends of the family do not observe the child's difficult behaviors; these outbursts are reserved for the adoptive parents, particularly the mother.

Individuals who attempt to "support" the adoptive family may, in fact, sabotage the family by laying blame on the adoptive parents for the child's difficulties. This is especially true when the adopted child has entered the adoptive family at a young age. Even though the infant may have experienced devastating separation trauma during his first several months of life, most people assume that these experiences don't matter because the child has no conscious memory of them. In reality, the younger the child is when he or she experiences trauma, the more devastating the impact on the child.

Adoptive parents cannot be expected to be superhuman, but they may feel guilty for things said or done in anger during explosive moments with an angry child. After all, the typical reaction to anger is more anger, and breaking this cycle can be exceedingly difficult.

Guilt can be expected if parents begin to resent the child or even fantasize about life without him in the family, if they begin to think, "How could I renege on my commitment to this needy child?"

Grief

Grief is about loss. For adoptive parents, Adams writes, "parents grieved for the child who might have been, or who was supposed to have been. That child was not going to be there in the way that parents expected, needed, or wanted."[14] One adoptive family said, "If we had our *own* child, we wouldn't have these problems." While this may or may not be true, the intense emotion associated with this disappointment over the loss of the dream child was very real.

Another part of the grieving process is facing the loss of one's self as a successful parent. Adoptive parents who find themselves in this stage of adoption breakdown speak of the loss of all sense of competency; they feel incredibly inadequate. They failed to achieve what they had hoped for. They possess an utter sense of hopelessness and helplessness as they face the reality that there was nothing more they could do to change the course of events for their child. "It was like I had to grieve the death of a child, but in reality, he was still living," says one adoptive father.

When Coping Fails: Stages of Disruption

When adoption-related crisis begins to build, there are a number of predictable patterns of behavior on the part of adoptive parents and the child. Of course, family members have struggled with their own emotional responses and challenging behaviors for some time, and they have relied on tried-and-true support systems to help relieve the family distress.

Unfortunately, adoptive families coping with overwhelming stress find that strategies that have worked in the past may prove ineffective now. For example, most parents in two-parent homes rely on one another for "tag team" parenting, sharing the responsibility of discipline, caring for sick children, carpools, and so forth. In an adoptive family in crisis, this option may not be viable because of an uneven motivation about the child's adoption or the child's adamant rejection of one of the parents.

When traditionally helpful coping strategies fail, parents may feel more and more out of control. The child often becomes the "identified problem" in the family. Parents (as well as others in the family) may begin to seek therapy for the child, or issue ultimatums to the child about his behavior. They may say something like, "If you do that one more time, you cannot be part of this family." If the situation escalates, temporary placement of the child outside the home may occur, or the parents may even consider termination of the adoption as the only recourse.

Researchers in the field of adoption have identified several steps in escalation that families commonly experience in prolonged crisis with their adopted child.[15] Understanding these family dynamics can give parents early warning signs within their own relationships. Once those signs are recognized, the family can seek services and support to stabilize the relationship.

The stages families experience as they spiral toward a disruption in a foster or adoptive placement are:

Step One: Honeymoon

Adoptive families typically experience pleasure and excitement at the onset of the adoption journey. Each member enters the relationship with high hopes and high expectations. This phase may last several months or, in some cases, many years if no major crisis has affected the family.

Step Two: Diminishing Pleasures

The atmosphere in the home begins to change. Adoptive parents begin to feel tensions in their interactions with the child. What used to be cute is now irritating and frustrating. The family remains hopeful that "this is just a phase." Often at this stage, adoptive parents do not share their concerns with anyone outside the family, thinking this phase will soon pass.

Step Three: The Child Is the Problem

The relationship with the child continues to deteriorate. Every negative thing the child does or says—from tantrums to misbehavior—becomes intolerable. The interactions continue to spiral downward. The child senses the tensions, which increases his anxiety, and this only serves to increase his negative behavior. The parents perceive the child is rejecting them and they overreact to even minor problems.

Step Four: Going Public

The problems within the family soon begin to impact the family's public life. The child's negative behaviors are no longer confined to the home, but are witnessed by family, friends, the school, and so on. Frustration and embarrassment often lead the family to turn to others for sympathy with a long list of the child's problems. Supportive people offer advice, which may line up with the family's view that the child is the problem and subconsciously feed the family's need to distance themselves from the child.

Step Five: The Turning Point

The family continues to crumble. The child is involved in a "critical incident"—[5]stealing, sexually acting out, truancy—which the parents long expected. The child has crossed the line, and the parents feel there is no hope for a healthy relationship. The family usually continues to live together, but with impenetrable walls of hurt, anger, and rejection blocking future happiness. No one has any emotional energy to regain healthy family life. Unrelenting conflict creates a barrier to any real relationships or intimacy. In some cases, adoption dissolution (termination of the finalized adoption) is inevitable.

Step Six: The Deadline or Ultimatum

Sometimes, the family's problems culminate in a crisis. The adoptive parents establish a deadline for the child's problems or behavior to drastically improve, or the child must leave. Often, these demands are unreasonable, such as demanding that clothing never be left on the floor or that the child never become angry or misbehave in any way.

Step Seven: The Final Crisis Ends the Adoptive Relationship

Jessica sat in the lobby of the girls' group home, waiting for her caseworker. She was coming there to live. She had been adopted as a three-year-old but now was back in foster care. "My parents told me if I came in late one more time, I would have to leave. I was late last night and here I sit today. In good times, my parents introduced me as their daughter. When we had a problem or fight, I became their adopted daughter."

The day comes when whatever demand made upon the child fails to be met. The final crisis erupts within the family. Even a minor incident can become "the last straw." The family decides to have the child permanently removed from the home, often immediately. Everyone affected by the dissolution feels considerable pain: the child feels angry, confused, and rejected and parents feel angry, guilty, and filled with grief.

Terry and Marie had two adopted children: a medically fragile daughter, Sydney, age eight, who was confined to a wheel chair; and a healthy, preadolescent son named Jeremy. Their daughter had joined the family at birth, and their son was adopted at age seven. Prior to his adoption, Jeremy experienced several years of sexual abuse by his caregiver. Jeremy's adjustment had been very difficult, even for these patient and nurturing parents. There were challenges with bed-wetting, destructiveness, constant control battles, cruelty toward family pets, and even some episodes of fire-setting.

Terry and Marie remained steadfast in their commitment to parenting Jeremy until a critical episode occurred in the family.

Five years after they adopted Jeremy, Terry and Marie were dismayed to learn from Sydney that Jeremy had been sexually abusing her. They felt the only way they could protect their vulnerable daughter from abuse was to place Jeremy outside the home. This was an agonizing decision for the adoptive parents, and, was yet another confirmation for Jeremy that adults could not be trusted.

The heavy toll of such a breakdown on both the child and the adoptive family can be crippling for all family members. Yet, certainly, adoption breakdown is not inevitable after the adoption of a wounded child. How can such breakdown be prevented? What are some strategies that can help parents recognize the danger signs early and act to prevent an adoption disruption? We'll explore preventive strategies in the following chapter.

Quick Reference

Key Point 1
What does it look like when adoptive families are in crisis? Initial crisis is experienced when individuals and families experience an upset in the equilibrium, or state of balance, in their lives. Both individuals and families struggle to return to a state of calm. If individuals or families are unable to reestablish equilibrium, another crisis may result. Three factors determine whether an individual or family system will experience crisis:

1. Exposure to unmanageable stress

2. Lack of resources to cope with the stress

3. An inaccurate perception of the stressful situation

Key Point 2
Adoption breakdown is a journey through a series of emotions. Families facing adoption breakdown may experience:

*   Denial
*   Frustration and anger

- Shame and guilt
- Grief

Key Point 3

When adoption-related crisis begins to build, there are a number of predictable patterns of behavior on the part of adoptive parents and the child. The stages of adoption breakdown are:

- Honeymoon
- Diminishing pleasures
- The child is the problem
- Going public
- The turning point
- The deadline or ultimatum
- The final crisis

Discussion Questions

1. What stressors are you experiencing with your child?

2. What other stressors are present in your life? In your family?

3. How are you coping with the stress you are experiencing?

4. How is your spouse coping?

5. What support can you provide for your spouse in coping with his or her stressors?

6. How do you ask your spouse to support your coping efforts?

7. What successes have you achieved in parenting your child since his placement?

8. How have you grown as a person since the adoption? How have you grown as a parent?

Chapter Eight

Managing the Crisis of Adoption Breakdown

By Betsy Keefer Smalley, LSW

"Hurt children are often so frightened by intimacy, they will go any lengths to avoid it. They are afraid to love people because people in their past, those who should have loved and protected them, hurt and abused them. Their deep assump tion is that their adoptive parents, like everyone in their past, will hurt and leave them."

—Greg Keck and Regina Kupecky

Molly was six years old when she joined her adoptive family, an infertile couple with no other children. Molly's adjustment had been somewhat bumpy, with virtually no honeymoon, but her adoptive parents were beginning to see signs of progress. At age ten, following years of splitting (see definition of splitting in chapter five), Molly began to display signs of attachment to her adoptive mother, Claire. She snuggled with her mother to read books and began to share more about her days at school.

One day, Claire called a post-adoption counselor because she was furious with her daughter. The school principal had just called to inform her that Molly would be suspended from riding the school bus for two weeks, due to disruptive behavior on the bus. Claire would be expected to drive Molly to school every morning for two weeks and pick her up after school. The mother was angry that she was paying the consequence for her daughter's misbehavior. She commented to her post adoption counselor, "The thing that makes me so angry about this whole situation is that things were going so much better. In fact, just before she left for school, we had a very special moment. Molly gave me a Mother's Day card she had made for me the day before in school."

The attention Molly had given her adoptive mother served as a trigger: It made Molly feel disloyal to her birth mother. Molly felt that it was "not fair" for her adoptive mother to receive recognition in place of her "real" mother. Molly felt like a bad, disloyal child. Her behavior on the school bus shortly after this display of affection reflected her feelings of worthlessness.

Common Triggers for Adoption-Related Crisis

While the stage may be set for crisis by the feelings and dynamics described in the last chapter, many times an event or critical incident occurs which "triggers" a reaction in the child or the adoptive family. The trigger could be a sound (police or fire sirens), a smell (cigarette smoke, particular foods cooking), or even changing seasons (anniversaries of past losses). Other critical incidents or triggers may be more predictable, and many can be anticipated. Some of the more common triggers are:

Birthdays

Many adopted children and adults share that they become preoccupied with thoughts of the birth family as their birthday approaches. They wonder if the birth family (particularly the birth mother) remembers them, if birth family members are safe and well, and if the birth family remembers the birthday. For some adoptees, the birthday may also be the anniversary of the separation from the birth family.

Of all of the triggers experienced by children separated from their birth families, the child's birthday may be the most predictable. Parents may notice that the child becomes moody two to three weeks prior to his birthday. He may withdraw from those around him. He may increase or escalate into anger as the actual birthday approaches.

He may have explosive reactions to family celebrations or other birthday events. Parents may diffuse this trigger in one or more of the following ways:

- Talk with the child three weeks prior to his birthday about his feelings and questions about his birth family. For example, "Now that you are a year older and can understand more, you may want to ask more questions about your birth family. Is there a question I can answer for you?" Or "I always think of your birth mother when it gets close to your birthday. Do you wonder about her too?"

- Do not plan elaborate parties or celebrations for the child's birthday if he has demonstrated an inability to tolerate this level of family involvement in the past. Remember that his birthday may be generating grief, and he may not feel like having a party.

- Encourage the child to develop a journal of letters that he writes every year just before his birthday to a birth family member, sharing in the letter what he is like at this age. Keep this journal with a picture of the child at each age as a history of the child's life that may or may not be shared with the birth family at some point in the future. Assure the child that the birth family very much wants the child to be successful and happy in life, and they would be proud of the person he is becoming.

- Update the child's life book with events that have occurred during the past year.

Mother's Day

Many adopted children struggle with issues of divided loyalties to birth and adoptive mothers as Mother's Day approaches. Strategies to "de-fuse" this trigger include:

- Help the child make a Mother's Day card for the birth mother. In an open adoption, the cards can be shared. If contact with the birth mother is not an option, the cards can be kept in a special album.

- Ensure that the child understands he does not have to stop thinking about or loving the birth mother after adoption. The child can love multiple people, including mothers, at the same time. He does not have to choose. In the same way that mothers can love more than one child, children can love more than one mother, all at the same time. Love felt for one person does not diminish love felt for another person.

- Understand that a child who does not have a conscious memory of a birth mother will still have a strong sense of loyalty to the psychological presence of the birth mother.

A bond to an idealized, fantasy birth mother may be even stronger than a relationship with a real person.

- Support and empathize with the child's grief for a lost mother. Mother's Day is a difficult day for any person who has lost a mother figure.

Moving

In our highly mobile culture, families often move between neighborhoods, communities, or even regions. Some children view these moves as adventures or challenges, and some are nervous about change. After all, the nature of stress is change, involving something unknown or unexpected. For children who have experienced traumatic moves and separations, moves can be triggers for crisis. They may experience irrational fears of being left behind or abandoned when the family moves, or the children may intensely grieve for lost relationships with friends, neighbors, or teachers as a result of the move. Some strategies to address this trigger include:

- Try to create an opportunity for the child to see where he is moving. Fear of the unknown is very threatening, but the known is less threatening.
- Allow the child to make as many choices and have as much control in the move as possible. Perhaps he can choose the paint color for his new bedroom, assist the family in making a list of things important to him about the new community or new house, or pack his own belongings to be sure they will not be lost to him.
- Encourage connections to the past so that losses are not complete. Plan opportunities for the child to visit his old friends and home following the move. Continuity is important, and this child has experienced serious, perhaps multiple, breaks in the continuity of his life.
- Try to help the child identify what his most significant attachments are in the old home. Remember that attachments are not always to people. Pets are an important part of a child's attachments, and pets should accompany the family to the new home unless absolutely impossible. If the child has a

strong attachment to a swing set the family has intended to leave behind, it may be worth the expense to move it.

Transition to a New School

As a child moves to a new school, even a planned move within the same school system from one level to another (elementary school transition to middle school), the child's anxiety about impermanence and change may be triggered. Some strategies to address this trigger include:

- Visit the new school prior to beginning classes to meet teachers or other key support people.
- Practice travel to and from the new school to reduce anxiety about becoming lost.
- Find a "buddy" or mentor, a peer who will offer support and information to the student changing schools.
- Offer empathy, not judgment, dismissal, or ridicule, to an anxious child.
- Assure that at least one parent is available to emotionally support the child as soon as he comes home at the end of the school day.

Illness of a Parent

Children who have been permanently separated from birth parents may become panicky when their adoptive parents become ill. Young children may have interpreted substance abuse or mental health issues in their birth parents as "illness." If so, they may believe their adoptive parents will cease to nurture and protect them if they become ill. Some strategies to address this trigger include:

- Allow the child to visit a parent in the hospital.
- Communicate with the child in a developmentally appropriate way (perhaps using play or puppets) about a parent's illness or hospital stay.
- Clarify that the ill parent will make necessary arrangements to assure the child's care while the parent is ill; for example, "Grandma will take care of you until I am better."

- If the prognosis is uncertain, be honest about this with the child or youth. Don't make promises or assurances that cannot be honored.

Death of a Grandparent

The loss of a grandparent is difficult for most children, but a child who is grieving other losses may experience an intensely painful grief response. Some strategies to address this trigger include:

- Allow the child to have closure and receive a "good-bye" blessing from the grandparent, if possible.
- Ensure the child has accurate information about why the grandparent has died.
- Empathize with feelings of loss.
- Assure the child that other family members will continue to nurture him, and they are safe and well.
- Help the child write a letter, draw a picture, compose music or poetry that commemorates the importance of the relationship.
- Frame a picture of the child with the grandparent for his room, or help child make a collage of pictures.

Death of a Pet

Again, the loss of a pet may trigger grief related to earlier losses. Some strategies to help a child deal with the loss of a pet include:

- Empathize with feelings of loss.
- Have a "good-bye" ceremony or funeral to help the child with closure.
- Frame a picture of the child with the pet for his room.

Graduation from High School

Graduation from high school signifies another transition to an unknown situation. This can be potentially threatening to a youth who has faced terrifying changes during unknown situations in his history. Some adopted youth believe that the adoption lasts only for the duration of childhood; that they will no longer be part of the adoptive family once they graduate from high school. Foster youth are painfully aware that their placement will end when they graduate from high school and must emancipate. Some adopted or foster youth may even sabotage emancipation by failing to complete graduation requirements. Some strategies to address this trigger include:

- Assure the youth that adoption does not end with adulthood; he will always be your son.
- Encourage a slow process of emancipation (living at home and going to local college) if the youth appears anxious.
- Understand that many adolescent adoptees make sweeping statements about their plan to move far away from the adoptive family (or plan to return to the birth family) following graduation. Learn that these are expressions of anxiety about emancipation. Assure the youth that his place within the adoptive family will remain secure after his graduation or emancipation.

Divorce of Adoptive Parents

Divorce signifies another loss of a parent. Many children of divorce believe that they have been the cause of the family break-up. A child who has lost one or more family members already may be convinced that he is responsible for the tension between his parents. Some strategies to address this trigger include:

- Provide information about the separation that is developmentally appropriate.
- Provide counseling for children of divorce with a therapist who is sensitive to adoption issues.
- Ensure the child understands he is not responsible for the loss of another parent; continue to work with this issue over time.
- Assure that the child continues to be "co-parented" even though adoptive parents are unable to live together.

Holidays

Any person who has experienced a loss feels painful memories about earlier holidays spent with a lost loved one. Some foster and adopted children may have experienced traumatic moves during the holidays, and these children will experience "anniversary reactions" of grief, perhaps including anger or depression, during the holiday season. Some strategies to manage the holidays include:

- Keep expectations for holiday celebrations to a minimum.
- Allow the child to choose the level of family connectedness he is ready to accept.
- Incorporate traditions the child remembers from earlier attachments or cultures.
- Select (or let the child create) a special ornament or memento to commemorate the importance of the birth family in the child's life.
- Empathize, don't criticize.

School Assignments

Sometimes teachers unwittingly trigger adoption issues by creating assignments related to family trees, personal histories, baby pictures, and so forth. These assignments can resurrect feelings of being different, anger about lack of information regarding personal history, or divided loyalties about which family to include. Strategies to cope with these types of assignments include:

- Provide education to school personnel about the impact of family tree/history and other assignments on adopted children.
- Assist the child in completing assignments in creative ways to acknowledge and celebrate his history honestly. For example, you might help him display his birth family in the roots of the family tree and the adoptive family in the branches.

The Child's Perspective

Many children with histories including abuse, neglect, or repeated separations believe they have caused the separations that have occurred in their lives. They may experience shame and guilt over imagined shortcomings that have resulted in rejection or abandonment from adult caregivers in the past. They assume it will be a matter of time until these shortcomings are discovered by the adoptive family, and they will be forced to leave yet another family.

Not surprisingly, many children who live with the constant dread of abandonment wish to take control of this perceived rejection by creating a family crisis, resulting in their eviction from the home. They essentially want to be in charge of the end of the family relationship. They want to abandon the family before they can be abandoned themselves. As overwhelmed parents sometimes issue ultimatums about rejections they do not want, children who are very afraid of rejection may assure parents they never wanted to be part of the adoptive family, that they hate members of the adoptive family, or that they will move far away as soon as they are eighteen and never return. They think, *"I will hurt you before you can hurt me."* Some of the things children say in these explosive exchanges with parents need to be "translated." What is said is not what is meant:

What Is Said	What Is Meant
You're not my real mother! You can't tell me what to do!	*Are you going to keep me? Are you really my parents?*
I hate you! I wish you had never adopted me!	*Do I really belong in this family?*
I want to find my birth mother and move in with her.	*I need to know more about my birth family. I have questions that are not being answered.*
I want to go to school as far away from you as I possibly can get!	*I am afraid to go away to school.*
When I am grown up, I am going to move far away and never see you again.	*Is the adoption over when I am grown up? Will I still be part of the family?*

When adoptive parents hear these angry outbursts, of course, they may react with hurt feelings, fear of losing the child they worked so hard to adopt, and anger at the child's rejection. Parents must retrain themselves to hear and feel the pain and fear hidden by the child's angry words.

Sometimes adopted children have reunion fantasies, believing that they will be returned to the birth family or to a beloved foster family if they are ejected from the adoptive family. They may even perceive they have been taken from the birth family *by the adoptive parents*, and the children may harbor resentment or anger toward the adoptive parents for the assumed "kidnapping."

In either case, much of the child's difficulty is related to an inaccurate perception of the situation in his life leading to his adoption, which is one of the three factors leading to crisis. The crisis for the child is almost always displayed through difficult behaviors—the language of children in pain. The following are challenging behaviors that adopted children may display as the crisis begins to spiral out of control:

- Destructiveness toward property
- Swearing
- Lying
- Stealing
- Aggressive behavior toward others
- Running away
- Control battles/resisting authority
- Substance abuse
- Food hoarding
- Sexualized behaviors

The Parents' Perspective

Adoptive parents may find that mental health or school professionals are not competent in addressing issues of adopted children or adoptive families. They may feel "blamed" for the children's difficulties and isolate themselves, rather than connecting with helpers or other adoptive families who understand the dynamics of their families.

Some adoptive parents may not feel they are "entitled" to be the parent of the child. That is, they may not feel they are the "real" parent; in fact, the child may be hurling this very accusation at the parent as a tool for manipulation. Unentitled adoptive parents often relinquish their power to be the authority in the home. In other words, they may function as tentative parents, fearful of, or threatened by, any or all of the following:

- Another angry outburst or confrontation with the child
- The real or psychological presence of the birth parent in the child's life
- Concern that the adopted child will feel he is not loved as much as birth children are (or would have been) loved

While some parents are tentative, they may be raising children who may need more guidance than most. This can be a disastrous combination, propelling many adoptive families toward crisis, particularly during the child's adolescence.

Survival Skills for Adoptive Parents

So how can adoptive parents cope with the challenges of parenting their children? Can crisis be prevented completely? Probably not, but parents can keep stress at a manageable level and increase their capacity to cope with that stress by employing some of the following suggestions:

- *Acknowledge the child's grief and let the child understand your losses.* Sometimes, parents believe they may trigger the child's grief if it is brought out in the open for discussion. However, the only way "out" of grief is "through." The child needs a safe environment in which to grieve his losses, and one of the most significant gifts an adoptive or foster parent can give a child is support to progress through the stages of grieving: denial, anger, bargaining, depression, and resolution.

- *Network with other adoptive families to avoid isolation.* Families who have not had personal experience with adoption may lack understanding about some of the feelings and challenges normally experienced by adoptive families. Many adoptive parents react to negative judgments of friends, church members, professionals, and even extended family, by withdrawing from social supports. It is essential to replace these supports with connections to other adoptive families who understand the dynamics and stages of adoptive family life.

- *Don't overreact to problems.* Not all problematic behaviors or feelings are related to adoption; many are developmental or are related to circumstances in the child's environment. Talk with other parents and/or knowledgeable professionals to determine whether problems are really related to adoption, or are a normal part of growing up. Remember, your child is a child first, an adopted child second.

- *Don't under-react to problems.* Get post-adoption services early, if needed. Adoptive families often need post-adoption support at key times in the life of their child. Families should be aware of available services prior to the onset of crisis. Don't wait until a crisis is in full swing before seeking adoption-competent help.

- *Talk openly about adoption in the family.* It is often necessary to *initiate* conversation, as children can be fearful of hurting the adoptive parent's feelings. Many adopted children will not talk with their parents about the psychological presence of their birth families, as they believe that to do so would be disloyal. It is imperative that adoptive parents raise the subject of adoption periodically so the child learns that adoption is not shameful or secretive.

Further, the child will understand his birth history more completely as he matures, so the conversation about facets of his history must continue as he is able to master more abstract thinking. Many parents assume they are done talking about adoption when the child is able to "parrot" his adoption story, often during the preschool years. However, while children can repeat the words of their adoption story, they will be unable to understand the concepts behind the story for many years. If adoption is rarely discussed in the family and the child is left to understand his history without parental guidance, he will likely embellish his story with unrealistic fantasies, typically of birth parents who are impossibly perfect (movie stars, sports stars, and so forth) or impossibly dysfunctional (bag ladies, and so forth).

- *Encourage the child to have positive feelings about his birth family.* To enjoy positive self-esteem, a child must feel good about his roots. Remember that parents are allowed to love more than one child. Children should be allowed to love more than one parent. Don't force your child to choose between you and the birth parent. No child should be asked to choose which parent to remain loyal to—children can love both families at the same time.
- *Get as much information as possible about the birth family and the child's history.* The trail gets cold quickly, so get as much information as possible at the time of placement. You can return to the agency at any point in the future to clarify information or to obtain additional information.
- *Always be honest in sharing information about the birth parent and the birth history.* If the information is very difficult, some facts may be deferred while the child is very young.

Facts should *never* be changed. As a rule of thumb, children should have complete information by the time they enter adolescence. Most adoptive parents err on the side of waiting too long before sharing information, rather than sharing information too early.

- *Be alert for signs of distress when losses or transitions occur.* Be sensitive to "anniversary reactions" and increased emotional stress around birthdays, holidays, and Mother's Day. Discuss feelings and fears openly. Watch for patterns when your child's behavior deteriorates. Journaling about situations that occurred just before a family crisis may provide clues to triggers that are activating fears. After two years of struggling with a son's intermittent negative behavior, his adoptive family finally noticed that the child's misbehavior occurred whenever a camera was introduced into a situation. When asked about his reaction to the camera, the early adolescent boy remarked that he usually moved from foster homes shortly after they took pictures of him. He associated the camera with losing a family.

- *Allow the adoptive father to become the primary parent during adolescence.* Much of the child's grief, anger about abandonment, and divided loyalties are directed toward the birth mother. This anger is often transferred to the adoptive mother through the dynamic of splitting (for a full explanation of splitting, review chapter 5). The mother/teen relationship can become very strained. The adoptive father should handle limit-setting whenever possible.

- *Avoid control battles.* You may need to lose a few battles in order to win the war. Parents can successfully work on only one or two behaviors at a time. Prioritize your battles, and be prepared to let a lot of other less important issues slide for the time being. Parenting shouldn't be one battle after another.

Jason's adoptive parents sought a post-adoption support group to provide support for themselves and a connection to other adopted children for Jason. Instead of feeling like they had failed in their role as parents, they learned they had the capacity to provide guidance and structure for a troubled child, and most importantly, a family for a child who had been left behind by seriously troubled birth parents. They sought respite care from time to time when Jason's rejection of them was overwhelming, and celebrated his success when he graduated from high school. The week of his eighteenth birthday, Jason's parents brought a birthday cake to the support group that had stood by them in their commitment to this child. As Jason's mother cut the cake, she said, "We are celebrating tonight. It hasn't been an easy road, but we have succeeded as Jason's parents because he is eighteen and he is alive."

Quick Reference

Key Point 1
Many times, adoption-related issues can be triggered by events, anniversaries, or even times of the year that remind children of losses or traumatic experiences. These adoption issues generate feelings, and those feelings lead to behaviors which in turn can lead to crisis within the adoptive family. Some common triggers for adoption-related crises are:

- Birthdays
- Mother's Day
- Moving
- Transition to a new school or graduation from high school
- Illness or death of a parent or grandparent
- Death of a pet
- Divorce of adoptive parents
- Holidays
- School assignments

Key Point 2
Parents can prevent or alleviate adoption-related crisis through strategies that anticipate and avoid triggers, promote communication and understanding that the child is now safe and protected, and/or express empathy and support as the child moves through his grief process. Specific strategies are outlined within this chapter for each of the common triggers listed above.

General Survival Skills for Adoptive Parents

- Acknowledge the child's grief.
- Network with other adoptive families.
- Don't overreact to behaviors; not all behaviors are related to adoption.
- Don't under-react to adoption-related issues.
- Get as much information as possible about the child's birth family and history.
- Communicate openly and honestly about adoption and the child's history.
- Remember the child is able to love more than one set of parents at the same time.
- Be alert for reactions to adoption-related triggers.
- Allow the adoptive father to become the primary parent during adolescence.
- Pick your battles.

Discussion Questions

1. How has the experience of fostering or adoption been different from what you expected when you began the application process?

2. How have your feelings about fostering or adoption changed since you began the application process?

3. What were your feelings when you first met your child?

4. Can you remember a time when you felt like giving up?

5. What strategies do you employ when you feel a crisis looming?

6. What triggers or patterns have you noticed that might spark a crisis for your child or your family?

7. What strategies will you employ to diffuse those triggers?

8. How do you define success as an adoptive or foster family? How will you know when your mission is accomplished?

PART FOUR:

The Child, the Family, and School

What is school like for a maltreated child? What does every day feel like for a child struggling with the damaging effects of abuse, neglect, and trauma? Why does getting through almost every day without a problem seem to be an impossible dream?

WHAT'S AHEAD

Chapter Nine

The Maltreated Child in School

By Timothy J. Callahan, PsyD

"School stresses me out; too much of everything all at once. I don't even know what's going on most of the time. But I love Mrs. Hall [teacher]; I wish she was my mom."

— Spencer, age eleven

Thirteen-year-old twins, Sam and Amanda, go to the same school. They are doing well, but that has not always been the case. Both were adopted when they were very young by Barb and Max, a young couple starting a family with big dreams and lots of love to give.

The children's early years with their biological parents were filled with neglect and domestic violence. When they were first adopted, both children were noticeably delayed in a variety of areas but quickly made up lost ground once in Barb and Max's safe and nurturing home.

When they started school, Amanda withdrew, while Sam disrupted the classroom with tantrums. Grade school was an academic struggle for both, but Sam received more attention from teachers because of his outbursts. Amanda was quiet, anxious, and overly compliant. According to her third grade teacher, "She doesn't seem to care about her work, she just wants attention."

Unlike his sister, Sam did not seem to want attention and he appeared to be "in his own world." Neither had friends; Sam, because he scared peers with his temper, and Amanda, because she felt she was not likeable.

When the school staff suggested special education for both kids during third grade, Barb and Max were concerned and confused; prior to school, both kids appeared to be thriving and hitting their developmental milestones. Since the start of school, both children appeared to be "going backward." Thorough assessments of each child indicated both could benefit from specialized instruction. Assessments revealed that both children, although noticeably bright, struggled to deal with the academic demands. They had difficulty settling down, focusing, and following directions. Although their teachers assumed that both were "capable of doing the work," assessment revealed deficits in memory and information processing. Both children, although different in presentations, lacked curiosity and, instead, responded to learning new things with overwhelming anxiety. When Sam was anxious, he acted out; when Amanda felt distress, she clung to the teacher.

Once the children were placed in smaller classrooms with more emphasis on working at their own paces and had more teacher-student contact, both children appeared less distressed, more focused, and motivated to achieve. School-based mental health services helped both kids learn distress management techniques, social skills, and positive self-talk. Barb and Max worked closely with the teachers, e-mailing daily and meeting face-to-face, whether things were going well or not. By the time the children were ready for middle school, they transitioned to regular classrooms.

Barb and Max became parent advocates to assist other parents who were similarly struggling with their children's adaptation to the school environment. Sam and Amanda both plan to go to college to be teachers.

A day in school is quite an adventure. For at least six to eight hours, the brain storms in response to a steady bombardment of cognitive, social, emotional, and physiological demands: people everywhere, swirling in a roar; the worry of homework not done; the test anxiety; the friends and rivals; the teachers and rules. Navigating the currents of the local social jungle is at least as strenuous as the ever-accumulating academic demands. In fact, school is a demanding, twelve-year ordeal with pressures that should be respected, appreciated, and understood. School activates as well as educates, refines as well as instructs, stimulates as well as socializes. School provides a critical theater in which to develop, grow, and learn.

School also stresses and strains and sometimes overwhelms. Today's schools seem increasingly to be playing catch-up, teaching to the test and serving as an unsteady launch pad for an uncertain future. Children who have suffered trauma, particularly the complex kind, often face the stressors of school with underdeveloped, hyper-reactive, and overtaxed nervous systems. As discussed in chapter four, children who have suffered attachment trauma may struggle at a variety of levels, from physiological to social. The areas of impairment most often seen in maltreated children are the same areas that define the school experience: namely cognitive, behavioral, emotional, interpersonal, and biological.[1]

This chapter will attempt to imagine what school is like for children who have suffered maltreatment. First, we will look at what is going on in their brains and everything that goes with it, including thinking, relating, behaving, and feeling. Next, we will identify behaviors commonly observed by teachers and peers, and consider the complexities of the teacher-youth-parent relationship. In the following chapter, we will discuss approaches, guidelines, and interventions that may help create a successful, safe, and satisfying school experience.

Of course, people are incredibly unique in their experiences, reactions, styles, and manners of adapting. Each child who has experienced complex trauma will, as any child will, respond to the stressors of school in his or her own way. We will attempt to make sense of this complex topic by combining experiences, behaviors, symptoms, and solutions into meaningful clusters, without forgetting the uniqueness of each person's way in the world.

The Nuts and Bolts of the School Experience

Some inherent features of the educational experience help us understand what school is like for a child who has been maltreated. Intrinsic in the school experience is the phenomenon of "uncertainty." Heather Geddes, in her book *Attachment in the Classroom,* refers to the concept of uncertainty as "the essential experience of school."[2] School is about learning something you do not know, something you are uncertain about. Securely attached children tend to approach uncertainty with interest and curiosity.

For maltreated children, however, uncertainty overwhelms, frightens, and freezes them in their track.[3] Since the learning process is, by definition, about not knowing something, we should not be surprised that kids who cannot tolerate the distress of uncertainty will struggle in school. We'll discuss more about managing the distress of uncertainty in the Affective Regulation section.

Another inherent feature of school is the teacher-student-task relationship, what Geddes refers to as The Learning Triangle.[4] A skill is taught through the connection between the teacher and student. Teachers are more than messengers for academic lessons; they are conduits through which learning takes place. For children who have experienced trauma to their primary attachment, the learning process depends on the perceived security of the relationship with the teacher. More about the teacher-student will be covered in the Relationships section.

Although we are amazingly resilient beings, our developing brains are affected by trauma, particularly early and chronic maltreatment. For children who have suffered early neglect and abuse, school can be an enormous struggle because the trauma has affected their brain development. For children who have experienced trauma later in development but are otherwise securely attached, learning is a distraction away from the emotional healing process. Either way, the underlying causes of poor academic performance are often overlooked, and the related behaviors take precedence as the focus of interventions.

We will now look at the specific areas of functioning that are most emphasized in school; the same areas most damaged by maltreatment.

How Cognition Functions

The brain in school is one cranked-up organ. Firing on all circuits, the brain is activated to the extreme when faced with the learning process. Full-out stimulation from the demands of reading, writing, and arithmetic leads to the "my brain is cooked" comment after a tough day in school. With most of the action going to putting on the brakes, the brain in school is constantly limiting as it learns, resisting as it refines, and inhibiting as it ignites. The higher brain literally restrains the instincts to fight, escape, or freeze. Of course, we cannot see what is truly going on with the brain in school. We cannot see the carving of neuronal pathways that bridge the gap between "no way does this make sense" and "I get it." We cannot see, let alone fathom, the complexity of the brain in the act of learning.

The stimulation is, for the most part, good for us, and our brains find learning satisfying. When life-threatening maltreatment interrupts the flow of development, such stimulation can overwhelm and overtax an already stressed nervous system. Research shows that neglect and abuse can negatively affect cognitive development.[5] Cognition is a complex brain function, made up of many processes. To improve functioning, we must determine specifically what is working well and what is not.

Cognitive functions include all the skills necessary to read, write, and calculate math. However, there are also very subtle and often overlooked cognitive processes, known as "executive" functions. They set the stage for all learning, regardless of specific school subjects. Executive functions act to oversee, guide, and manage cognitive, emotional, and behavioral functions.[6]

Maltreated children may have difficulty not only with the subject matter, but also with executive functioning.[7] Because these functions are less apparent than the behaviors masking them, it is crucial that we look closely at executive functioning before jumping to less accurate causes. We will focus on the following executive functions: attention, working memory, self-monitoring, time/planning, and cause/effect.

Executive Function #1: Attention

Attention is the gateway for all learning. Despite the simple directive to "pay attention," the act of attention is an incredibly complex brain process. Attention is made up of other abilities, including initiating, switching, inhibiting, working memory, monitoring, and organizing.[8] The brain powers up in response to a demand, such as a question from the teacher. Alerted by a surge of electro-chemicals, the brain *initiates* a plan to attend. Attention requires taking focus off something and *switching* onto something else. Once attention is turned to the teacher, maintaining the focus, despite a variety of distractions, is no small task. In order to attend to the task, the brain must *inhibit* distractions, particularly the ones with emotional value. If the student maintains focus despite distractions, he must split his attention into listening and keeping a memory of the instructions, known as "working memory."

Executive Function #2: Working Memory

Working memory is the capacity to hold information in mind, in order to complete a task. It is essential for multi-step activities, such as math.[9] Without a working memory, we would forget instructions seconds after the teacher delivered them. Teachers often describe children with working memory delays as having trouble remembering things, losing track of what they are supposed to work on, and requiring constant prompts and reminders.[10] If a student is able to initiate, switch, and split attention while inhibiting distractions, and remember what he is supposed to do to complete the assignment, then he is ready for the next critical executive task, self-monitoring.

Executive Function #3: Self-Monitoring

Monitoring refers to the ability to self-check your work as you go.[11] In school, children with delayed self-monitoring often can be observed rushing through work, failing to check for errors, and making careless mistakes. It is tempting to jump to the conclusion that the child is willfully unmotivated to self-monitor, and for some kids that may be true. However, for children whose brain development is affected by exposure to complex trauma, the capacity to monitor may be outside of the realm of willpower. While some children undermonitor themselves, others overmonitor. Maltreated kids, who are hyper-vigilant to anticipated threat and humiliation, may find themselves trapped in an inefficient self-checking cycle. For neglected and abused kids, self-monitoring is less about checking work than assessing safety and self-worth.

Executive Function #5: Time and Planning

The past cannot exist without the ability to remember, and the future is empty without the capacity to imagine. The "time-machinery" that enables these abilities is brain-based. Time is divided into seconds, minutes, hours, years, decades, centuries, and millennia. We unconsciously assume time is as real as the sky above. However, if someone has a different concept of time, not by choice but by brain arrangement, he will stand out as different or even disturbed. Teachers may describe such children as unsettled, impulsive, chronically late, moving at their own pace, unorganized, and unable to plan or set goals. This behavior is particularly apparent when time dominates required activities, such as in school. It is difficult to plan the future without reflecting on the past. If the memory functions necessary for such reflections are not well developed, the child will struggle to anticipate future events, set goals, and develop steps ahead of time to carry out the goal-directed tasks.[12]

Executive Function #6: Cause and Effect

Neglect and abuse delay cause-and-effect processing and, specifically, seeing accurately how our actions impact the world.[13] When the infant cried in need (cause), there was no comfort response from the caregiver (effect). Over time, a child learns there is no connection between what they do and how others respond.[14]

Affective (Emotional) Regulation

Beyond academic stressors, interpersonal pressures that provoke emotional stress abound in the school setting. Difficulty regulating emotions is a common feature of attachment trauma.[15] As we discussed in chapter 4, we learn to tolerate and regulate our emotions through our attachment with our caregivers. Maltreated children whose development has been hijacked by neglect and abuse struggle to understand, control, and express their feelings. School likely evokes uncomfortable emotions such as distress, frustration, and anxiety.

Distress Tolerance

Distress is the way the body communicates need, whether hunger, security, certainty, validation, or love. When a child's attachment is secure and the caregiver consistently acknowledges and satisfies needs, the child learns to tolerate distress at the nervous system level. He learns to trust that his distress will be relieved. The securely attached child learns from his caregiver to tolerate, identify, describe, and regulate his own emotional states. Distress for a well-attached child may be unpleasant but not catastrophic.

For maltreated children, distress may feel overwhelming and even life threatening. Rather than a temporary imbalance in need, distress is experienced as endless and overpowering pain. The only relief for some maltreated kids is to "freak out."

Temper tantrums, wailing, screaming, and throwing chairs across the classroom, vent pent-up feelings of distress. Maltreated children who come from a base of fear will have difficulty "talking" themselves down from the fight, flight, and fright instincts. Similarly, they may have difficulty describing their feelings and come up blank to a teacher's well-meaning inquiries such as "What's wrong? Do you feel okay? Can you use your feeling words?"

Delays and deficits in a child's capacity to regulate distress are amplified in the school setting. Uncertainty is distressing and therefore the learning process, by definition, is distressing. The learning process will overwhelm a child who cannot tolerate distress of any kind. Maltreated children may find the distress unbearable and likely will learn ways to avoid it in the future. Kids eventually may become apathetic, distracting, disturbing, and oppositional to avoid the overwhelming pain. Often the defiant and unresponsive teen is the same child who freaked-out catastrophically only a few years before. School staff likely will be unsuccessful motivating a student who is unmotivated because of distress. The student will only be helped by learning to manage his distress.

Many of the skills necessary for reading, writing, and math are built from the foundation up. Children who have spent their years in school avoiding the distress associated with the learning process are likely to have major gaps in their academic foundations that affect all future learning. Uncertainty accumulates over time, and so do the distress and avoidance strategies. By the time a child is an adolescent, he may feel that learning is impossible and hopeless.

Teachers and parents may become frustrated with the student and mirror the teen's feelings of helplessness. Helping maltreated kids learn specific and effective ways to manage their distress will help create a more fertile ground for any academic skill development.

Performance Anxiety

Neglect and abuse make the emotion of fear the predominant base from which all things stem. Maltreated children's nervous systems are on alert for anticipated danger, ever-ready to dump huge amounts of stress hormones into their nervous system in preparation for fight or flight or fright. Fear-based, maltreated children who struggle to cope with distress tend to be particularly anxious when put on the spot to perform. Geddes observes, "For many pupils, performance anxiety can be behind their difficulties and behavior and if this is not recognized, patterns of behavior can persist which exaggerate difficulties. Consequently, behavior becomes the issue rather than the learning need."[16] For many children, and particularly those who have been traumatized, behavior is simply the way they appear to others when they are attempting to endure distress. Teaching ways to control performance anxiety will have more positive impact on the learning process than teaching academic skills alone.

Emotional Regulation and the Interpersonal

School is filled with all kinds of people with all kinds of feelings. Maltreated children may find it difficult to read others' emotions. A traumatized child, like a combat veteran who returns from the horror of war with a hypersensitivity to anticipated dangers, might punch someone in the face over a misunderstood comment.

These kinds of behaviors make it hard for others to read the emotions of the maltreated child, particularly if the child has learned to look angry and menacing to ward off potential threats.

If we were deprived of the nurturance we need to develop, recognize, and express feelings, we would struggle daily to understand and be understood by others. The aloneness that comes from chronically feeling out of place drives some children to give up on others. They resort to isolation and antisocial behavior. We will discuss interpersonal issues later, but for the purposes of this section, it is important to remember that the emotional life of a maltreated child is complex and riddled with suffering, confusion, and isolation. From this understanding comes a rather obvious solution: provide a simple, safe, and inclusive social atmosphere where respect and dignity of the individual dominates.

Behavioral Control in the Classroom

Of all the favorite commands adults give kids, there are few more impossible than "Behave yourself!" It is up there with "Pay attention!" and "Be spontaneous!" To behave ourselves, we have to work some real magic with our brains. Overriding primal instincts to fight or run away consumes enormous amounts of energy. Maintaining awareness of rules and regulations requires enormous memory capacity.

Yet, we can observe behavior and, consequently, it's the easiest thing to target. It is also the easiest to misunderstand and over-interpret. Behavior problems get the attention of the teacher and school officials much more quickly than possible underlying cognitive, emotional, or relationship problems. Behavior is often a solution, a strategy to impact others in some way. It is an attempt to find equilibrium, meet a need, or temporarily relieve distress. For kids who have been traumatized by dangerous and unpredictable chaos, their behavior in school may appear senseless, dangerous, and chaotic. Attempting to control behavior without understanding its function will likely only obstruct the learning process.

Research indicates that behavioral disturbances and unsuccessful school adaptation are significant features of maltreated children.[17] Children identified as needing special education for behavioral and emotional disturbances were found to have experienced major disruptions in relationships with their primary caregivers, compared to children without the behavioral disturbance.[18] Behaviors displayed by maltreated kids vary across a spectrum of type and severity, however patterns do emerge. Some common classroom behaviors displayed by attachment-traumatized kids include:[19]

- Disrupts classroom activities by talking out loud; excessively seeks attention
- Argues with teacher; attempts to control authority; dominates environment
- Does not follow directions; does more or less than directed; goes at own pace
- Displays hyper-vigilant, distrusting, heightened state of anxiety
- Reacts catastrophically to not getting his way; suddenly overreacts to unseen triggers
- Exhibits moodiness

- Shows difficulty in tolerating frustration, distress, disappointment
- Does not contribute to classroom activities
- Deliberately omits parts of assignments
- Tends to get in trouble when not supervised
- Possesses limited organizational skills; cognitive impairment
- Attempts to split parent-teacher relationship (triangulation)
- Does not appear to enjoy self or others, lacks mutual joy
- Resents monitoring by staff, even though it is necessary for safety
- Demonstrates social impairments, lacks sense of personal boundaries
- Shows no apparent remorse following misbehavior or apologizes without changing behavior
- Resists taking responsibility for actions, blames others
- Does not respond well to rewards and punishments do not work well
- Destroys toys
- Purposely slurs words
- Self-injures, picks at self, accident-prone
- Bullies others, insensitive to others' feelings
- Shows hypersensitivity to criticism

Some misbehaving is just what kids do sometimes, and there is nothing particularly meaningful behind it. But for traumatized children, more often than not, behavior is strategic and functional (although not necessarily conscious).

As we discussed earlier, neglect and abuse delay cause-and-effect processing. Over time, a child learns there is no connection between what he does and how others respond, unless he resorts to extreme behaviors that adults cannot ignore. When we instruct a child to seek positive instead of negative attention, we are missing the point. For the child, attention at any level is better than being invisible.

There are just as many unseen micro-processes behind behavior as there are behind cognitive and emotional functioning. Research suggests that maltreatment disrupts the development of the underlying processes necessary for adequate behavior control.[20]

Maltreated kids tend to have difficulty controlling impulses and appear to act without thinking. When we think about time distortions, emotional instability, and minimal executive overrides, it makes sense that a traumatized child may appear impulsive.

Maltreated children also tend to have pathological ways to self-soothe, such as venting, aggression, self-injury, hoarding and gorging food, or risk-taking. Oppositional behavior for maltreated kids may serve a variety of self-protective functions, including "camouflage," deflection away from deficits, and armor against being overpowered.[21]

Traumatized children's behaviors may be attempts to reenact the trauma drama. Reenactment is the unconscious way we work through past traumas in the theater of the present, to resolve unmet needs and return to balance and well-being. (For further discussion about reenactment as it affects the adoptive/foster family, see chapter 5.)

Ultimately, maladaptive behaviors displayed by traumatized kids are efforts to elicit care-giving behaviors from adults. They need adults to act like adults, and they will test us to the extreme to ensure they will be kept safe in an unsafe world.

Some traumatized children are overly compliant as a strategy to avoid danger. Such children are hyper-aware of what is expected and then contort themselves to be what others want them to be. It makes sense that the overly compliant student may "fly under the radar" in school; this is the intent of the strategy. It is important that children learn to control their behavior. However, it is unhealthy for kids to devote so much energy to obediently pleasing others. Children who overuse this strategy need to know that love is not conditional on compliance.

Relationships at School

We are social creatures. Our lives depend on our connections to others. Our first act is to connect to our mother's womb. Hopefully, we remain anchored and attached to the world around us throughout our lives through our relationships. We come from, live with, and learn from each other. It is how we are made.

School, as we all know, is much more than a place to learn skills and gain knowledge. School is a social phenomenon, a theater in which we learn to be with others. We learn academic skills through a relationship with the teacher. The teacher-student bond echoes the parent-child attachment, particularly for the young and maltreated.

We also build relationships with peers. Navigating through the peer jungle requires good interpersonal awareness and skill. Research shows that neglect and abuse affects children's ability to trust others, read interpersonal cues, and be sensitive to personal boundaries.[22]

Traumatized children may not be able to attune to others' feelings. Similarly, maltreated kids tend have difficulty seeing another's point of view. Teachers and peers may think the maltreated child is self-absorbed and insensitive. When we consider the fundamental role the parent-child attachment plays in a child's social development, it is glaringly apparent that a child who has experienced attachment trauma faces the social stressors of school ill-equipped, compared to a securely attached child.

Teacher-Student Relationship

It's easy to misunderstand the subtle but important quality of the teacher-student relationship as an anchor for the process of learning. For young kids, the relationship is the soil in which the learning process is planted. As children mature and develop, they rely less and less on the teacher-student relationship. They approach tasks more directly. Eventually, they approach tasks independent of the teacher; they become their own teachers and the teachers of others.[23]

For children who have been exposed to neglect and abuse, the teacher-student relationship may remain a necessary base for the learning process long into adolescence.[24] For many maltreated kids, tasks may seem meaningless unless anchored to a secure relationship.

The teacher-student relationship is the conduit through which students acquire a skill, whether reading, writing, or math. For some children, the harmony has to be "extra right" for learning to take hold. We will focus on the teacher-student relationship in more detail in the next chapter when we look at school interventions and strategies.

Relationships with Peers

Quality relationships with friends and acquaintances are critical to our health and happiness throughout our lives. Building and maintaining peer relationships are fundamental life skills that will serve the developing person in a variety of contexts—school, work, romance, or leisure. School is a social theater, and to survive, let alone flourish in it, children need to develop social skills. Early caregiver-child attachment experiences forge the building blocks of interpersonal functioning—sensitivity, empathy, trust, expressive verbal skills, the capacity to tolerate the distress/frustration, and the ability to read interpersonal cues.[25]

Maltreated children may struggle because traumatic attachment experiences have delayed and distorted these building blocks. No one properly tuned into the child's emotions during critical periods of brain development, so he will struggle to be attuned to others' feelings. Sharing and mutual play cannot easily occur unless they're activated by a reciprocal caregiver-child relationship. Distrust and fear, although very effective for defending against danger, can be toxic qualities in relationships. Menacing glares scare away predators, but also classmates.

When adolescence kicks in around age thirteen, peers become the primary arena for development. Eric Erickson, a major theorist in the field of developmental psychology, observed that each stage of development has certain characteristic milestones and accompanying crises. So does adolescence. The teen years, Erickson observed, are primarily for trying on different identities while figuring out how to belong to the pack.[26]

Adolescence is the time we practice being independent, primarily by rebelling against adult control. Maltreated teens experience the same drive to define themselves, belong to a peer group, and rebel against the status quo. However, the added confusion and pressure from previously unmet needs, such as safety and love, push up from the bottom. The adolescent drives of the maltreated teen take on a desperate quality. Maltreated kids tend to keep themselves in the focus of adults, testing to ensure the caregivers will do their job this time. For the maltreated teen, rebellion against adults functions not to establish independence, but to bring adults closer.

Maltreated children, like any children, want friends, but they may find themselves alone and isolated, looking in from the outside. Some kids have difficulty engaging and making friends, while others cannot keep them. The effects of trauma, such as distrust, misinterpretation of cues, emotional instability, and apparent self-absorption, strain relationships. Quality relationships with friends can help heal attachment trauma, but peers may not be able hang in long enough for the healing to take hold. Social skills groups, in which kids learn and practice all the nuances of interpersonal interaction, can be effective in improving functioning.

Self-Concept and School

As we discussed in chapter 4, having a coherent, continuous, and core sense of self is critical to functioning as a self-reliant and fully adaptive person. Maltreatment affects the development of self-concept.[27] Secure attachment with caregivers helps the child develop a worthy, lovable, and competent sense of self. Maltreatment creates a self-concept infused with the opposite feelings. Maltreated children may not feel that they are worthy of love and respect. They may feel inadequate, helpless, and powerless. They likely are in a state of ever-present shame. Neglect and abuse are so destructive because they damage the child's dignity.

If a child feels deeply inadequate and unworthy of praise or even success, he will struggle with school, academically and socially. Some maltreated children cope with the awful feelings of inadequacy by not even trying. Sometimes the only way to keep a shred of dignity is purposely not to attempt to be successful; to find some comfort and control in knowing that if you don't try, you won't fail.

Some maltreated children may attempt to cope with inadequacy by being overly dependent on teachers or peers. Others may be oppositional, resistant, and isolated. The key for school staff is to keep the focus on dignity, while reducing feelings of inadequacy, shame, and self-loathing. Understanding the effects of maltreatment helps us avoid the false assumption that a child is simply unmotivated or not interested in being successful.

Quick Reference

When we mix uncertainty with a few cognitive delays and a good dose of fear, shame, and distrust, and then heat them up in a peer pressure-cooker to unlock the emotional unrest, we have quite a scenario for suffering. Often there is a multidimensional, multilayered developmental process that teachers and caregivers easily overlook:

Key Point 1:
Children who have been neglected and abused may struggle to catch up in several developmental areas, including cognitive, emotional, interpersonal, and behavioral.

Key Point 2:
School is a stressful experience filled with uncertainty, cognitive demands, relationships, anxiety, and frustration. School is also about the joy of learning, brain development, and bonding with friends and teachers.

Key Point 3:
Schools have increasing difficulty offering individualized, flexible approaches

for children who do not fit the typical student profile. Maltreated children and their caregivers, as well as teachers and peers, may suffer unnecessarily because traditional methods do not meet the complex needs of complex kids.

Key Point 4:

Determining the specific need or delay (cognitive, emotional, or behavioral) of a child is the key to any intervention. Once we understand the underlying, specific reason for the student's problems, appropriate interventions will likely effect swift, positive change.

Key Point 5:

Behaviors and attitudes overshadow many of the unseen causes of poor school performance, including cognitive, emotional, and interpersonal processes. Understanding, appreciation, and empathy will open up more doors for effective change than any particular management technique or intervention.

In the next chapter, we will look at some specific ways educators and caregivers can help a maltreated child benefit from and succeed in school.

DISCUSSION QUESTIONS

1. What are some reasons why school may be overwhelming to the maltreated child?

2. Why is the teacher-student relationship important in the learning process?

3. Discuss the disadvantages of aiming interventions exclusively at behavior.

4. How does maltreatment affect a child's understanding of cause and effect? Why is cause-and-effect processing important?

5. What is distress tolerance and why is it so important in the school setting?

Chapter Ten

School Interventions for the Maltreated Child

By Timothy J. Callahan, PsyD

"If a child can't learn the way we teach, maybe we should teach the way they learn."

—Ignacio Estrada[1]

Billy is a second grader, cute and precocious, with a talent for math. He frequently is the source of his teacher's neck pain. He's currently in foster care, following years of neglect by his biological parents. "He goes from smiling calm to screaming rage in seconds, and without any provocation," his teacher, Ms. Allen, reported to his foster parents in a team meeting. "He is typically cool as cucumber, but sometimes he acts like a wild little animal."

His foster parents report they do not see such explosive behavior at home. After some discussion and review of behavioral observation data from Ms. Allen and her aide, the team concludes that a Behavioral Intervention Plan would be helpful. Billy's behavior, however, seems to worsen with every behavior modification strategy. After three months of increasingly disruptive behavior, the team meets to consider further options, including alternative placement or medications. His foster parents and child protective services caseworker urge the team to keep trying to work with Billy in the current setting and to hold off on medications until they try less intrusive methods.

One benefit of Billy's behavior plan is that it tracks patterns of behaviors over time and circumstances. Billy's foster mother notices in the charting data that Billy's explosive spikes occur primarily at the beginning and end of class. His teacher agrees with the observation and adds that Billy seems to need extra reassurance from her at the start of class, so much so that he delays the start of the lesson. She similarly observed he "sticks around after class, just talking about stuff, and he's often late for the next class." The team decides to hold off attempting to fix the behavior problems. Instead, they recommend spending extra time getting to know Billy, his history, and his perception of things.

After a month of focused observation and increased student-teacher interaction, it becomes clearer that Billy was having bursts of terrible anxiety, specifically when faced with new learning or changes in routine. Billy's teacher, aide, and school social worker developed a plan to address his anxiety by helping him learn to tolerate distress better. He learned and practiced relaxation and self-soothing strategies at school and home. Positive and effective self-talk helped him override his fears. Also, his teacher put aside five minutes every morning to check in with him just to "chat."

After six weeks Billy's explosions disappeared, and he spent less time gaining reassurance from his teacher. Billy gained skills in managing distress, particularly the stress of feeling uncertain and lost. Billy's early life of maltreatment very likely made it difficult for his nervous system to tolerate and control surges in distress. Although the time spent helping him manage his distress temporarily distracted him from his lessons, Billy learned a set of skills that will serve him any time he faces uncertain and new situations.

Maltreatment, particularly the early and chronic type, damages children in ways that may leave no long-term visible scars but insidiously leave hidden wounds on the entire developing being. Maltreatment disrupts a child's development of functional domains, from thinking and feeling to behaving and relating.[2] These are same domains required for school success. If underdeveloped, they will strain the child's ability to adapt and respond to academic and social demands.

The school environment can activate and jump-start the maltreated child's cognitive, emotional, behavioral, and social development unlike anything else. It provides children with opportunities to learn, read, and write, and also to develop abilities such as distress control, behavior management, and emotional regulation. School is a major theater where kids learn how to interact with one another.

School can be a healing experience for children who have been delayed by maltreatment. The healing process, however, requires an attachment to the teacher and opportunities to develop the building blocks that were delayed from the trauma. Unfortunately, schools are busy teaching subjects, not children. Teachers have less time and opportunity to develop meaningful bonds with the kids. They must teach to state and federal standards instead of addressing what the child may need. Some kids first need to learn how to handle the distress associated with uncertainty before learning how to approach something as uncertain as math calculations.

As we learned in the previous chapter, there is much more going on behind cognition, emotions, behaviors, and relationships than we observe on the surface.

Maltreated kids face academic and social stressors with gaps in some of these foundational skill areas, gaps that surface in the classroom in indirect and obscure ways. Readiness is critical.[3] When a teacher teaches "over" the child's readiness, behavior problems are likely to develop.

Managing the maltreated child's behavior without understanding what is driving it often leaves the child feeling frustrated, and the teacher and parent feeling hopeless and powerless. If we can uncover and focus on the specific deficit or delay affecting functioning, we can avoid attempts to fix everything, or something that does not need to be fixed. We uncover what we most need to know about a child by spending time with him, listening carefully, pouring ourselves into the relationship, and looking for opportunities to repair the effects of maltreatment. We can serve as the anchor that was missing when the child most needed it.

Guiding Principles for Working with Maltreated Children

Classroom strategies and interventions are most effective when they flow naturally from a core set of beliefs and principles. Techniques, even ones based in research, won't be effective unless they are anchored to an overarching philosophy. If we employ a technique or strategy without knowing the world of the maltreated child, we will likely do more harm than good.

For example, relying on a behavior modification system for a child who is misbehaving in order to escape feeling invisible will be counter-productive. "Good" behavior to a maltreated child may be less effective in getting attention than "bad" behavior.

A more effective approach, in this case, would be to focus less on behavior and more on the relationship, aiming the strategies toward helping the child feel more connected and recognized. The following are some guiding principles to keep in mind when working with maltreated children:

- Traumatized children operate from an instinctual base
  of fear; behaviors are often survival strategies to avoid
  anticipated threat.[4]

- Traumatized children may experience life as chaotic, unpredictable, and dangerous; they may feel incapable of having any impact on their situations and have no idea what to do to make their lives better.[5]
- To such kids, adults are not trustworthy or capable of keeping them safe.[6]
- After years of maltreatment, kids adapt with whatever they have available. Behavior problems such as oppositionality, aggression, refusal, shutting down, lethargy, and low motivation are likely coping strategies.
- Teachers are caregivers who spend almost as much time with the child as the parents; teachers can act as caregivers to help heal the wounds of maltreatment.[7]
- There is much suffering in these children's lives. Teachers need to remember to come from a base of compassion, nurturance, and understanding.
- Dignity and safety preside over everything else.
- Life is the teacher. Parents, teachers, and counselors are sympathetic participants/observers who act as coaches or mentors.
- Any intervention needs to be based on the four basics goals of attachment: proximity, security, safety, and self-regulation.[8]

Guiding principles enable us to filter our approaches through lenses that view the maltreated child with the dignity, understanding, and respect he deserves.

From Parent-Child to Teacher-Student

The teacher-student relationship is important because, for humans, the relationship with caregivers is the tie that binds and anchors everything, including learning. We are designed to learn about the world first through the parent-child relationship. The attachment to our caregivers is the entry point for all learning.

From the anchoring experience of "oneness" through what Allan Schore calls the "mutual gaze,"[9] the caregiver slowly introduces the infant to the world of objects. For example, while holding and lovingly gazing into the infant's eyes, a caregiver introduces a rattle. The rattle then begins to take on reality and meaning as the caregiver shakes it and gets the baby to reach for it. The baby grabs it and applies the only strategy he knows, namely, putting it in his mouth. He interacts with it curiously, activating visual-motor brain connections as well as language from the ongoing parent-child "baby talk."

When the caregiver introduces another object of a different form, like a block, the infant attempts to apply the "mouth strategy" only to find out that the block won't fit in his mouth (at least let's hope not). Another tactic must be attempted. He may swing his arm in frustration and accidentally knock the block away. Now the object has meaning because he knows how to impact and interact with it.[10] He'll approach the next object introduced by either putting it in his mouth or hitting it.

As more and more objects are introduced, the infant begins to develop a repertoire of strategies for interacting with the world.[11] It is this essential process that creates the foundation for any future learning.

Healthy adaptation involves the ability to perform six tasks:[12]

1. Assess what the environment is calling for.

2. Inventory existing strategies.

3. Apply one strategy that appears to be the best fit.

4. Watch to see if it works.

5. Modify the strategy.

6. Add the newly modified tactic to the existing repertoire.

As children develop, they rely less on the parent to introduce objects. They curiously seek out things themselves. Toddlerhood is the period in which the child curiously explores and tests an unknown and uncertain environment. As long as the exploring toddler can look back and make sure his anchor is watching, and therefore tethering him to the world, he can venture out and learn to interact with objects on his own. Healthy development should result in kids being increasingly less dependent on relationships with adults to learn about their world. For children who were deprived of necessary attachment security, the exploring and learning processes are delayed, distorted, and impaired.

When a child begins school, he extends the relationship-dependent learning process from the parent to the teacher.[13] If he has had relatively safe and successful learning experiences interacting with his world through the parent-child relationship, he likely expects such a relationship with his teacher. If the parent-child relationship is shaken to its core by neglect, abuse, or exposure to general awfulness, the child may anticipate such dangers with the teacher.[14]

Kids in search of a secure base may appear to push the teacher away through defiance or refusal to complete tasks. They may battle for control. They are, in fact, not pushing away, but pulling toward. Human children elicit what they need from those in charge of their survival. For maltreated kids, they need the adults to behave like adults and make the world safe. What better way to get us to forcibly assert our adulthood than by challenging our ability to be in charge?

Children who have been seriously and chronically mistreated can be very complicated and difficult to understand. Such children take time and investment to know them as individuals.

Strategies for Teachers

Teaching is hard work. Teaching traumatized children with symptoms of attachment disorders makes the job even harder. As classrooms balloon to over thirty students, the ability to meet an individual child's needs becomes strained. For some maltreated children, the goal of school is to engage adults in a relationship, not necessarily to learn how to do math.

A teacher who attempts to teach an academic skill inevitably will become frustrated with a child who constantly seeks attention. A child who is seeking a surrogate caregiver for attachment inevitably will become frustrated with a teacher who constantly rejects his attention-seeking in favor of skill-building. The frustration gridlocks progress in any direction: behavior problems, teacher burnout, strained relationships between the teacher and parents and the caregiver and child. For schools, the only apparent alternatives are to remove the child from the classroom, recommend medication, place him in alternative programs, or suggest home schooling.

As discussed so far, many of the behavior problems displayed by maltreated children camouflage the real driving forces. The following are some practical techniques that may enable the teacher to teach and also be effective with children who need to heal attachment trauma:

- *Avoid yelling.* The more matter-of-fact, the better. Raised voices trigger fear and stress hormones. Keep anger and frustration out of voice tone.[15]
- *Be in control without being controlling.*[16] The teacher manages

the teacher-student relationship. He sets the tone, rhythm, cadence, and emotional quality. Teachers need to make it clear in their interactions that they are in control of the classroom so that everyone will remain safe.

- *Look for opportunities to teach/model interconnectedness, societal expectations, and the need and benefit of complying.* Model, as well as teach, social skills.[17]
- *Understand the function of a behavior before attempting to manage it.*[18]
- *Use natural consequences when possible and safe*[19] Help kids see the impact their behaviors have on others. Meaningfully connect behaviors with consequences. Use restitution when possible.
- *Look for opportunities to repair the teacher-student relationship following a misbehavior-consequence cycle.* Successful interactive repair will reduce the chances that the child will experience toxic shame.
- *Communicate with parents regularly and frequently.* Communications should never go through the child.[20]
- *Enforce a zero-tolerance policy for violence.* Threats of violence, arguing with the teacher, and blatant disregard for instructions cannot be tolerated.
- *Teach reading, writing, and math, but also executive skills.* Teach the child focusing techniques, self-monitoring, memory techniques, cause-and-effect, impulse and time management, as well as social skills, distress and frustration control, and self-motivating techniques.
- *Be consistent, repetitive, and predictable.*[21]

When Individual Attention Is Called For

Effective school-wide and classroom management strategies address many of the problems that develop in the classroom.[22] Children whose disruptive behaviors mask underlying developmental delays need individual attention to jump-start the developmental areas that have been affected by chronic and early maltreatment. We will look at a few critical areas that, if addressed early and often, will help the maltreated children catch-up to their classmates.

Distress Tolerance

Distress tolerance is one of the most critical developmental abilities and yet the most easily overlooked. A teacher can teach distress tolerance by first modeling good stress management, remaining calm, keeping perspective, and talking through the perceived crisis. A distressed teacher will spread anxiety and ignite the nervous systems of children who are on alert for fear and danger. In the same way, a calm teacher will help create a relaxed atmosphere where learning may be challenging but not catastrophic. Just as a frightened child needs to hear reassurance from his attachment figure, so students need to hear their teacher say, "It is going to be okay, we'll get through this together."

Teaching and practicing stress reduction techniques can be effective ways to help children learn to tolerate and regulate distress.[23] Calming the body will reduce the intensity of the fight-flight flare-ups and allow for more room to talk oneself down from the drive to freak-out. Breathing exercises, visualization, positive self-talk, and progressive muscle relaxation can have a positive impact on academic success, by creating an atmosphere where remaining calm is a valued and achievable skill. These techniques can be taught and practiced as a classroom, in smaller groups, or individually. With the increasing pressure on students and teachers to achieve standards, making stress-reduction part of the daily classroom experience will likely help all of the students.

For some children, relaxation techniques are helpful but not sufficient to reduce their overwhelming distress. For such kids, it is important to determine the source of the distress. Sometimes the child may bring in distress from home, from the past, or from the unknown. Sometimes the distress stems from the uncertainty of learning something new, or not understanding what the teacher is teaching. Either way, the best way to decipher the true underlying cause of the distress is by getting to know the child, spending time talking about how he feels and thinks, and fusing the bond for future learning.

The teacher can gain a great deal of data from observations, but at times formal assessments can be very informative. School psychologists and school mental health staff can help shed light on specific delays and deficits through a variety of testing tools. Their most important tool, however, is observation of the child in a variety of contexts. By observing the child, they may identify some deficits that are easily overlooked, specifically, executive functioning delays.

Executive Functioning Delays

As discussed in the previous chapter, crucial behind-the-scenes processes known as "executive functions" oversee, guide, and manage cognitive, emotional, and behavioral functions. They include attention, working memory, self-monitoring, time perception, and cause-effect interpretation. Complex trauma can significantly affect the proper development of these functions.[24] Teachers can help children stimulate, activate, and refine these critical processes. Let's take a closer look at attention span, memory, and cause-effect processing.

Attention: Attention is a complex process made up of micro-abilities, such as initiating, switching (see chapter nine), and inhibiting. Teaching children practical ways to focus their attention will create fertile ground for future learning. Depending on the child's age and developmental level, teachers can make focusing techniques fun and meaningful by approaching them as another skill to be learned. Attention span is not an obstacle to learning, but rather the focus of it. Marcia Tate, in her book *Shouting Won't Grow Dendrites: 20 Techniques for Managing a Brain-Compatible Classroom*, outlines some ways teachers can "hook" students' attention:[25]

- *Need*—Discuss with students why they need to learn the information. Obvious as this may sound, the "why" is often left out of the lesson.
- *Novelty*—Mix it up in class; occasionally rearrange things in the classroom environment; use multimedia technologies, and so on.
- *Meaning*—Connect information to real life.
- *Emotion*—Help students connect emotionally to the lesson. Teach with enthusiasm and passion for the subject.

Tate also recommends that teachers use short-term memory activities during the morning hours, when children tend to be more focused; present new material in multisensory ways; and provide opportunities for students to move.[26]

Memory: Trauma affects memory development and functioning, and much of school involves memory.[27] If a child has difficulties with memory, performance and/or behavioral problems can develop.

Teachers can help children to remember better through memory devices such as mnemonics. Mnemonic devices work by associating something that's easy to remember with whatever is being memorized.[28]

Common mnemonics include *ROY G. BIV* (colors of the rainbow: red, orange, yellow, green, blue, indigo, violet), and *EVERY GOOD BOY DESERVES FUN* (musical notes, E, G, B, D, F) and *MY VERY ELEGANT MOTHER*

JUST SERVED US NINE PIZZAS (planets of our solar system).

Mnemonics work, and children who struggle to remember will benefit from learning how to use such memory aids. There are many creative and effective ways to improve memory. Rather than focusing on a child's motivation or behavior, a teacher and caregiver will get much further by helping a child develop a repertoire of memory-enhancing aids.

Cause-and-Effect Processing: Maltreatment can affect a child's ability to understand his impact on others. He may struggle to make sense of the cause-and-effect nature of the world. Such children need matter-of-fact feedback about how their behavior affects others. As long as shame and judgment are kept out of the picture, most kids will benefit from knowing how others perceive specific things they do. This feedback requires much sensitivity. And, of course, any feedback will go over better when there is a bond with the one giving the feedback. A child whose mother did not provide feedback during critical periods of his development will not know how he is perceived by the world. He often inaccurately interprets how his behaviors impact others.

Telling a child, "You don't need to do that to get my attention" is less useful than "I notice when I talk with other students, you tap your pencil really loudly. Are you worried that I'll forget about you when I talk to others? It is okay, I won't forget you."

We've reviewed only a few of the many things teachers can do to teach the behind-the-scenes skills. The point here is to open our minds and eyes to what is truly the obstacle to the teacher-student-skill process, and avoid jumping to the false conclusion that the problem is behavioral or motivational in nature. It is best to assume skill deficit first and bad attitude last. In due time, if skills remain undeveloped, attitude problems will develop.

The Parent-Teacher Relationship

For any student, open and regular communication between parent and teacher helps the student to be more successful in school. For neglected and abused children, the communication between caregivers and teachers is all the more important.[29]

"Triangulation" is a phenomenon where the child splits the teacher from the parent. It is an effective strategy primarily designed to maintain control over and test the adults in the child's life.[30] Sometimes the splitting is simply an effort to test a parent's loyalty. There is much comfort and security for both the child and the caregiver when a parent comes to a child's rescue. Sometimes the splitting is an effort to test the teacher's loyalty. Either way, the triangulation is more than a manipulation; it is an effort to get adults to act like adults.

When adults can be split by the child's triangulating strategies, the child may temporarily feel empowered. However, in the long run, when the adults are so easily controlled, maltreated children remember how adults in their past did not act as adults who would or could keep them safe.

As important as maintaining regular and open communication is, it is not easy to accomplish. Everyone is so busy that well-meaning teachers and caregivers let time slip by, and before they know it, the school year is over. In addition, it is easy to drift from regular communications when things are going well. When the child acts up, communications often resume. This crisis style of communication often stresses the teacher-parent relationship, infusing the communications with tension and blame. The teacher and caregivers may disagree about what is happening with the child; however, they need to work out those conflicts outside of the child's awareness. The teacher and caregivers need to present a unified front. Teacher parent communications are most effective if they occur whether or not the child is doing well.

Regular communications can occur in a variety of ways: daily progress sheets with room to exchange feedback, weekly e-mails, phone calls as often as possible, and periodic face-to-face meetings. For children whose maltreatment has resulted in attachment disorders, the communications between teacher and caregiver should never go through the child, no matter how convenient it seems. Communicating via the child is a breeding ground for splitting.[31]

The key to the teacher-parent relationship is to consistently demonstrate to the child that the adults can be trusted to keep him safe. If adults fulfill their primary obligation of taking care of them, kids can relax and be kids.

Special Education and Alternative Placement

Sometimes children display behaviors, symptoms, and delays that severely interfere with their ability to benefit from school. Traditional approaches in the classroom may not fit the needs of all children all of the time. Some children with special needs benefit from accommodations designed to increase their opportunities for scholastic success. Accommodations range from modified schedules to smaller classroom, from extended time for tests to alternative educational programs. Children who have experienced complex trauma may need certain accommodations, at certain times, to function better in school. Teachers and school staff may be able make some accommodations without formal procedures. However, for children who are disabled by their special needs, there are legal supports that protect their civil rights and ensure an appropriate public education.

The Office of Civil Rights and the Office of Special Education and Rehabilitation Services, both within the U.S. Department of Education, are two governmental bodies that oversee the constitutional supports for students with disabilities. The Individuals with Disabilities Education Act (IDEA) spells out procedures for providing specialized instruction, including the Individualized Education Plan (IEP).

An IEP is a legal working document between parents and the school district that outlines how the specially designed instructions, including accommodations and additional services, are implemented.[32]

An IEP can be very helpful for a traumatized child who has developed severe behavioral and emotional disturbances. Smaller classrooms with one-on-one instruction provide children with opportunities to build a bond with their teachers and learn at their own pace. Additional services, such as occupational, speech, and mental health therapies, can be very helpful in addressing developmental delays and emotional disorders. School-based counseling services are an invaluable form of support, validation, and guidance in a traumatized child's natural school environment.

Each state's department of education has its own specific methods for implementing the laws that ensure appropriate education for children with disabilities. Interested readers are encouraged to investigate the special education services available within their local and state educational systems.

Quick Reference

Schools can play an enormous role in helping children damaged by maltreatment to heal, grow, and get back on a healthy course of development. The academic and social stimulation in the school experience can help jump-start nervous systems delayed and disrupted by maltreatment.

Key Point 1:

We develop and learn about the world through the caregiver-child attachment. When the attachment is disrupted, so are the functional domains we so very much need to learn, namely, cognitive, emotional, behavioral, and interpersonal processes.

Key Point 2:

Just as we learn about the world and ourselves through our relationship with our caregivers, we learn a skill through the teacher-student bond. After the bond is formed, teaching becomes more penetrating and meaningful.

Key Point 3:
Maltreated kids need to have a safe, anchoring relationship with their teacher. This connection can counteract the awfulness of previous experiences with adults, and teach the behind-the-scenes skills missed during the first years of development.

Key Point 4:
Sometimes children are not at a place where they are ready to learn. They need to acquire basic skills first, such as tolerating distress, controlling their attention span, and understanding their impact on others.

Key Point 5:
Teachers can act as attachment figures and teach maltreated children what they should have learned in infancy and early childhood.

Key Point 6:
Schools and teachers, children and their parents, are under severe pressures to meet federal and state standards, with increasingly less funding. Consequently, teachers often teach subjects to pass tests, instead of teaching children to succeed in life.

Key Point 7:
Children whose needs are not being met by traditional educational methods easily stand out in school, often being accused of being disruptive or disturbed. Many of these children will improve their misbehavior by forming a connection with their teacher and learning how to participate adaptively in the school experience.

Key Point 8:
Teachers can create a positive school experience for a child recovering from neglect and abuse by following a few guiding principles, forming a relationship with the student, and teaching to the child's needs through that relationship.

Key Point 9:

For children disabled by maltreatment to the degree that it interferes with their education, laws exist that ensure they receive accommodations and specialized instruction.

Key Point 10:

Schools can heal as well as teach. They can also contribute to the problem if they view the maltreated child's way of adapting to trauma as an obstacle to teaching instead of the focus of it.

Key Point 11:

We all need to advocate for dignity and respect for the individual child.

DISCUSSION QUESTIONS

1. Discuss why attempting to manage the behaviors of maltreated children without understanding the behavior's function is often futile.

2. Why is readiness so critical for the maltreated child's school success?

3. What does it mean to "be in control without being controlling"?

4. What are executive functioning delays, and why is it important to identify such delays in the maltreated child?

5. Discuss why the current pressures to meet state and federal standards may leave the maltreated child behind in the school setting.

PART FIVE:

Strategies for Successfully Parenting Traumatized Children

You cannot create an environment of healing for your wounded, traumatized children unless that healing environment exists for you as well.

What's Ahead:

Living with Children with Attachment Trauma: Understanding the Terminology, Diagnosis, and Parenting Strategies

By Timothy J. Callahan, PsyD

"Enjoying your child and sharing in the awe of discovering what it means to be alive, to be a person in a wondrous world, is crucial for the development of your child's positive sense of self."

—Daniel Siegel[1]

Elle wasn't even aware she was picking a hole in her thigh. She was nervous about the party—her twelfth birthday. "Everyone's coming," she hoped. But fifteen minutes after the official start time, no one was at the door, no bright presents, no party dresses. Her mother was nervous as well. Elle was her pride and joy since she adopted her from a hellish environment ten years ago, and her heart broke watching Elle alone on the couch. Elle began to cry when she noticed the blood. Her mother instinctively yipped, but then squeezed out, "It's okay, honey, you're just nervous." But it wasn't okay. Elle felt like a dam was bursting inside. She ran to her room. She felt a surge of rage, crazy rage, the kind of rage that explodes all over the place. She punched herself in the head so hard she saw stars racing around her head, just like in the cartoons. When her first, and only, guest arrived, Elle was in restraint in the upper hallway, both parents taking hits and kicks.

The children's unit at the hospital was familiar with Elle, this being her sixth visit since the family moved to town four years ago. Medications only seemed to slow her down, which was valuable for maintaining a semblance of a peaceful family atmosphere. But the medications also took away Elle's sparkle. Her treatment team reviewed the list of symptoms and presenting problems, including mood swings, explosive rages, self-harming behaviors, and injuring siblings and animals. Her impairments affected her performance at school, where she frequently was in trouble for defiance and fighting. What was not discussed was Elle's bright wit, her penetrating insights, the way her laugh lit up the room, or that beautiful sparkle in her eyes. Her parents sobbed at the discharge meeting when the attending psychiatrist suggested a residential facility in the eastern part of the state.

Elle felt like she was different, really different, as if no one would or could ever understand her. She settled on that thought. An ugly despair rose up and she screamed, "I hate myself, I want to die." She loathed herself as much as anyone could, but the funny thing was that she didn't even know why. Elle tried to do well and make her parents proud, but something inside, like a big mean bully, kept messing everything up. She felt in danger and on alert all the time. Elle's parents suggested she "keep it together and calm down," but what they didn't know was that she was holding back a volcano with all her might. In a moment of bitter hopelessness, she thought, "They'd all be dead if I wasn't keeping it together."

Elle cut herself badly the first day she got home from the hospital. The next morning, her parents agreed to the residential treatment. Elle thought, *Nothing good can happen, not for me, ever.*

To outside observers, including parents, teachers, peers, and providers, behaviors of attachment-traumatized children can bewilder and frustrate, frighten and unsettle. To outside observers, the child's apparently deliberate attempts to ruin family fun, his compulsive need to control and lie, his explosive reactions to minor slights or demands, his hoarding of food, his stealing, his cruelty to animals, his bullying of siblings and peers, and the ever-present manipulation, stretch even the most capable person's patience.

Parents of children who display symptoms of severe attachment disorders often are perplexed as to why their child would put raw meat in his sister's bed, microwave the kitten, and falsely report sexual abuse. They observe their child to be charming and sweet to strangers, but cold and hateful toward those that love him most.

Hope fades as the parents learn that the child's promises and apparent guilt over misdeeds never translate into behavior change. Some parents are so frightened by their child's sadistic behaviors and apparent lack of remorse or conscience that they conclude the child is evil. But the child is not evil; he is misunderstood, untethered, and bewildered by incapacity to adapt. His brain and being, once safe and secure, will perform amazing feats of growth, but it takes time to heal. Understanding his experience the best we can allows and guides the healing process.

Our goals in this chapter are to: (1) understand the experience of a child with attachment trauma, (2) know the terminology used by the professionals with whom families work, and (3) gain effective parenting strategies.

Behaviors are outward reflections of underlying and unseen feeling states. Since we cannot read people's minds, we must interpret and infer a person's intent from observed behaviors. For example, road rage is inflamed when we attribute the slowness of a driver to an intentional desire to obstruct us. Once we discover the driver is an elderly person just attempting to be safe, our rage fades. Understanding the child's world, seeing it from his perspective, helps us make sense of his behaviors, even those that are bizarre and illogical.

Attachment-traumatized children who display severe, persistent behavior patterns, appear to share certain feelings about themselves and the world.[2] They tend to:

- Experience themselves as bad and incomplete
- Have a limited and fragmented sense of self and autonomy
- Experience deep, obscure, and overwhelming shame
- Have intense feelings of rage without easily identifiable threat
- Feel overwhelmed with pervasive anxiety, but without identifiable threat
- Experience overwhelming despair
- Feel compelled to isolate themselves
- Feel driven by destructive and self-destructive forces outside of their control

Understanding the Concept of Attachment Disorder

The term *attachment disorder*, although frequently used, has no clear, specific, or consensual definition[s].[3] Increasingly, attachment disorder is used to describe an array of behavioral and emotional problems, but only the diagnosis of Reactive Attachment Disorder of Infancy or Early Childhood (RAD) is recognized. RAD was added to the Diagnostic Statistical Manual (DSM) in 1980 and refined in subsequent editions. The DSM-IV-TR describes RAD as a disorder that involves "markedly disturbed and developmentally inappropriate social relatedness in most contexts, beginning before the age of five years."

- RAD is not accounted for solely by developmental delays and does not meet criteria for Pervasive Developmental Disorder (PDD). Children with PDD display severe and pervasive impairments in multiple developmental areas—impairments that are evident in the first years of life and not the result of trauma from maltreatment.
- The disturbance is associated with grossly pathological care, such as persistent disregard of the child's basic emotional and physical needs or "repeated changes of primary caregiver that prevent formation of stable attachments."[4]
- RAD has two types of presentation, *inhibited* and *disinhibited*.

A child with *inhibited* type RAD, for example, is resistant to comfort, withdraws from others, is watchful as if anticipating a threat, and shows a mixture of approach and avoidance toward caregivers and others.

A child with *disinhibited* type will, for example, strike up a conversation in the waiting room with a stranger. In an engaging, charming manner, he will discuss deeply intimate aspects of his life—aspects he refused to reveal to those who love them. Such children appear to be attaching to others but the connection is superficial; such children make friends easily but cannot maintain the friendship.[5]

RAD can be a stigmatizing label and much care should be taken to rule out other overlapping disorders, including conduct and oppositional defiant disorders (ODD), Post-Traumatic Stress Disorder (PTSD), other anxiety disorders, pervasive developmental disorders, mental retardation, and severe forms of attention-deficit hyperactivity disorders (ADHD)—before rendering such a severe diagnosis as RAD.[6]

There is a growing concern among clinicians, theorists, and researchers that the current RAD definition in the DSM-IV-TR is too narrow.[7] O'Conner and Zeanah (2003) have suggested the concept of an *attachment spectrum*.[8] An attachment spectrum includes RAD at the severe end but also contains a range of other attachment-related impairments along a continuum of severity and type.

The following are behaviors that are typical for children who fit the severe end of the attachment spectrum, including RAD. Caution should be taken to avoid assuming that any one or cluster of symptoms indicates a disorder:[9]

- Intense lying, often about obvious things
- Poor response to discipline
- Discomfort with making eye contact, except when lying
- Physical contact, too much or too little
- Lack of mutual enjoyment
- Body functions impairments, including eating, sleeping, urinating, defecating
- Discomfort with increased attachment
- Superficial charm, indiscriminate friendliness
- Poor communication skills
- Difficulty with cause and effect
- Lack of empathy
- Tendency to see things in extreme
- Habitual disassociation or hyper-vigilance
- Desire to tease, hurt other children
- Propensity to act innocent, despite being caught transgressing
- Dangerous behavior without any awareness of risk
- Deliberate intent to break or ruin others' things
- Lack of apparent guilt or remorse
- Cruelty to animals
- Stealing
- Sneaking, hiding, and hoarding food
- Seeming inability to learn from experiences
- False reports of abuse
- Absence of painful feeling when hurt, refusal to let anyone help
- Demanding attitude instead of asking
- Bossiness with adults and peers alike
- Extended tantrums

- Tendency to be accident-prone
- Manipulation of others by acting cute and charming
- Inappropriate friendliness with strangers
- Preoccupation with fires
- Preference for violent cartoons, television, movies

The Debate About RAD Diagnosis

There is much debate regarding the prevalence of attachment disorders for children who have been severely maltreated. Severe maltreatment is prevalent, with victim rates of 12 per 1000 children reported nationally, and countless cases unreported.[10] It's easy to assume that attachment disorders must be similarly prevalent.

The DSM-IV-TR, however, describes the prevalence of RAD as "very uncommon."[11] A 2006 taskforce report on RAD indicates that "a history of maltreatment should not imply any disorder."[12] The report suggests that "many emerge without any long-term mental disorders, let alone a disorder as severe as RAD. Resilience to trauma and adversity is not limited to the extremely healthy or robust.

Rather, resiliencies are a common and relatively normal human characteristic." Yet there is an apparent rise in the use of the diagnosis of RAD to describe troublesome behaviors by children in foster or adoptive care, a rise that may be due more to over-diagnosis than prevalence.[13] So, what can parents do?

The Process of Assessment

As we've noted, attachment trauma can create problems in functioning along a wide continuum of severity and type of presentation. Our resilient nature helps most maltreated children overcome many of the effects of attachment injury. For those children who display impairment in functioning and are suffering or causing suffering, parents should take care to thoroughly assess and rule out non-attachment related factors, such as current environmental stressors (changes in placement, custody hearings) and any other overlapping diagnosis.

A thorough assessment entails multiple sources of information, such as parent and school reports, as well as multiple observations of interactions with parents.[14] Assessment should take into account behavior patterns over time and across contexts and situations. Attention should be paid to the family and caregivers, and not solely the child. Also, cultural issues must always be considered. Diagnosis of attachment disorder should never be given simply because the child was maltreated, growing up in an institution or in foster or adoptive placements.[15] A thorough assessment is crucial not only to clarify the nature of the presenting problems, but to also point to the appropriate intervention.

Parents interested in seeking an assessment for their child should look for mental health providers who are licensed and who have training and experience with children with attachment trauma. It will take some homework and networking to find the resources available in any particular community. The Association for Treatment and Training in the Attachment of Children Web site (http://www.attach.org) is a good place to start. The organization's Web site provides information about what is current in the field and may direct parents to local providers.

Attachment Therapies

The confusion and controversy regarding the term *attachment disorder* is minor, compared to the current debate over so-called attachment therapies. No clear or agreed-upon definition of the term *attachment therapy* exists.[16]

There are many different types of therapy that focus on attachment, ranging from the traditional to the radical, and Web sites touting the effectiveness of a particularly unique attachment therapy are on the rise. "Holding therapies" have drawn the most attention, following the suffocation death of a ten-year-old girl during a therapy session in 2000; several similar deaths have occurred over the past seven years.[17] In a cautionary 2006 report, a task force, assembled by the American Professional Society on the Abuse of Children (APASAC) and the American Psychological Association (APA), attempted to cut through the controversy and concern by setting guidelines and recommendations regarding attachment disorders, assessments, and treatments.

The report describes the field of attachment as "young and diverse" and contends that "not all attachment-related interventions are controversial." The report also indicates that many treatments have not been scientifically determined to be safe and effective. The report is firm in its position that the following treatments or attachment parenting techniques are unproven, potentially dangerous, and should not be used:[18]

- Physical coercion
- Psychologically or physically enforced holding
- Physical restraint

- Physical domination
- Provoked catharsis
- Ventilation of rage
- Age regression
- Humiliation
- Withholding or forcing of food or water
- Prolonged isolation
- Exaggerated levels of control and domination over a child

The report clarifies that these recommendations do not include reasonable use of behavior management techniques, time-outs, grounding, rewards/punishments, and occasional restraint to prevent injury. It should be noted that holding in general, such as hugging, playing, and touching, is an essential aspect of a healthy parent-child relationship. Parents should not confuse this healthy affection with the risky coercive or compression holds mentioned in the report.

Before parents consider involvement in attachment-focused therapy, the task force recommends that parents seek traditional, first-line treatments that focus on "caregiver and environmental stability, child safety, patience, sensitivity, consistency, and nurturance."[19] Many proponents of the intrusive attachment therapies argue that more traditional interventions, such as family therapy, cognitive-behavioral approaches, and parent skills training, are not as deeply effective as attachment therapy. Research, however, indicates that the common characteristics of successful attachment approaches include the core features of traditional therapy—namely, short-term, behavioral, and goal-directed focus on the parent-child relationship.[20]

The field of attachment treatment is in its infancy (or possibly toddlerhood), and the future looks encouraging. But for now, parents must be discriminating consumers of all things attachment related. It can be argued that, historically, it has been a scientific challenge to determine the effectiveness of any psychotherapeutic interventions. Parents should look to attachment models that are grounded in research and that treat the child with dignity, kindness, and respect. Attachment interventions should help parents provide a secure and responsive base, increase attunement, and deepen the relationship. Avoid interventions that are designed to provoke rage or confrontations.

The task force report cautions against any approach that predicts that a child may become a psychopath or predator if left untreated. Models that portray the child "as pervasively manipulative, cunning, or deceitful are not conducive to good treatment and may promote abusive practices."[21]

Parenting Principles That Lead to Success

Alice and Sam adopted Justin after fostering him for two years. Justin had improved significantly while in their care. He caught up on the verbal, cognitive, and social skills that were postponed by years of neglect and abuse by his birth parents. He no longer wet the bed. His temper tantrums, well known around the neighborhood, had subsided. Special school accommodations had resulted in good academic progress and less behavioral acting-out.

The day after the adoption was finalized, ten-year-old Justin attacked Alice with a kitchen knife. She was unhurt but deeply concerned. Justin had a history of rages but was never known to attack anyone. He became withdrawn and irritable. Sam observed, "He seems to be testing us, like he needs to make sure we'll keep him, no matter what." The school called, requesting a meeting due to Justin's disruptive and aggressive behavior. When Alice and Sam required a much-needed break, no babysitters were willing to watch him because of previous explosive incidents. The recent family reunion became a disaster when Justin allegedly bullied the younger cousins and subsequently "freaked out" when confronted about his behavior.

Alice and Sam's twenty-year marriage had weathered many trials and tribulations, but this seventy-pound little boy was putting the union at risk. They argued more than ever. Alice felt a distance growing between her and Sam. She cried when Sam breached the topic of giving Justin up for adoption. After a long and tearful night of discussion, Alice and Sam recommitted themselves to Justin, reaffirming that "he is our boy. No matter what, we'll make this work."

Alice and Sam sought support and knowledge. They found a community of parents and service providers who were dedicated to helping children with attachment trauma adapt and thrive. After years of reading, research, assessments, therapies, support groups, special classes, and programs, they learned how to parent more compassionately and effectively. They committed to a family atmosphere of shared fun, peacefulness, and mutual respect, avoiding at all costs the lingering presence of rage, fear, or resentment. Matter-of-fact limits and clear expectations took months to fine-tune, but they eventually freed the household of the daily chaos. Justin's behavior was difficult to understand at first, but by being open, empathic, and attentive, Alice and Sam found they began to feel more attuned with Justin's experiences. Probably the hardest thing they had to do was to take care of themselves, keep their own joy, and not allow Justin to ruin their days. In the end, Alice and Sam were grateful they hung in there. Justin turned out be an amazing person.

Parents face unusual challenges in parenting a child who has suffered attachment trauma. Extra care and support is crucial for all involved. Knowledge and perspective, and understanding and informed approaches, are particularly necessary when helping children adapt and thrive in the family environment. In many ways, parenting a child with attachment trauma is similar to parenting a nontraumatized child but in more concentrated form. The key appears to be a willingness to spend lots of time with the child, interacting, playing, and guiding. The more the time spent with the child, the more opportunities there are to reorganize and reactivate the child's brain.

Alice and Sam made the leap to understanding parenting as an art form that requires passion, disciplined perseverance, and adherence to certain principles. Daniel Hughes, in his book *Facilitating Developmental Attachment*, outlines some key principles to consider when parenting a child of trauma:[22]

- *Family Atmosphere:* In Justin's case, his parents committed themselves to maintaining an atmosphere of relative peace and enjoyment, mutual fun, and respect for individuality and dignity. Alice and Sam learned strategies to keep resentments from accumulating, and ensured that everyone went to bed free of anger and tension.

- *Expectations and Structure:* Alice and Sam lived in chaos for years. They felt desperately out of control. Children, who early in their lives had no one to structure their world, tend to crave the security of limits. Yet they fight to the death to push through or around the structure. Expectations should be clear and firm, and enforced in a calm, consistent, and matter-of-fact manner.

- *Emotional Attunement:* Alice and Sam listened carefully and observed Justin's patterns in a loving, curious way. They devoted themselves to attempting to understand his experience and empathize with his feelings. Since attachment trauma affects the child's emotional connection to the world around him, it is critical for parents to help rebuild the connection through attunement, understanding, and validation. Over time, and through efforts to help their child identify and express feelings, Alice and Sam helped Justin regulate his emotions more effectively.

- *Practice:* Alice and Sam consciously viewed Justin as a person who lacked skills and needed practice, rather than jumping to the conclusion that he behaved in purposefully resistant ways. Not completing a chore, for example, was a source of much frustration for Justin's parents. Instead of employing punishment, Sam showed Justin how to wash and dry the dishes. They did it together and then Justin went solo. A natural consequence for not completing a chore is to practice it until the skill is developed.

- *Regression:* Attachment-traumatized children may appear, at times, to act younger than their age. Justin, for example, sometimes talked like a baby and acted like he wanted to nurse. Alice and Sam learned that periodic regression was the way Justin attempted to work through the trauma. They used these regressions to provide him the nurturance he did not receive when he was younger.

- *Parental Self-Care:* Alice and Sam initially struggled to attend to their own psychological and emotional needs because it seemed selfish. Over time, however, they realized that because parenting an attachment-traumatized child can be grueling work, if they were to be there fully for Justin, they must be healthy. Healthy parents attempt to maintain their joy and not let the child set the tone, despite the child's effort to ruin the good times. Humor, patience, perspective, openness to support from others, and realistic expectations are key virtues for parents to practice.

Arthur Becker-Weidman, in his book *Creating Capacity for Attachment: Dyadic Developmental Psychotherapy in the Treatment of Trauma-Attachment Disorders,* suggests parents take a P.L.A.C.E. approach with their children: **P**layfulness, **L**ove, **A**cceptance, **C**uriosity, and **E**mpathy.[23] Fun and play are one of the first things to go when there is undue stress in the family. Playfulness and humor are healing and can help reestablish the bond following tough times. Loving the child unconditionally accelerates and deepens the attachment process. Learning to accept and validate the child's viewpoint and feelings enables parents to understand and react more effectively.

Spending time with our children and investing ourselves fully in the art of parenting are the most effective ways to counter the effects of early chronic mal-treatment. Children with attachment trauma need more of our concentrated time than children who have not been maltreated.

Parents need to be constantly aware of themselves—what they say and how they say it. More so than we think, maltreated children listen attentively to what is being said between parents. They are vigilant to anticipated threat or abandonment.

Parents are often the target, but not the source, of a child's wrath, so it is important to rise above the instinctual reaction to respond personally and emo-tionally to a child's attacks.

Simple things, such as being glad to see the child when he comes home from school, playing games, reading bedtime stories, painting fingernails, or brushing hair, have enormous impact on building attachment.

Parenting children with attachment-related problems can be very reward-ing but also very exhausting. Parents need support, and they should not hesitate to seek assistance or therapy for themselves, individually, as a couple, as a fam-ily, and/or in a group of other parents.

Quick Reference

Children's symptoms from attachment trauma can be bewildering, frustrating, and even frightening to parents, teachers, peers, and therapists.

Key Point 1:

The impact from early and chronic maltreatment can be deep and pervasive, affecting fundamental functions and processes.

Key Point 2:

Children whose symptoms cluster into a diagnosable syndrome share certain experiences and display common behaviors. Reactive Attachment Disorder of Infancy or Early Childhood (RAD) is the recognized diagnosis used by mental health professionals to describe the symptoms associated with attach-ment trauma.

Key Point 3:

RAD is a rare and rather controversial disorder, frequently misapplied and over-applied to children who are in fact suffering from other disorders, or are simply acting out in foster or adoptive care.

Key Point 4:

Much care should be taken to research treatment for attachment disorders. Parents should understand what types of interventions are available and avoid any approaches that are coercive, dominating, humiliating, harsh, or conceptualize the child as psychopathic or pervasively deceitful.

Key Point 5:

Parenting is an art with certain guiding principles. Parenting children with attachment disorders requires incredible patience, knowledge, passion, love, empathy, and skill.

Key Point 6:

Parents must take care of themselves emotionally by seeking support and keeping their humor and perspective.

Key Point 7:

Children are resilient and their brains are capable of incredible healing. The traumatized child can bond, grow, and thrive.

DISCUSSION QUESTIONS

1. Why is it important for you as a parent to understand the life experiences of a child with attachment trauma?

2. Why is it important for you as a parent to understand the common feelings shared by attachment-traumatized children?

3. Looking at the list of behaviors that are typical for children who fit the severe end of the attachment spectrum, do you identify any of those behaviors in your children? How have you tried to manage these behaviors? What do you need the most help with?

4. Before seeking an assessment or treatment for your child who might have an attachment disorder, what other steps and actions should be considered?

5. Discuss the principles of parenting to consider when parenting a child with attachment trauma. What principle might be most helpful for you right now?

Chapter Twelve

Taking Care of Yourself: The Parent's Neglected Task

By Betsy Keefer Smalley, LSW

"Affix your own oxygen mask first. When that is in place, you may help your child."

—Flight attendant, any airline

Nancy and John Turner had two adopted children: Robin, a fourteen-year-old, domestically adopted child; and Randy, a twelve-year-old, adopted child from Asia. Both children had been adopted at a few months of age. John experienced serious problems with his heart and was in the hospital to have a pacemaker implanted. Nancy, understandably, was a "bundle of nerves." In fact, both parents were extremely tense and preoccupied with the health crisis facing their family. It is not surprising, then, that they did not notice the impact of the health crisis on their adopted children, who were panic-stricken that they would again lose parents. Robin became so anxious at the prospect of losing her father that she ran away from home, from a situation she feared would end in yet another abandonment. Now Nancy had a dangerously ill husband in the hospital and a truant daughter, only fourteen years old, out in the world, unprotected and alone. The stress and worry were overwhelming for Nancy, making her feel as though she were living in a pressure cooker. Nancy's coping ability was even further strained by the expectation that she meet the needs of her younger child, Randy, who was very frightened for both his father and his sister.

All parents feel stress. Raising children is a challenging job, certainly not one for wimps. The challenges of adoptive parenting increase the level of stress for any family, and adopting or fostering traumatized children increases stress even more. As we have seen in earlier chapters, stressors on the adoptive or foster family include the following:

- Unmet expectations regarding adoption and family life
- Feelings of failure, guilt
- The impact of adoption or foster care on other relationships (with spouse, other children in the family, extended family, close friends)
- Coping with a child's needs or challenging behaviors
- Dealing with multiple service providers (or the lack of adoption-competent service providers)
- School issues
- Difficulty in finding substitute caregivers to provide occasional respite or relief
- Managing either openness in adoption or the challenges associated with closed adoptions (see information on psychological presence in chapter two).

The level of stress, as we have seen in chapter seven, is one of the three factors that can propel a family or individual into crisis. The second factor in crisis control is coping. Let's explore some principles of self-care that will increase the adoptive parent's capacity for effective coping.

Principles of Self-Care for Foster and Adoptive Parents

Recall often that you are not the source of your child's problems.[1]
Many adoptive parents have to work hard to remind themselves (and others) that their children came into the adoptive family with histories of abuse, neglect, abandonment, separation from significant others, predisposition to mood disorders or other mental health issues, behavioral difficulties, learning and developmental lags, and insecure attachment. The adoptive parents are *not* the problem, and they are not in charge of "fixing" their children. Heather Forbes, an adoptive parent and post-adoption service provider, said, "You are responsible for providing a stable environment in which the child can be in charge of his own healing."[2] A significant challenge for adoptive parents is accepting that healing will likely be a long-term process. The "solution" of permanence in a nurturing family may take years, or even decades, to take root in a maltreated child's psyche. Adoptive parents were motivated to help wounded children, and frustration with the daunting amount of time, energy, and commitment this requires is understandable.

Adoptive parents should not assume complete responsibility for behavior and attachment issues that developed prior to their connection to the child. They can control their own attitudes, responses to the child, and parenting strategies, even when it is not possible to control, hurry, or manage the child's adjustment process.

When educators, mental health therapists, extended family members, and friends of the family are judgmental and unsupportive, parents feel a lack of validation for the hard work they are doing. But when parents themselves join in on such inappropriate blaming and lack of validation, the guilt and shame can be intolerable.

This overpowering guilt, rather than the child's difficult behaviors or his insecure attachment, is the culprit underlying the inability of some adoptive parents to continue their commitment to their adopted children.

Parents can learn to cope with difficult behaviors, or even with the child's rejection. It is much more difficult for parents to deal with their own self-rejection or blaming. Have you ever noticed that the more you try to be a good parent, the guiltier you feel? Silly, isn't it? We can experience those negative reactions when we haven't taken time to become centered, to understand and reflect on what our mission is—what we're called to be in life. Rather than exercising our desire to do something good, regardless of the results, we become manipulated by guilt, the reactions of others, and a distorted sense of duty. Robert Wicks, author of *Riding the Dragon,* tells us, "Moreover, at the critical moment when children [sic] really do need us to walk the extra mile with them, we pull back because we are just too tired to go on."[3]

So, what are some healthier responses to these feelings of guilt and fatigue?

- Learn to clarify for other "blamers" that you are not responsible for the difficulties your child experiences. Help them to understand that you are working hard to help him resolve his emotional wounds, and that this will take significant time. Remind them that you have the commitment and patience to help the child regain his trust in adults, particularly in you, his parents.
- Remind your spouse that he or she is not the problem.
- Most importantly, believe this same truth yourself.

Maintain a sense of humor.

Adoptive parents who can maintain humor in the face of parenting challenges will find it much easier to cope. Humor can serve as an aid to coping as well as an effective way to reframe a relationship challenge.

> John and Nancy Turner joined a support group for adoptive parents facing extreme problems with their children. Eight other adoptive families also attended the same group, which served as a lifeline for post-adoptive parents coping with troubled children. Some parents had children with frequent school suspensions for behavioral outbursts; some were dealing with children who had issues with lying, and so on. Just before Christmas, one creative adoptive father wrote a parody of a "Christmas newsletter" for the entire group, bragging obnoxiously about each family's child, inflating their difficult behaviors into assets. This parody of our culture's annual boastful newsletters about children and families brought mirth and a strong connection to other struggling parents during a troubling holiday season.

Connect with other foster and adoptive parents.

Find support from another adoptive parent. You definitely cannot safely vent your own rage and frustration to your child, probably not to a professional, perhaps not to your spouse. But another parent will understand.

There are both informal and formal support networks for adoptive families.

Informal groups include online chat rooms for adoptive or foster parents, such as www.chat.adoption.com; magazines for adoptive families, such as *Adoptive Families Magazine* (www.adoptivefamilies.com); and play groups or friendly connections with other adoptive families.

Formal support networks include post-adoption support groups, foster family support organizations (local, regional, and national), conferences such as state adoption or foster care conferences or the North American Council for Adoptable Children (NACAC) conference every summer. For additional information regarding the NACAC conference, visit www.nacac.org/conference/conference.html. To find other formal support networks for adoptive families, see Appendix Two at the back of this book.

Stop comparing yourself to other families.

Debra McMahon writes in *Adoptalk*, a newsletter published by the North American Council for Adoptable Children, "They [other families] do not live your life, and they are not raising your children. Get comfortable with compromising and being different. Your child may talk, think, achieve, behave, and live differently from other children. Instead of measuring your family's worth by other people's standards, set expectations for your family based on your children's capabilities and your family's reality."[4] Remember that you are comparing your "insides" to other families' "outsides." Of course, this is a very unfair comparison!

Find an adoption-competent family therapist.

Many families find that they require assistance from a professional in learning to cope with the challenges of parenting their adopted or foster children. It is essential when looking for a skilled therapist to do your homework and find a counselor who is "adoption competent."

Many mental health professionals have had limited training in understanding the dynamics of adoptive family life and many have a troubling tendency to look for pathology within the family whenever a child is experiencing extreme behavior or attachment issues. This blaming approach will be counterproductive in working with adoptive parents. Remember, adoptive parents are not the problem! To find an adoption-competent therapist within your community, contact a post-adoption program, if available. If post-adoption services are not accessible in your community, contact an adoption agency in the area. Even if that agency did not facilitate your adoption, they will most likely be aware of therapists who are experienced in helping adoptive families. Further, talk with other adoptive or foster families in the area and ask about their experiences with various counselors.

At a minimum, a therapist must:

- Be knowledgeable about adoption and the psychological impact of adoption on children and families
- Be experienced in working with adopted children and their families
- Know the types of help available for adoption-related issues and problems
- Have received training in working with adoptive families[5]

Interviewing Prospective Therapists

Parents should contact prospective therapists to give a brief description of the concern or problem for which they need help. The following questions may help you select the therapist who can provide the most useful assistance:[6]

1. What is your experience with adoption and adoption issues?

2. How long have you been in practice, and what degrees, licenses, or certifications do you hold?

3. What continuing clinical training have you had on adoption issues?

4. Do you include parents and other family members in the therapeutic process?

5. Do you prefer to work with the entire family or only with the children?

6. Do you give parents regular reports on the child's progress?

7. Can you estimate a timeframe for the course of therapy?

8. What approach to therapy do you use?

9. What changes in the daily life of the child and family might we expect to see as a result of the therapy?

10. Do you work with teachers, juvenile justice personnel, day-care providers, and other adults in the child's life, when appropriate?

If there is no therapist in your community experienced in working with adoptive families, you have two choices: you can travel to a community with adoption-competent services or you can find a skilled family therapist and ask them to do some reading or training to become more familiar with adoption issues and adoptive family development.

Stay regulated. Don't jump into the child's fear.

"When your child collapses into his fear, don't go with him," says Heather Forbes.[7] Recognize "how your own internal peace impacts the external peace," says adoption therapist Juli Alvarado.[8] Create peace within yourself so the atmosphere of the home becomes calm. At times, traumatized children induce their negative feelings in adoptive parents because they don't know how to manage or regulate their feelings themselves.

As we discussed in chapter 4, parents need to create a "secure base" for the child. The parent must be secure in who he is, a person who can teach and model how to regulate his emotions.

Of course, there will be times when the parent has reached the limit of his capacity to cope. After all, no parent is superhuman, and all parents can have feelings, including anger and fear, triggered by a child's defiance or emotional outburst. In those situations, the parent may need to say to the child, "I am leaving the room because I don't want to do or say something I don't mean. I will be back as soon as I am calm again, and we can talk about how to solve this problem." This type of response to conflict demonstrates for the child:

- I am taking responsibility for my own emotional state.
- I will not abandon you as others have.

Find outlets for your own emotional, spiritual, and physical needs and design opportunities to enjoy them.

While immersed in parenting demands, it is easy to allow your other significant relationships to "slide off the table." In order to keep your own cup of energy full, you need to replenish it. Your adopted child may be unable to fill your cup. While you wait for his "cup" to be full enough that he can share with you, you must nurture your relationships with those people who can meet that need. Your spouse, supportive extended family members and friends, your pastor, or members of your church family may provide the nurturing you need in order to nurture your needy child.

Exercise can release tension and increase coping ability. In fact, endorphins released by the pituitary gland following exercise can be helpful in combating depression. While you may feel you do not have the time or energy to exercise, it is likely that you will feel more energetic, rather than depleted, following physical activity.

Take advantage of activities or hobbies that can give you more energy or renew your sense of well-being. Author Robert Wicks explains, "Too often we don't avail ourselves of the type of activities that renew us."[9]

Whenever we board an airplane, the flight attendants admonish us to put on our own oxygen mask first, before helping others. In the same way, we need to engage in those activities that give us emotional "oxygen" before we can nurture needy children. Spouses can provide significant support for these renewing activities through "tag-team" parenting. Spouses can help exhausted partners renew themselves by assuming parenting responsibilities so that the partner can take advantage of an activity or interest that energizes that person.

Try to schedule some down time every day. "If you have no down time—a time without distractions or demands—you cannot benefit from moments of reflection and calm that may help you to center and stay balanced," says Debra McMahon.[10] Some suggestions include:

- Quiet walks by yourself
- Time and space for meditation (prayer, time alone to consider the purpose of your work with this child)
- Spiritual or recreational reading—including the diaries and biographies of others whom you admire
- Opportunities to laugh, through movies or cheerful friends
- A hobby, such as gardening or music

Do a role check. Is one parent carrying most of the load?[11]

Many couples struggle with the level of energy and commitment required to parent a child who seems to reject all of the parents' efforts to provide nurture. If one parent becomes depleted, an unfair burden may fall on the shoulders of the other parent.

Occasionally, one parent over-functions as the nurturing parent or as the disciplinarian. In these situations, one parent (assuming he or she is more committed to the adoption or has learned more about children who have been traumatized) does not allow his or her partner to participate fully in the parenting role. A helpful technique is to explore and list which parenting tasks each parent does very well and which parenting tasks are problematic or disastrous. The parents can then engage in "role differentiation," deciding which parent will be the primary parent for particular tasks in caring for a child. This enables the parents to work as a team, share the load, and use their individual strengths to benefit the entire family.

Choose your battles and win the war.

When you have conflict with your child regarding his behavior, evaluate whether the issue is really something that matters right now. Will it matter in five years? If his homework isn't complete, it matters today, but it likely will not matter in a few years. Her decision to get her eyebrow pierced may not matter next year, but her choice to engage in premarital sex could have devastating results. Learn to "separate the wheat from the chaff" and focus on the issues that could have permanent or long-lasting effects on the child's life.

Prioritize what you can accomplish and keep your list realistic and short. Work on one behavior or issue at a time. If you attempt to change five behaviors at once, you and the child will both be frustrated and overwhelmed. After one issue is resolved, you can move on to the next, most emergent challenge. While choosing your battles, you need to decide which can be deferred until later and which need to be addressed immediately.

Teach and correct in ways that enhance, rather than diminish, attachment. Discipline is about guidance and coaching, and it is best accomplished through rewards, including lots of attention for positive behavior (even small improvements deserve attention and reward). Punishment, a negative consequence for poor behavior, is sometimes necessary. However, if you rely as much as possible on discipline rather than punishment, you will enhance your child's secure attachment. Punishment tends to undermine attachment.

Stop, drop, and roll.
Juli Alvarado, an adoptive mother, treatment foster parent, and adoption therapist, teaches parents of traumatized children to "stop, drop, and roll."[12] She encourages parents to refrain from frightening an already frightened child in a confrontation by following these steps:

1. **Stop** talking. Don't scream at your child, belittle him, or use sarcasm. Remind yourself to close your mouth.

2. **Drop** into your breathing. Relax and focus on your own breathing instead of the conflict you are experiencing with your child.

3. **Roll** back into your relationship with your child. Allow the repair in the connection between you to occur. Focus on what you want to teach and model for your child in the moment, not on what he has not yet learned. Move into understanding rather than blaming.

Identify who owns the problem.
When a family problem occurs, parents should decide who owns it. To assist with this decision, parents should ask themselves these four questions:[13]

1. *Are my rights being disrespected?* Rights include the right to be respected as a person, respect for your property, the right to have a life apart from your children, the right to enjoy friendships and other relationships, and the right for privacy and time for yourself.

2. *Could anyone get hurt?*

3. *Are someone's belongings threatened?*

4. *Is the child too young to be responsible for this problem?*

If the answer to *any* of these questions is yes, *you* own the problem.

If the answer to *every* question is no, the *child* owns the problem.

Whoever owns the problem is responsible for solving it. However, because traumatized children often lack good problem-solving skills, parents will frequently need to provide guidance in negotiating a solution. Remember, however, that you are not responsible for solving problems owned by the child; you are only responsible for coaching him in how to problem-solve.

Take a break—find respite care.

All parents need a break from the demands of children. Parents of traumatized children have especially heavy demands, yet may have fewer options for relief. Some parents feel they cannot trust another caregiver to pinch-hit. Or they may be unable to find a caregiver with the skills to manage their child's behavior. Or they may feel that their child's needs are so extreme, it would be damaging to leave the child. Yet, the energy expended in finding an avenue for some relief will pay big dividends in increased patience, renewed energy, and commitment. Your child will receive the recurring message that, while you may go away from time-to-time, you can be counted on to return. Let's explore some guidelines to increase success with respite care:

There are several varieties of respite care, or relief from parenting responsibilities. **Informal respite care** includes the "tag-team parenting" mentioned earlier: asking a trusted family member or friend to supervise the child while you take a break, a paid babysitter, or another adoptive parent you have met in a support group or adoptive parent association. Informal respite care is a wonderful option and the type most parents have used when they need to be away from their children for an appointment or a time to be child-free. To take advantage of informal respite care, you must find a sitter you can rely on.

Formal respite care: As you explore your informal options, you may not find many "takers" who can handle the challenges presented by your child. If that is the case, formal respite care may be available through post-adoption service agencies, foster care organizations, programs for developmentally delayed children, or community service organizations. Formal respite services provide trained, experienced caregivers who are accustomed to caring for children with special needs. There is typically a fee for these services, but the fee gives you the peace of mind that a skilled caregiver is supervising your child. To investigate formal respite services in your community, contact an adoption or foster care agency or the local United Way.

When to use respite care: Respite care can be planned or available for emergency situations following a family crisis. Planned respite opportunities are highly preferable to respite following a family "meltdown." Emergency respite may save the day when parents are at the end of their rope, but it sends a message of abandonment to a child who has experienced too much of this in his history. Planned respite, on the other hand, is expected and anticipated by both the child and the adoptive parent. Planned respite may occur one weekend a month, every Monday night as "date night" for mom and dad, or even a camp for adopted children during the summer months.

Be creative: You may be able to design your own respite program by collaborating with one or more adoptive families who agree to take turns giving one another some relief. One community with a local college formed a respite program for adopted children. The pre-adolescent children brought sleeping bags to the college gym and slept on the floor one Saturday night each month. Two adult staff supervised the children with the help of numerous college students studying social work, psychology, and education. The students received an internship in their fields of study while volunteering with the adopted children; the adopted children had a great time and were able to discuss some of their issues and feelings about being adopted in support groups; and the parents had one weekend each month to recharge their batteries.

Don't forego planned respite care, formal or informal. Adoptive parents should avoid "pile-ups."[14] You may find it preserves your own sanity to arrange a "child care" day periodically to pay bills, do taxes, get your own health needs addressed by professionals, and so on.

Remember that the child's progress will not always be consistent.
There will be times when the child's behavior regresses, when problems you considered resolved will reappear. "That's because human growth is never constant.

People move forward and acquire new skills, then appear to slip back and lose them again. Remember, though, that the regressions do not go back further than the peak of the last growth spurt," say Regina Kupecky and Dr. Greg Keck, authors of *Adopting the Hurt Child*.[15] While this "backsliding" can be disconcerting, it is most often temporary. It is part of the process of healing.

Look for patterns in your child's outbursts. If you understand his triggers, you may be able to prevent an explosion altogether, or lessen the intensity significantly.
Does your child experience a crisis annually as her birthday approaches? Is early May, with Mother's Day around the corner, always a battle of divided loyalties for your child? Does September's return to school or the beginning of summer vacation signal trouble? Do you experience "arsenic hour" every evening just before dinner?

When you have some understanding of what sets off your child, you can develop strategies to intercept some of these triggers in a way that prevents crisis (see chapter eight for more information to identify and intercept triggers).

Keep in mind that children use behavior to express feelings because they haven't been successful in communicating feelings through language. Look for the feelings behind the behaviors and learn to address the issues and feelings underlying the triggers. With your help, your child will learn to regulate his emotions more effectively and express feelings with words instead of behavior.

Use family meetings creatively.
Hold family meetings regularly. Family meetings are designed to negotiate solutions for family problems so children learn to solve problems in ways that respect the needs of all members of the group. Family meetings give children control by participating in family decisions such as planning vacations or special field days for the family. Another function of family meetings is to have fun! The following guidelines will help you design successful family meetings that accomplish all of these goals:[16]

- *Time and frequency of meetings should depend on the age span of the children involved*. Obviously, younger children will need shorter meetings with activities as well as discussion.
- *Have an agenda*. Post a sheet of paper somewhere in the house so family members can add discussion issues to it.

- *Plan the time.* The parent should decide which items to cover during the meeting. Allow time to problem-solve and negotiate decisions.
- *Take turns.* Let everyone take turns being responsible for different tasks during the meeting—leading the meeting, reading the list, taking notes, and so on. It may be helpful to have a "talking stick." Only the person holding the "talking stick" may speak. This assures each person can complete what he or she wants to say before passing the stick to another family member.
- *Take notes.* Recording the agreements and established plans helps to prevent confusion and future disagreements about the decisions made.
- *Let everyone participate.* Allowing the children to speak first helps them feel significant and fosters responsibility.
- *Limit complaining.* While family members should be encouraged to respectfully offer their opinions and input, the meeting should not become a "gripe session." Use open-ended questions to refocus the group on solutions. For example, "Okay, now that we know this is a problem, what can we do about it?"
- Do what you agree to do, and follow through with agreements until the next meeting. If changes are needed, negotiate those at the next meeting.
- Use family meetings to celebrate each other and successes. Talk about positive things and express appreciation to one another for some help or act of kindness. Ask people to share what's going well for them right now.
- Plan family fun. Use family meetings to plan a family activity or outing that everyone will enjoy.
- Use family meetings to help create predictable routines and structure for your household. Traumatized children do well with structure and an unhurried routine (and so do their parents).

Find ways to have fun with your child.

Parents, particularly those with children who display difficult behaviors, can be drawn into a steady stream of correction. The correction can escalate into nagging or other negative messages sent to a child who already believes that he is unlovable and unkeepable. One way to interrupt this negative cycle is to work consciously on ways to increase your positive interactions with the child. This is not only fun for everyone, but, more importantly for long-range benefits, it enhances attachment.

We often hear about "love at first sight" between two adults—a "magic" that occurs and all appears to be wonderful. Although that initial attraction may have sparked the relationship, it will not carry the couple through fifty years of marriage. Adoption is similar. A photo or first meeting may spark the relationship into being, but it will not suffice for parents to withstand the "terrible twos" or turbulent teens. It will take maturity and planning on the part of the parent to remain in the adult role when the child is exhibiting difficult and challenging behaviors.

The child must sense unconditional love from his parents, especially during these times. Children can sense, and will negatively react to, an adult who regards them in a negative light. Of course, parents become upset over things their children do and this generally does not harm the parent-child relationship in the long run. However, a parent's feeling of long-term negative regard for a child almost always predicts collapse of the parent-child relationship.

Increase your positive interactions.

The positive interaction cycle is initiated by the parent. It involves anticipating the needs of the child and acting to meet those needs. It is not tied to the child's performance, such as a reward for cleaning his room, but is offered because the parent operates on a philosophy of "big people take care of little people."

Many adoptive parents wrongly believe that the child should "take the first step" in forming attachments with them. A lack of trust, and ambivalence about new attachments, may make this impossible for many adopted children. Adoptive parents should regularly approach the child in a nonthreatening, gentle manner to initiate social interactions. Parents must be prepared to continue to engage the child in a meaningful and pleasurable interaction without expecting the child to reciprocate in kind.

Unlike rewards or sticker charts, this positive interaction process is interactive. It involves an exchange between the parent and child. The exchange may be brief, as in "Here, let me help you fix your barrette," or an extended activity, such as playing a game of Monopoly or hiking.

The parent could offer to comb the child's hair, play her favorite game, go for a walk, get a new pair of sneakers, or read the child a favorite book or poem.

Positive interaction involves many of the things that occur naturally in families, such as blowing bubbles for a toddler to pop with his fingers or teaching the child motions to a "finger song." In planning these types of activities, it is important to keep in mind the following principles:[17]

- *You must genuinely participate in the interactions without emotional reservations.* If you are not comfortable with a planned activity for some reason, it is best to find another activity that will be more suited to your comfort level.
- *Consider the personal preferences of others who will be participating.* It is appropriate at times to stretch individual preferences and encourage family members to try new things, but be certain that it is not too much of a stretch.
- *"Less is more" is a good principle to follow.* It is best to keep activities quick, fun, and to the point. It is best to have a number of simple activities "under your belt" before you attempt longer, complex ones.
- *Talk to your child's therapist or caseworker about the intended activity.* They may have insight into your child's background or functioning that would help you plan for success.
- *Think of your child's triggers before you decide to complete a particular activity.* A child who has a history of sexual abuse around bedtime may not respond well to a bubble bath and snuggle time before bed.
- *Try to make it easy for the child to follow the rules of any games used in the activity.* It is important that the child begin to have fun "obeying" the adult.
- *Try to make things noncompetitive, if possible.* Change the goal of games to be group oriented, such as "Let's see how many Jenga blocks we can all build. When we make it to twenty, then we will eat the ice cream," or "Let's see if the whole family can find all these words in this word search puzzle."

Positive interaction requires that the parent be able to "wipe the slate clean" over and over again without holding any grudges or frustration from past failed attempts. Some children will take a long time to respond to a caring adult. They may have been so disappointed in adults' maladaptive attempts to take care of them that they may need lots of "proof" that it will be better this time. That proof may mean the adult has to reach out over and over again without much response on the part of the child. The adults need to keep themselves healthy during these trying times and have a support system that will meet their needs with other adults. Children should never be responsible for making adults happy or fulfilled.

Positive interaction may also require that the adults break some of their own parenting rules. Rules such as "You must do all your homework correctly before playing outside," or "You must eat all the food on your plate before you may get up from the table," may lead to night after night of negative interaction cycles. Parenting children with attachment issues requires a flexible approach to parenting and the ability to start each day anew. Positive interaction allows, even encourages, the parents to put some fun back into the parenting process. Try a "Dessert Before Dinner" night! If the parent/child relationship has been strained lately, arrange to pick the child up at school for a lunch out at a fast food restaurant; this provides some time alone for you and the child to have fun. Parenting should not be drudgery. If the situation has degenerated to this level, you will have to mindfully design opportunities for fun with the child.

Reframe your definition of success and celebrate small gains.

Be sure that your expectations of yourself are realistic. Many parents give up because they are more disappointed in themselves than they are in the child. No parent is perfect, and there will be many days when you realize you have made mistakes. Fortunately, few of these mistakes are fatal. When there has been a difficult episode with your child, repair the relationship as soon as possible. Talk with the child about what triggered your anger, what triggered his reaction, and how both of you can avoid a similar episode in the future. Conflict is an expected part of relationships, particularly with those people we care about most. Be sure to recognize the parenting strengths and successes you have noticed in your family and yourself.

Use positive self-talk or learned optimism. "Some people predict worst-case scenarios, apparently so that they will not feel so bad if terrible things happen," says Deborah Gray, author of *Nurturing Adoptions*. "Actually, they waste energy and momentum that could be used to solve problems. I have asked families to use their resources in a positive way rather than wearying themselves with gloomy predictions."[18]

Avoid "catastrophising." Parents often fall victim to dire predictions of the future based on the child's current level of functioning: *He'll wind up living in a refrigerator box under a freeway overpass. She'll have three children by the time she's twenty, and they'll all have different fathers. He'll be on the roof of a parking garage with a loaded rifle.* Mark Twain recognized the total foolishness of worrying when he wrote, "My life has been filled with terrible misfortunes . . . most of which never happened."[19]

"Families who are raising children should have a sense of what success looks like and feels like for this specific child. They need to have a specific, reality-based future point," explains Deborah Gray. "Often families of children with special needs will need the objectivity of their social workers and/or therapists to form realistic expectations and a path toward realistic goals for their child. A projected age of twenty-five years old is a good benchmark age. Working backward, figure out what will have to happen to ensure the best likelihood of that positive development for their child by the time he reaches twenty-five."[20]

At age four, Gretchen was adopted from the foster care system, following two years of serious neglect by her single birth mother and two years in a foster family with an older couple. Her elementary years were fairly uneventful, but middle school was anything but calm. Gretchen developed a serious drinking problem and was hospitalized for treatment. The psychiatrist treating Gretchen had almost no experience with adoption issues. He held out little hope of recovery for the adoptive parents, assuring them that Gretchen would probably never improve, as her birth mother "was probably an alcoholic."

Fortunately, the adoptive parents had the good sense to remove her from this "treatment" and take her home. Gretchen recovered from her alcoholism and graduated from high school. At that point, she decided not to attend college. Her well-educated parents had three older sons by birth, all with graduate degrees. They were extremely disappointed that Gretchen was not using her intelligence and predicted that she would not be a successful adult without a college degree.

A year later, Gretchen became pregnant by her rather unsavory boyfriend. The adoptive parents were beside themselves and felt they had failed to provide Gretchen with the tools she needed to be a well-adjusted adult. In spite of extensive catastrophising by the adoptive parents, Gretchen decided to parent her baby as a single mother and she unloaded the unsavory boyfriend.

She pursued a career in real estate and is now a highly successful business-woman in her midthirties. The years of stability she enjoyed with her adoptive family enabled her to break the cycle of child neglect and be a wonderful mother to her son, who is now a young pre-adolescent.

While the adoptive parents had many years of questioning their level of "success" as parents because Gretchen did not fit the mold established by their older sons, they are now extremely proud of their daughter's independence and stability. Gretchen is certainly to be commended for her many positive attributes and accomplishments, and these adoptive parents have every right to be very proud of their significant contributions that enabled this young woman's achievements.

Quick Reference

Key Point 1:
Raising children is a rewarding but stressful business. Adoptive and foster parents are vulnerable to even higher levels of stress related to raising their children. Some of the added stressors for adoptive and foster families include:

- Unmet expectations regarding adoption and family life
- Feelings of failure, guilt
- The impact of adoption or foster care on other relationships (with spouse, other children in the family, extended family, close friends)
- Coping with child's needs or challenging behaviors
- Dealing with multiple service providers (or the lack of adoption-competent service providers)
- School issues
- Difficulty in finding substitute caregivers to provide occasional respite or relief
- Managing either openness in adoption or the challenges associated with closed adoptions (psychological presence)

Key Point 2:
Even when exposed to high levels of stress, individuals can prevent crisis through effective coping strategies. The following list of coping strategies can assist

adoptive and foster parents in preventing stress from escalating into crisis.

- Recall often that you are not the source of your child's problems.
- Maintain a sense of humor.
- Connect with other foster and adoptive parents.
- Stop comparing yourself to other families.
- Find an adoption-competent family therapist.
- Stay regulated. Don't jump into the child's fear.
- Find outlets for your own emotional, spiritual, and physical needs and design opportunities to enjoy those.
- Do a role check. Is one parent carrying most of the load?
- Choose your battles and win the war.
- Stop, drop, and roll. (Stop talking. Drop into your breathing. Roll back into your relationship with your child.)
- Identify who owns the problem.
- Take a break—find respite care.
- Remember the child's progress will not always be consistent.
- Look for patterns in your child's outbursts. If you understand his triggers, you may be able to prevent an explosion altogether, or lessen the intensity significantly.
- Use family meetings creatively.
- Find ways to have fun with your child—increase your positive interactions.
- Reframe your definition of success and celebrate small gains.

Discussion Questions

1. Have you created expectations for yourself that are impossible to reach? Do you accept blame for your child's difficult behaviors? Have you acknowledged gains the child has made since joining the family?

2. Are there renewal activities or relationships you have neglected because you feel you don't have time or energy? How might you change that?

3. Can you identify a reliable babysitter or respite provider to allow you some child-free time?

4. How can you and your spouse plan for some tag-team parenting to give each of you some time alone or with other significant persons?

5. What positive interactions might you design to increase your attachment to your child?

6. Can you identify or create a support system of adoptive or foster families?

Chapter Thirteen

A Story of Hope: The Rest of the Story

By Grace Harris

This chapter shares the journey of adoption for John and Grace Harris. Many adoptive parents will relate to that first phone call, the first visit, and those first feelings of embracing a love like no other.

—Jayne Schooler

My heart caught in my throat when the screen on my phone showed that it was the Department of Social Services. The kind, effusive voice of Michelle, our social worker, came over the line. "I'm calling to tell you about a sibling group of three: two girls and one boy, ages one, two, and three," she explained. "They are of Italian descent. There seem to be some significant needs between them. The way this works, as you know, is that you need to let me know in twenty-four hours if you and John plan to move forward on this or not."

I had been asked to decide within twenty-four hours if our lives would forever change from a family made up of John, Captain (our dog), and me, to a family with three children under the age of four! The emotional surge I felt when she described the three children made it seem impossible to say no. To do so would be like rejecting these children who had experienced a very traumatic life already.

Yet, our home was set up for only two children, and only the same gender, as they would have to share a room. But if we said no would this be our last chance to build our forever family? What would happen to these children? Though I didn't know their names, I couldn't help but start to "see" them in my mind . . . and wonder. And worry. And feel responsible.

Eight hours later, when John and I sat down to talk about it, we were excited.

We were laughing; talking over one another; asking dozens of unanswerable questions. However, in the end, we could say only "no." We simply were not able to take on these three young children under the age of four. But we felt like we were abandoning them, as if they had already somehow been entrusted to us.

Calling Michelle and explaining our answer was hard and emotional. I felt guilty; I felt we were being picky and cruel. But she welcomed our response. She helped me see that actually we were practicing good parenting skills. We knew our limits and capacities and made a sound decision based on that, even when we were emotionally spent.

After this first experience, we received three more similar calls about adoptable children. Each time, we experienced the same rush to respond. The decision to say "no" was haunting.

Several months later, we got news of a different sort from our social worker. "You remember those three children ages one, two, and three that I told you about back in March?" she asked. Of course I remembered; I had thought about and prayed for them numerous times. "Well, there was a bit of misinformation there," she continued. "The older two children, brothers, ages three and four, are available for adoption. We think that you and John just might be the right family for them."

I had a very hard time focusing and hearing what Michelle was saying as my heart raced, and I thought, "We have another chance to provide a home and become a family with two of these kids!" I found out that there were three brothers who were now two, three, and four. The youngest sibling was in the process of being placed in a pre-adoptive home, since the Department of Social Services (DSS) could not find one family to take all three siblings. The older two had been in foster care together for the last year. The DSS was seeking a family who would commit to keeping the three boys in touch with one another as brothers.

As before, we had twenty-four hours to decide if we wanted to move forward with the process. John and I knew right away that this was an opportunity we wanted to take. We met with our social worker and the children's social worker. We saw these beautiful little boys in pictures. The black-and-white, close-up facial pictures of the two older brothers and a series of colorful, chaotic pictures of the three brothers stood out most in my mind and heart. John and I carried these pictures everywhere. We immediately became attached to these two older souls with dark, haunting eyes and precious grins.

Getting Acquainted

We had one week to make an initial commitment to place these children in our pre-adoptive home. We were able to talk to their foster mom on the phone. We learned about their daily routines, needs, and interests, and the dynamic, loving family with whom they had lived for the past year. We observed each of the boys in their preschool and kindergarten classrooms. Their school social worker, Jennifer, filled us in on Josh's role of walking his three-year-old little brother, Brent, into the classroom after they got off the school bus at 7:30 in the morning. He helped him get settled in his class and sat at the table with him for what usually became three to four bowls of cereal. Only then would Josh turn and leave the room, walk himself to his own four-year-old classroom, and put his own things away in his cubby.

Brent was the lone child at the table, eating his cereal, while all the other children and the teachers were already on the carpeted area for circle time. One of the teachers came over and tried to coax Brent along to hurry, but when he finished that bowl he asked for another.

Eventually, Brent joined the other children in the group, and we watched from across the room as he snuggled up in the lap of one of the teachers. He mouthed the words to the songs they were singing. Too quickly, it seemed, the social worker motioned for us to follow her into Josh's classroom.

The children in Josh's room were also doing their morning greetings, singing, and repeating silly rhymes. At first, Jennifer could not locate Josh in the classroom to point him out to us, but then she got down on her hands and knees and looked under the furniture. There he was, huddled under the table in the far corner of the room. She had told us that Josh struggled with participation the classroom, but that he had made a great deal of progress from hiding much of the day to being able to engage off-and-on with children, activities, and teachers. One teacher in particular, Mr. Mike, spent naptime talking calmly to Josh and telling him stories, because Josh would not sleep.

As Jennifer talked, we watched Josh stealthily make his way closer to the circle over the next ten minutes. He ended up hanging over the top of the stack of mats at the edge of the circle, mouthing the words to the "kindergarten rap." He even did some of the hand motions. I had tears streaming down my face, and when it was over it was all John and I could do not to break out into a round of applause!

What a journey that four-year-old had made before our very eyes, to risk almost-inclusion with the others. As soon as the rap was over, he bolted back under a table halfway across the room.

Within a week, we met the boys on one of their regularly scheduled play dates with their younger brother, who had now been placed in a pre-adoptive home. Because these were three very active children, it was common to have extra workers on hand, so the boys' social worker simply introduced us as her friends who were going to join in the play that day. I immediately gravitated to Brent, age three, and we spent the entire time swinging. Josh and John swung on the monkey bars and played chase. Josh would check in, take over swinging Brent, and then bolt across the dirt to find his younger brother. He played with him, introduced him to various parts of the playground, and stayed close by to make sure he could manage the slide or the tree trunk.

Those first two-and-a-half weeks with the boys is a set of still shots in my mind. Today, six years later, I can remember every exchange, locations of visits, what we did, what the weather was like, and the first time Brent spontaneously grabbed my hand and pulled me to play on the swing set with him. I remember how Josh raced around the playground near our home, begging our dog, Captain, to chase him. It all seems so fragile, so precious, and so heart-breaking.

Preparing for the Boys' Move

The boys moved in with us in early December 2002, following our harrowing realization that, though they had lived with this foster family for well over a year, they had never been told that it was a temporary placement. My fear and indignation as a soon-to-be-mom, and as a social worker, was fierce. It led to a dogged determination to support these two little tough and tender souls. The DSS had a contract with a phenomenal agency called The Center for Family Connections, which works with people touched by adoption. They assisted us all in planning a transition time over a series of weeks, instead of the regular plan of a number of days.

We were to take time to build the boys' story for them and share it with them in small doses. That step would be followed up with ten weeks of visits and shared experiences, and then a move-in date of December 6th. I came to see this as more of a "move out" in their minds, instead of a "move in," as they experienced a dramatic loss all over again. We were coached on how to anticipate this further trauma for them and how to develop connections for and with them. We were guided on how to maintain contact with their foster family, instead of leaving that part of their lives behind.

We found that it was the fear and discomfort of the adults that often kept things from being shared with the children. Josh and Brent had already lived through the neglect, abuse, and trauma that we were afraid to mention to them. They were survivors!

Since no one had spoken to them in almost a year-and-a-half about their biological parents, Mommy Sarah or Daddy Bob, I was quite certain that they had created some explanation in their own minds to try to understand their birth family situation. I also knew from my own studies and experiences as a social worker that children tend to blame themselves. They assume there is something wrong with them that led to the separation. We wanted to help Josh and Brent learn the truth of their mom's great love for them. It was surely love that prompted her to take them to a police station because she knew that she could no longer provide the home, protection, and care they needed. She made a plan for them. She wanted to be sure they would be safe and cared for.

I also knew that adopted persons often feel a great sense of not fitting in, of not belonging, and of missing parts of themselves, as if they didn't exist at particular times in their own lives. For instance, without baby pictures and stories of first steps, words, and illnesses, children grow up feeling a void—as if they were not born, did not grow as an infant, or have that first tooth come in. It's almost as if they are invisible in their own memories, because there was not someone else there to verify it or review it naturally with them, as children in intact families usually experience. I wanted to fill this gap as much as possible. We began work with many experts, other adoptive parents, and adults who are adopted persons. We sought to learn how to honor the boys' entire lives and not just the part we were privileged enough to share.

Memories of the Transition

During this ten-week transition, there were a couple of particularly poignant times. One was strategizing a way for the boys to meet Captain, our twelve-year-old mutt, who was very much a central part of our family. They had pictures of him in their little scrapbooks I'd made to introduce us. They also had pictures of our extended family, community of friends, and church. When the DSS social worker gave the boys their scrapbooks, she told them that she had at last found their forever family. They carried the scrapbooks around with them as extra appendages for weeks.

A social worker suggested that we take some special dog treats for each child. She instructed us to ask the boys to hold on to them and keep them safe until the next week, when they were to meet Captain in the play area outside the foster home—in their "territory." I wrapped fun ribbons around four different treats for Captain and delivered them to the kids midweek. You would have thought I was Santa! They were as excited over those treats as they might have been if I had brought *them* a treat!

Saturday morning arrived and John, Captain, and I drove up to the home. We ended up bringing one child out at a time to interact with Captain, who was a small-to-mid-sized, sweet dog. Brent had talked big about loving dogs, but we thought he'd end up being scared. In the end, he was terrified, and only with Josh's careful help was he able to fling the treat close to Captain before running away. But he was so proud of himself for "playing with Captain" and talked of nothing else for days. So began the great love affair between Captain and these boys.

Captain was almost instantaneously a symbol of safety and warmth for Josh. We taught the boys how to play Frisbee and tug-of-war, feed him, and pet him gently. This connection was a gift and a glimmer of hope when connection with the boys was difficult.

The first time we brought the boys to our home, we picked them up at their foster home early in the morning and didn't return them home until early evening. Because they had already met Captain, we decided to drive up to our house (which they'd seen in their scrapbooks), get out of the car together, and walk to the backyard.

We played outside in the tree house with trucks and balls, and we played Frisbee with Captain for quite a while. When we all decided that we wanted to go in, we sat on the back patio in a circle, holding hands/paws on a blanket I'd left out for that purpose, and placed the leaves and berries we'd each picked from the backyard in the center. John and I talked about how we were about to enter our first home together as a forever family, and then we all said together that we are becoming a forever family. We prayed and asked for the gift of connection and love and then ran inside.

By early afternoon, when my parents came in to meet them and spend the day with us all, Josh grabbed my father's hand and walked him around "their house." He took him into *their* bedroom, pointing out the bunk beds and toys. Brent started walking around in my mom's shoes later that evening, and we enjoyed homemade chocolate chip cookies we baked together. We felt grateful for what was becoming our forever family.

Moving In

John and I drove on a very cold and snowy night to pick up the boys. We had planned a thank-you party for the foster family for taking such wonderful care of these two precious souls and for entrusting them to our care. On the way home that night, surrounded by suitcases and piles of their things, Josh asked us a haunting question. He asked us where he and Brent would go when they were "done at our house." At first, I didn't quite get what he was asking, but then it dawned on me—he did not understand that forever family meant *forever*. I felt like my heart might shatter, as my eyes filled with tears. His assumption was that all of life was fluid; that there was no permanency, even in where and with whom he and Brent might live. This tore at my innate sense of stability and my dreams for the forever family I had created in my heart and mind.

Just as all relationships develop, take shape, and grow over shared time together, so our forever family strengthened through weeks and months. We discovered shared interests of jigsaw puzzles, reading, "extreme sports," and board games. We juggled new schools, new routines and expectations, and simply living together. We shared the loss of John's grandparent, a dear friend whom the boys had become close to in our home, and Captain, our dog of fourteen years. Sharing these losses, as well as many days of joy, pleasure, fun, and simple routine, allowed each of us to begin to connect in unique and often beautiful ways.

Of course, we also faced many predictable challenges related to fear and to behavior at school, church, in public, and at home, even though we were working at least weekly with a team of mental health professionals. We found a sincere embrace within our extended families and a strong local community for the boys and our family that sustained us over time.

But as the boys learned to trust and connect to us as parents, they experienced deep threats, terror, and apprehension. Josh went through more than a year of waking in the morning in a "flight" mode of anxiety, terror, and out-of-control feelings, words, and behaviors. He experienced some relief from these fears with the help of numerous professionals and a great deal of support from John and me.

Then Brent, who had just turned five, entered a stage of incredible self-hatred, including blame for those close to him, as well as significant unsafe behaviors. We were frantic for some support and answers. His behavior threatened to derail our forever family and our home. It was no longer just loss in a general sense or uncertainty and trouble with transitions. It all seemed to have morphed into bolting and running away, vicious streams of yelling, blaming, and belittling himself, and even impulsive acts of attacking us and destroying property. After months of this chaos and violence in our home, at church, and at school, a psychiatrist said, "Oh, Grace, what you are describing is Reactive Attachment Disorder." I wept in relief that there was some explanation for this seemingly unrelated constellation of behaviors challenging our family.

Though it was the end of searching desperately for an answer, it was just the beginning of trying to understand this broad spectrum of behaviors. We learned that RAD originates in the lack of affective tuning for an infant with a caregiver, and from days, weeks, and months of not having basic human needs met. Daniel Hughes' book *Building the Bonds of Attachment: Awakening Love in Deeply Troubled Children* became my constant companion.[1] I devoured page after page, sustained by the disturbing and hope-filled story of a little girl and her foster/adoptive mom on their journey of connection.

As is often the case, as the mother I was the target of all of the berating remarks, yelling, pinching, hitting, and kicking. The wounds are deep for me from that season of our lives together. I felt devastated from being fully rejected and attacked; yet, ironically, Brent was trying to save himself.

His greatest unconscious fear was of trusting me and connecting to me deeply. He fought to protect himself, because he had been taught over and over at a very young age that those you trust and depend on will leave you.

We've practiced Hughes' parenting paradigm of "acceptance, curiosity, empathy, love, and playfulness" for over three years now, but it still often seems elusive and pie-in-the-sky. This approach to parenting is based on the parent always holding onto the truth of the trauma the child has experienced, and responding to the child in a way that is absolutely accepting, no matter what.[2] We do this better some days than others but know unwaveringly that it is the pattern we are striving for.

Most parents probably experience a moment when it becomes clear that their child is a separate being from them. The parent will never really know what it is to be *them*. This seems to be much more obvious for parents who have adopted, especially in situations like ours. We look very different from each other, as our children are biracial and we are Caucasian. They also have a sense of otherness that accompanies their trauma and fear. Sometimes it feels like we live with neon signs on each other that say, "You are not me/I am not you." This truth applies to biological families as well, but our chosen togetherness does not replace the otherness.

The whole concept of a "forever family" is a miraculous thing, really. I find myself connected not only to Josh and Brent, but also to their little brother and his family, their foster family, and teams of support people who have worked with us over the years. I also feel connected, in spirit, to their birth parents. I am forever grateful for the gift of life from the birth mother and father and for the mother's love and care for all three of the boys that ultimately ensured their safety. Though the otherness remains a part of our family, it is the togetherness that usually shines brighter in our interactions and conversations as a forever family.

You may be entering your own journey of becoming a forever family. You may be an adopted person. Or you may be someone, like the unforgettable teams of people we've been blessed with, who supports families struggling to connect. Whatever your interest in this book, I have to leave you with a few stories that I think will illustrate the fragility and extraordinary strength of this growing tapestry of connection between us.

Brent, age three and Josh, age four

Josh and Brent were very excited to go on a road trip to Georgia for Christmas, thirteen days after they had moved into our home. Late that first night, after hours of horrific screaming, crying, and even bolting in a parking lot, we discovered they had no idea we'd be spending the night away from their wonderful new bunk beds! They didn't know what a hotel was, nor did they like it very much.

The next morning, as we were driving through the beautiful rural areas of Connecticut, Brent began yelling, "Fake! Fake!" Josh quickly joined in the chorus and it took us a while to figure out what they were saying. We soon understood that they had never seen a live horse, cow, or goat on the side of a road. They thought they were fake! We pulled over to the side of the road. We sat there for a long time, listening to the boys count, and start over again. We laughed as they giggled at a cow swishing her tail or a horse raising its head in our direction.

Josh, age five

I had just settled Josh in the building-block area of his school room. As I headed out the door to work, the teacher overheard his friend ask him, "Why isn't your mom black like you and me?" Josh looked up from the tower he was building, shrugged his shoulders and said, "I don't know, but her favorite color's black!" And they resumed their play.

Brent, age four

One day, John was singing the chorus, "You can't always get what you want . . . you try sometimes, but you just might find, you get what you need." We later heard Brent singing it as "You always can't get what you want." Unfortunately, it seemed to reflect his understanding of the world very clearly.

Josh, age six

For Mother's Day, 2004, Josh drew a picture of himself and me together, entitled "Me and My Mom." At the bottom of the huge piece of artwork, he had typed "Mom, I love you because you are my favorite mom and because you got a dog! Love, Josh." This would melt any mom's heart, especially a serious dog-lover like myself, but the phrase "You are my 'favorite' mom" is not lost on me.

So was it making too much out of this "favorite mom" phrase to think he's actually comparing me to the two other moms he's had in his short six years of life? I can't know for sure, but, regardless, it was a gift that spoke deeply to my soul and one that reflected that Josh is counting me as his mom. This miracle of becoming a forever family never loses its sweetness.

Brent, age eight

Brent had been working on writing in his third grade class, often struggling to write different sentences instead of repeating the same one over and over. My best friend came to visit from out of town.

The last morning of her stay, Brent spent his time before church writing a two-sided page about how much he loved her, how happy he was that I had been able to be with her, how much our dog loved her, and so on. He mentioned memories of her that he could only have heard me talk about, since they occurred long before he was born or we were a forever family. He acted like he had been there and valued her presence. He independently wrote a beautiful note to her and simply signed his name at the end.

The journey of becoming and sustaining a forever family is a beautiful, heartbreaking, and precious thing. I am reminded almost daily of the fragility of each person in our family, as well as our great strengths and connectedness, as we continue to navigate life together. Some days I marvel that this "works" at all. On other days, I am deeply moved by the free affection Josh bestows on me, or John's deep awareness of all things "daddy," evident in Brent's stories and writings. May we live generously and compassionately with one another, claiming one another as cherished and accepted.

Speaking to the Heart, Equipping Parents for the Journey

by Jayne E. Schooler

Today, challenged by the "Cry of the Orphans" ministry, hundreds, perhaps even thousands, of families are beginning their incredible adoption journey. Churches are developing orphan care ministries, looking for effective ways to make an impact. As I hear the stories of churches and individuals from all over the United States responding to a call from God to care for orphaned children, I feel such incredible joy. God is speaking to hearts all over the country. Some are stepping up to foster abused and neglected children. They are making permanent commitments to them. Still others are looking to see how they can reach out to a needy child thousands of miles away.

After spending six months overseas in 2008, my heart was deeply moved by the plight of orphans. I viewed firsthand the incredible needs of these beautiful children living in very difficult orphanage circumstances. I just didn't stop in for a quick tour, but spent many hours over many months working with and training staff and social workers on best practices in child welfare. I spent many hours with the children, teaching them English, going on walks and picnics, swimming, and simply loving them. Most orphanage caregivers were doing the best they could under extremely difficult conditions, but life every day in many places was about merely surviving. I literally heard the cry of the orphan.

As God speaks to the hearts of so many, I not only feel joy, but also I feel a growing burden. We must not only speak to the *hearts* of interested prospective parents, but we also must help *equip* them for the journey. We want children to come to homes where their parents truly understand the brokenness from which they come and the emotional, psychological, and spiritual needs that arise from such difficult life experiences. We must recognize these people who are answering the call, and the passion that moved them to step up. We must understand how to equip them for the journey.

Who Is Adopting/Fostering These Children?

> Live creatively, friends. . . . Stoop down and reach out to those who are oppressed. Share their burdens, and so complete Christ's law. (Galatians 6:1-2, MSG)

So, what is the law of Christ? What does it have to do with foster care and adoption?

Families making the decision to move forward in response to God's call on their lives are unusual people. They live by a higher principle of life. Let me share the story of Kevin and Cindy:

Sixteen years ago, Kevin and Cindy felt called to become foster parents. Shortly after going through the licensing process, they received a phone call from the agency, asking if they would take three-month-old Katie. Katie, the agency told them, was a medically fragile baby, born prematurely to parents who could not care for her. They responded immediately—yes!

Delicate and petite Katie was placed into their home the next day, right from the hospital. That first evening, had Kevin not known infant CPR, Katie would have died in his arms.

The weeks turned into months, the months into years, as they continued to care for this extremely ill child. Trips to the hospital were part of their weekly routine, not to mention doctors' visits and hours of in-home care. Finally, the agency decided to move forward and seek permanent custody, thus opening the door for Katie's adoption.

As an adoption worker, I was required at that permanency hearing to testify as to Katie's "adoptability." The attorney for the biological family got down in my face, nearly yelling, asking me, "Who would adopt a child like this? What's wrong with these people? Why do they want to do it?" I simply responded to him by explaining that Kevin and Cindy love her deeply.

After the hearing, I went back to my office. A message my pastor and husband, David, shared recently in our church, came to mind. I sat down and wrote that attorney a respectful letter. Here is what it said:

Dear Sir,

I didn't reply adequately in court to you today as to why Kevin and Cindy are choosing to make Katie a permanent part of their family. Let me tell you why. Kevin and Cindy live by a higher principle in life. It is called VRS.

V stands for Voluntary. No one is forcing them to make this lifelong commitment to Katie. They are doing it out of supreme love for her.

R stands for Redemptive. Redemption means to restore dignity to a person whose life situations are difficult, painful and heartbreaking. Such were Katie's.

S stands for Suffering. Suffering means the loss of something for the sake of another. Kevin and Cindy have paid a high cost. Emotionally, physically, financially—in every way they have suffered. They would not call it that, but that is exactly what it is.

This is why Kevin and Cindy are adopting Katie. This is their life principle—Voluntary Redemptive Suffering.

We recently joined the family to celebrate Katie's sixteenth birthday. What a glorious day it was as we reflected on the incalculable ways God had provided for this precious child and encouraged the family in uncertain times.

Kevin and Cindy represent the thousands of people coming forward to foster and adopt. They are among those who live by a higher principle of life—VRS—the law of Christ.

Live creatively, friends. . . . Stoop down and reach out to those who are oppressed. Share their burdens, and so complete Christ's law. (Galatians 6:1-2, MSG)

What Is Needed to Equip These Parents for the Journey?

Families who are fostering and adopting a deeply wounded child have a desire to make a difference in a child's life. There are a number of ways to equip those families for such a journey:

Reality-based training that leads to experiential understanding prior to the arrival of their child.

Most prospective foster and adoptive parents are required to attend training classes prior to becoming licensed or adopting. It is critical that these training sessions are not treated as something to get out of the way, but as an opportunity to learn and understand the unique parenting needs of a wounded child.

Post-adoption support, resources, and training, designed to help parents with unfolding needs.

Not only do parents need preparational training, but they also need access to post-adoption support groups, relevant resources, and additional training to manage the behaviors of a traumatized, wounded child.

Connections with experienced adoptive parents who can act as mentors and coaches.

One of the beautiful things I have seen with foster and adoptive parents is that they relate to each very well. Often, they don't need to finish sentences because there is such a strong sense of identification. For new families, the connections made with experienced parents normalize the journey and strengthen a brand-new but fragile family bond.

Connections with safe people who understand the unique challenges of parenting wounded, traumatized children.

One adoptive mother recently told me that she is failing the mission. She feels completely incompetent to meet the parenting demands of her eleven-year-old daughter, who joined their family two years ago. Her daughter had been in six foster homes in two years. I asked with whom she had shared these feelings of failure. "No one," she told me. I was the first person outside her immediate family that she felt safe enough to share what was really going on. I was brokenhearted for her. I didn't live in her town, not even in her state. I was there for a few days to do training. What this struggling mother needed more than anything was a safe place, a listening ear, a person on an ongoing basis with whom she feels safe enough to be real.

A committed group of like-minded people who will maintain their commitment to each other in the best of times and in the worst of times.

I cannot think of a better group of committed people to help support adoptive families than the church. We are called to share one another's burdens. This calling requires a pastoral staff and group of lay people who have educated themselves on the unique needs of adoptive and foster families. It is a calling to an ongoing conversation about the needs of children around the world, the creation of an environment where those children and their families find a safe haven of love, support, and commitment.

We must continue to speak God's heart regarding the orphan. As we speak God's heart, may we equip well those who respond.

Assessing Attachment-Readiness and Capabilities in Prospective Adoptive Parents

By Deborah Gray

The following article has been excerpted from Chapter Nine: "The Role of The Child Welfare/Social Worker" in Deborah Gray's 2007 book, Nurturing Adoptions: Creating Resilience after Neglect and Trauma. *Those reading it as a printout will find it on the Internet at http://www.perspectivespress.com/ parentassess.html. Adoption agencies have the author's permission to print out and use this tool in their staff training on adoption assessment.*

Home studies should not be expected to identify only "perfect families." All families have areas of weakness. The home study should act as an educational tool that will help families be successful. It is also a screening process that acts to remove families who are markedly unsuitable for parenting children who will need extra help from sensitive parents. The 2 percent of prospective families who should not adopt children are also the ones who take inordinate amounts of time away from the child welfare system. Identifying unsuitable families before, not after placement, allows for significantly more time for post-placement training and support for families, completing adoptions, and recruiting more families.

The interview template which follows should only be used in the form of a *face-to-face interview*, not in the form of questions soliciting written responses. The template incorporates some of the research and theory behind the Adult Attachment Inventory. This format presents home study questions from an attachment point of view. It adapts concepts from attachment research and literature to the home study process.

Home Study Interview Questions

1. Describe the relationship you had with your mother as a child. Describe the relationship you had with your father. List five adjectives that describe your mother and five for your father.

The social worker should write down these descriptive adjectives, and then ask for examples of situations or events that demonstrate those qualities. Social workers should be looking for a description of parent-child intimacy. They should also be judging the general quality of the description. The narrative should be smooth, coherent, and have a firm basis in reality. Words and facial expressions should be consistent. If people cannot remember any examples to support the qualities that they mention, then start tracking the quality of sensitivity in their relationships.

2. Can you detail some times in which you really needed to depend on your parents? How did they respond? How did this affect you at the time? What do you think of it now? Would you parent in the same way or differently?

The examples should fit the answers to the questions. Any contradictions indicate the presence of something that should be explored further. One big red flag to watch for is the interviewee trying to turn instances where the parents were not there for them into an advantage.

3. Can you describe times where you felt lonely or rejected by your family? Were they aware of your feelings? How did you interpret their actions as a child? And now? Would you parent in the same way or differently?

Ideally, people should be able to describe painful experiences in a way that demonstrates an understanding of their parents' points of view. They should have an idea of why something happened, and also be able to acknowledge the effects of painful experiences on their own development. The person being interviewed should be able to do this without becoming overwhelmed with bitterness or any other emotion.

4. What is your current relationship like with your parents? How often do you see them or talk on the phone? If they are not living, what was it like when they were alive and how did their loss affect you?

Answers to this question should contain information about:

- The degree of reciprocity/attunement that they had as children
- Descriptions of how painful family situations were acknowledged and repaired versus being ignored
- Smoothness and coherency in the descriptions
- Insight into how those first relationships shaped their present lives

5. Were you ever frightened of or hurt by your parents? How was this dealt with in your family? How do you think this affected your childhood and who you are today?

Parents-to-be who describe bitter memories of abusive, insensitive, or abandoning parents, and who also show little resolution will need to work these issues out before placement. They will need a referral for therapy. Watch for positive indicators as well. People who experienced childhood abuse may have been buffered by positive attachment figures, like grandparents, who were sensitive and responsive. Descriptions of their alternate caregiver's sensitivity, with a sense of resolution about why their parents were not there for them are good signs. The more people are able to describe the reasons behind parents' actions with appropriate, regulated emotion and insight, the better. An appropriate answer to this question looks like this:

"My mother would not listen to me when I was upset by my family's sudden move. She ignored my tears and said, 'Pack.' Now I know that she had just had a Caesarean section a week before, was hormonal, in pain, and had to move our whole family, including a new baby. My dad had to choose between flying to the new city within forty-eight hours and losing his job. We had to follow him. As an adult, I have concluded that we must have been behind on rent. That's one reason why we moved so quickly.

"My mother never apologized, though. I think that I would do things so differently. I would at least try to explain what was happening and let my daughter know that I cared about her feelings. That would have helped a lot. My grandma let me cry at her house and took me to my school and around our neighborhood so that I could say good-bye to my friends and my teacher."

Notice that this sample contains an honest description of pain and a conclusion about her mother's point of view. It also includes a description of a sensitive parent figure, the grandmother, who provided support during an overwhelming situation. She went on to describe how she would do things if she were the parent. The example is relatively brief and easy to follow. It is clear that this person has the ability to use her own life stories as a source of empathy for others.

6. Give me a ten-minute description of your life, including main events and the major decisions that you have made. Start either at the present and go backward, or begin at birth and go forward. What are your earliest memories?
This type of narrative should demonstrate a person's sense of mastery over most of the events in life, or their ability to take responsibility for personal decisions and actions. Answers to this question will also highlight the contrasting attitude of blaming others. It will show thinking that is shame-based, and also reveal whether people view themselves as helpless victims or in a grandiose way. Listen for the inclusion of instances of seeking out support and acknowledging helpers, as these abilities act as important attributes for adoptive parents.

Look for a coherent life narrative. The narrative should be relatively smooth and should not have gaps. Emotions, as conveyed both through facial expressions and with words, should match the person's story. Pay special attention to life narratives that do not make sense! Why is the person lacking integration? If you, as an adult, find the person emotionally confusing, a child will certainly have difficulties using this parent as an emotional guide.

7. Tell me about your best friends. How did you meet them? How long have you known them? What do you do together? How often do you get together? How do you work out problems in relationships?
Get a sense of how connected the person is to their community and also the quality of their relationships. Check to see how long-term their relationships are. Loners who cannot work with others are not good choices as adoptive parents. They cannot instruct a child who needs help learning how to resolve problems and become more trusting. When angry, does this person cut people off permanently? Certainly this trait comes back to haunt social workers, in the form of disrupted placements.

Scrutinize people who have the following characteristics, as they are potential child abusers.

- They are charming.
- They are willing to accept an especially needy child.
- They have intense but short-term relationships, and no one

knows them well over an extended period of time.
• The person seems too good to be true.

If you observe these traits, look for a hidden price tag. Sexual predators and antisocial personality types gravitate toward the most vulnerable members in our society. They tend to be especially charming throughout the home study process. Check these people's histories thoroughly. Make certain that they have a clean, well-researched record. Take seriously minor charges, such as fraud, assault, drug or alcohol abuse, and domestic violence, and examine especially carefully all charges that are accompanied by great rationalizations.

Pay attention to red flags in the history that indicate instability: sudden firings, financial irresponsibility, frequent moves, lies, multiple marriages, affairs, and a lack of continuity in relationships. These form the symptom clusters predictive of personality disorders. It is important to remember that a caseworker cannot simply befriend every family. The home study process must effectively screen out predatory adults.

8. Do you consider yourself to have been a physically or emotionally abused or neglected child or teen?

Ask about any abuse that may be a part of the person's background. If there is abuse, when did it start? Did it involve the person's nuclear family? How have they come to understand it; what are they doing to resolve their relationships and gain safety? Were there multiple traumas? Does the person have night terrors? Does the person have flashbacks? Are they bothered by loud noises? Would a screaming or aggressive child bring out reminders of the abuse?

Remember that there is a difference between Type I and Type II abuse. Type I abuse is short-term and does not result in traumatic stress reactions. It stands out as an unusual and unique experience. Social workers often have optimistic views, taken from accounts of parents who have been successful in spite of abuse and in the absence of counseling. These views are usually based on people with Type I abuse, as they were impacted less.

As described in Part One, Type II abuse involves multiple events or long-standing abuse, with extreme stress. People with Type II abuse who have had no or poor treatment outcomes pose a risk for high-stress children. These parents can easily fall back into a behavior pattern of dissociation, flood with old trauma, and suffer from anxiety and depression. People with Type II abuse tend to incorporate numbing and dissociation, substance abuse, rage, mistrust, interpersonal relationship problems, suicidal ideation, and uncompleted grief into their personalities (Veitch, 1998). Even children with no histories of maltreatment find these personality states alarming. Children tend to form disorganized attachments with these adults. These individuals often have complex trauma. These homes are not healthy enough for adoptive placements.

9. Have you had periods of depression, or do you think your moods swing more than most people's? Do you think you have anxiety problems?

Please ask these questions in person, not just on a form. It is easy to check "no" on a form. It is much more difficult to lie in person. Many people have experienced periods of anxiety and depression but have responded very well to counseling and medications. These people do quite well with children after placement. They certainly should not be screened out of adoption. Check into the mood issues in a person's history. Are there periods of depression? How have they been handled? What is different now? Did they show resolution over losses from infertility? Are the losses related to infertility being confused with a long-term mood disorder?

Be wary of people with ongoing problems with depression, anger, or anxiety. Depressed parents will have attachment problems with any child, even a healthy newborn. They are simply not capable of doing the difficult emotional work that is required in the placement of a toddler or an older child. People with anger management problems make children feel as if they are still in a hostile environment. This signals them into fight, freeze, or flight mode instead of attachment. Anxious parents cannot help children calm down. They instead reinforce a wary, paranoid outlook on life. Encourage angry, depressed, and anxious applicants to get treatment for these issues first, and then proceed with the adoption process.

10. Are you comfortable letting others help you with this child? Do you mind working with professionals?

Parents need to embrace the team mentality. Children described in this book are best placed as special-needs adoptions. Parents should expect that they will need to coordinate a helping team for such children. They will have to develop resources that help their children. Mistrustful, angry, highly anxious, or depressed individuals will not be able to meet these children's needs, as they will not understand their need for advocacy and the use of teamwork within a community.

11. Are you able to accept lots of acting out and controlling behaviors in children as a probable scenario for the beginning of placement? For children who have trauma histories, will you be willing to get therapy, a necessary part of children's medical care?

Many parents naively believe that the child they are adopting from foster care or from an orphanage overseas will be a withdrawn, sad child who will be gradually drawn out in their home. Of course this is frequently not the case. Parents need to be informed of the long-term consequences of sexual abuse, physical abuse, trauma, and exposure to domestic violence. In particular, physically and sexually abused children are among the most aggressive children seen in clinical samples. Professional adoption workers must include, as part of the home study process, a discussion of the essential trauma-specific therapy that will probably be a part of their child's future. Research clearly shows that children who receive trauma therapy, especially when it includes a cognitive-behavioral approach, do enormously better as compared to children whose parents omit this therapy.

12. Will you be able to provide more structure and nurture for children who need this approach, rather than using the parenting style that most closely fits your own personality?

Successful parents of children who have experienced neglect, prenatal exposure to substances, or maltreatment almost always run highly structured and nurturing homes. While the structure may be gradually relaxed as children develop more internal structure and emotional maturity, success does require that parents use consequences rather than emotional outbursts or lectures.

13. What resources available in your community will help you support a child who has been neglected, abused, and/or otherwise traumatized?

This question includes the opportunity for some educational work so that families understand the differences between children adopted later in childhood or after maltreatment as compared to children who have a healthy start. It gives families time to think and talk about these differences in an individualized manner. It also gives them time to ask and answer a variety of questions and do their own homework. For example, does their insurance have mental health coverage for families? If not, could they change their policy to one that does? When is the open enrollment period? Have they located a mental health provider who takes their insurance and could see them with their child? Does the child need occupational therapy to remediate the effects of neglect? What is the monetary and time commitment of these therapies? What will they give up in order to make time and money available? Parents need either to have a rich assortment of resources already in place, or to be well connected to their communities so that they can acquire these extra resources. Cover the potential needs of a child similar to one they would like to adopt in a specific manner, detailing the necessary community resources. For example, help them locate respite care in a specific manner during the home study process.

Many people assume that their friends, relatives, neighbors, or religious community will help them. This often is not the case, and it is also one of the saddest disappointments for parents adopting children with special needs. Most people have busy lives and do not readily volunteer their time to these commitments — especially long term. Parents need to ask potential supportive people to commit to meeting the child's prospective needs, in specific terms, in advance. I have given several trainings where close friends have come in with the prospective adoptive parents. The parents had asked for support in advance, and, as a result, their friends had time not only to clear their schedules in preparation for the child, but to receive training.

About 30 percent of adoptive parents are single parents (AFSCAR, 2006). Social workers should help single parents work on identifying their future support systems throughout the home study process.

14. What resources are available for children with learning issues through the school district?

In a study in the state of Washington, the average foster-adopted child was two full years behind grade level by the eighth grade. Will the school in the parents' district help their child immediately and effectively? Do the parents understand an IEP process?

This information is part of the educational effort of the home study. It should include providing or assisting in locating resource numbers and references for the education services in the parents' school district. Even if the family is lucky enough not to need these services, they will be informed and can support other families who do need them.

15. How will you individualize and meet the needs of this child or children?

Parents need to have enough time and space for each child in the family. Educate parents about the differences and the special needs of children adopted after stressful beginnings. Sometimes one parent has deferred to the other in a decision to adopt such a child. They have a tacit understanding that they will still enjoy eighteen holes of golf weekly after the placement. These issues of entitlement should be recognized and addressed during the home study process. It is unrealistic to believe that one parent can plan and implement the entire childcare and community resource plan alone, without coming to resent the other parent.

Ask parents who are already too busy or too financially stretched to make a list of the activities they will drop. Give each parent a sheet of paper, and ask the partner to list what the other should drop. This leads to a healthy discussion about compromising as they barter with the partner's lists. Ask them to begin the dropping process before the placement. Single parents do this exercise with a close friend or relative. Sometimes parents are taking on too much. This constitutes one common reason behind poor placement outcomes; families accumulate too many stressors and adopt too many children.

Families should be able to individualize the needs of all existing members and reflect on how they are already meeting those needs, as well as how they will continue to meet everyone's needs after placement. This gives them a sense of the resources that they have. They should then talk about how they will meet a new member's needs, in specific terms.

16. For what type of child do you think you would not be able to meet the needs? Can you tell me about this?

Parents need to explore what they could not see themselves handling. This exercise gives the social workers enough information to help parents avoid these and related situations. Be certain to listen to parents and help them plan for placements that realistically fit their strengths. For example, parents may say that they are planning to have children share rooms and they could not handle sexual acting out behaviors. This should lead to a discussion about placement issues so that the family's wishes are met as closely as possible. It should also lead to a conversation about what to do if acting out did occur.

In conclusion, this section's approach and information is a necessary addition to home studies in the twenty-first century, helping families prepare realistically for the parenting ahead for those who adopt traumatized/neglected children being placed today. It should be considered a best practice technique for today's adoptions.

Building a Support System and Finding Resources

By Betsy Keefer Smalley, LSW

"With one day's reading, a man may have the key in his hands."

—Ezra Pound

Every year, new resources become available for adoptive parents, dealing with many issues and challenges. The following is an extensive list of books, newsletters, Web sites, and support groups that will guide families to the help they need.

Newsletters and Magazines

Adopted Child
P.O. Box 9362
Moscow, ID 83843
208-882-1794

Adoption Today
246 S. Cleveland Ave.
Loveland, CO 80537
970-663-1185
http://www.adoption.org/adopt/adoption-today-magazine.php

Adoptive Families
2472 Broadway, Ste. 377

New York, NY 10025
800-372-3300
http://www.adoptivefamilies.com

Adoptive Families Newsletter
SEARCH Institute
Thresher Square West
700 South Third St., Ste. 210
Minneapolis, MN 55415
800-888-7828

Fostering Families Today
http://www.fosteringfamiliestoday.com.
Helpful for foster families and adoptive families of children with special needs.

The Iceberg
P.O. Box 95597
Seattle, WA 98145-2597
E-mail: Iceberg_fas@yahoo.com
Supports families with members with Fetal Alcohol Syndrome or effects. This newsletter has stories, advocacy, and research findings.

Raising Black and Biracial Children
RBC
1336 Meadow View Lane, #1
Lancaster, CA 93534
E-mail: RBCeditor@aol.com
Supports parents of African-American, interracial, and transracial adoptive, and foster families.

Society of Special Needs Adoptive Parents
604-687-3364
E-mail: snap@snap.bc.ca
A newsletter covering issues related to parenting children with special needs. Also provides a book on parenting children with Fetal Alcohol Spectrum Disorder that can be downloaded. (Fee: $25/quarter for families; $35 for groups.)

Information/ Resources

Adoption Assistance Hotline
Sponsored by NAATRIN (National Adoption Assistance Training Resource and Information Network) through NACAC (North American Council on Adoptable Children).
800-470-6665

Tapestry Books
P.O. Box 651
Ringoes, NJ 08551
Phone: 877-266-5406
E-mail: info@tapestrybooks.com
http://www.tapestrybooks.com
An online source of books and literature for adoptive parents and adoptees.

Web Sites

Adoption.com
http://www.adoption.com
A comprehensive Web site covering all aspects of adoption, including travel tips, advice about interacting with your newly adopted child, care for yourself, and much more.

Adopt US Kids
http://www.adoptuskids.org

Adoption Learning Partners
http://www.adoptionlearningpartners.org
Created by the Cradle, a private adoption agency in Illinois, this resource provides web-based education for all members of the adoption triad.

American Public Human Services Association
http://www.Aphsa.org

Association of Administrators of the Interstate Compact on Adoption and Medical Assistance
http://www.aaicama.aphsa.org
Enhances the administration of the Compact and strengthens protections for children adopted interstate or moving interstate.

Association for Treatment and Training in the Attachment of Children (ATTACh)
http://www.attach.org
ATTACh recognizes and promotes healthy attachment and its critical importance to human development.

The Center for Adoption Medicine
University of Washington Pediatric Care Center
4245 Roosevelt Way NE
Seattle, WA 98105
206-598-3006
http://www.adoptmed.org

Child Trauma Academy
http://www.childtrauma.org
CTA translates emerging findings about the brain and child development into practical applications in how we nurture children. The site contains articles related to attachment and trauma as well as free online courses.

Child Welfare Information Gateway
http://www.childwelfare.gov/
Many articles and resources for both parents and professionals.

Child Welfare League of America
http://www.cwla.org
An association of nearly 800 public and private nonprofit agencies that assist more than 3.5 million abused and neglected children and their families each year with a range of services.

Evan B. Donaldson Adoption Institute
http://www.adoptioninstitute.org/index.php

Provides research abstracts and promotes advocacy for adoption.

International Adoption Medicine Program, University of Minnesota
www.med.umn.edu/peds/iac
Created by the first clinic in the U.S. to provide for the health needs of internationally adopted children. The site provides a wealth of information about medical needs of children adopted internationally. Recommendations for pre- and post-placement evaluations.

Interstate Compact for the Placement of Children
http://www.icpc.aphsa.org
Establishes uniform legal and administrative procedures governing the interstate placement of children.

The Kinship Center
http://www.kinshipcenter.org
An organization devoted to the preservation of and support for foster, adoptive, and relative families.

Love and Logic
http://www.loveandlogic.com
Dedicated to making parenting and teaching less stressful and more fun. Seminars are offered throughout the country.

National Child Traumatic Stress Network
http://www.nctsn.org
A national resource for developing and disseminating evidence-based interventions, trauma-informed services, and public and professional education.

National Council for Adoption
http://www.adoptioncouncil.org
An advocate for state laws that promote sound adoption policy; a resource for federal officials and policymakers about appropriate federal adoption initiatives and reform; a diplomatic resource for sound international adoption policy; a source of adoption facts and education.

National Resource Center for Special Needs Adoption
http://www.nrcadoption.org
Information and resources to aid with special-needs adoption. Web links to other helpful organizations and publications with a particular emphasis on working with special-needs adoption.

North American Council on Adoptable Children
http://www.nacac.org
Committed to meeting the needs of waiting children and the families who adopt them.

National Indian Child Welfare Association
http://www.nicwa.org
The national voice for American Indian children and families. The most comprehensive source of information on American Indian child welfare.
http://www.siblingsupport.org
A national directory of workshops designed to support siblings of children with special needs. There is a state-by-state directory on the Web site.

Tapestry Books
http://www.tapestrybooks.com
An online bookstore offering books about adoption for parents and children.

Support Groups

Adoption Network Cleveland
4614 Prospect Ave., Ste. 550
Cleveland, OH 44103
216-881-7511
Triad member support group—help with searches for birth or adoptive families.

Center for Adoption Support and Education (C.A.S.E.)
4000 Blackburn Lane, Ste. 260
Burtonsville, MD 20866
301-476-8526
http://www.adoptionsupport.org

Families for Russian and Ukrainian Adoption (FRUA)
P.O. Box 2944
Merrifield, VA 22116
703-560-6184
http://www.frua.org
Support network for families who have adopted or are in the process of adopting from countries in the former Soviet Union.

Korean American Adoptee Adoptive Family Network (KAAN)
P.O. Box 5585
El Dorado Hills, CA 95762
916-933-1447
http://www.KAANet.com

Korean Focus for Adoptive Families
1906 Sword Lane
Alexandria, VA 22308
http://www.koreanfocus.org
Support organization for families with children from Korea.

National Adoption Center (NAC)
1500 Walnut St., Ste. 701
Philadelphia, PA 19102
215-735-9988
http://www.adopt.org

National Council for Single Adoptive Parents (NCSAP)
P.O. Box 567
Mount Hermon, CA 95041
888-490-4600
http://www.ncsap.org
Founded to inform and assist single people who want to adopt.

National Foster Parent Association (NFPA)
7512 Stanich Ave., No. 6
Gig Harbor, WA 98335
253-853-4000

800-557-5238
http://www.nfpainc.org
Purpose is to bring together foster parents and agency representatives to improve the foster care system.

Sharing Transracial Adoption Resources and Support (STARS)
1403 Valley Rd.
Lancaster, PA 17603
717-808-3472
http://www.starsfamily.org

Respite Care

Access to Respite Care and Help National Resource Center
800-473-1727

ARCH National Respite Coalition (NRC)
4016 Oxford St.
Annandale, VA 22003
703-256-9578
Organization for secure, quality, planned, and crisis respite services to strengthen and stabilize families.

Organizations

ATTACh
2775 Villa Creek #240
Dallas, TX 75234
214-247-2329
International coalition of professionals and laypersons working to promote identification and intervention for those with attachment difficulties.

CHADD—Children and Adults with Attention Deficit Disorder
8181 Professional Place, Ste. 201
Landover, MD 20785
800-233-4050
301-306-7070

http://www.chadd.org

Child Help
15757 North 78th St.
Scottsdale, AZ 85260
480-922-8212
National Child Abuse Hotline: 1-800-4-A-CHILD
http://www.childhelp.org
Organization dedicated to helping victims of child abuse and neglect.

Council for Children with Behavioral Disorders
Care of: Council for Exceptional Children
1920 Association Dr.
Reston, VA 22091

Federation for Families for Children's Mental Health
1021 Prince St.
Alexandria, VA 22314
703-684-7710

The Kinship Center
http://www.kinshipcenter.org
An organization devoted to the preservation of and support for foster, adoptive, and relative families.

National Alliance for Mentally Ill Children and Adolescents Network
2101 Wilson Blvd., Ste. 302
Alexandria, VA 22201
703-524-7600

National Clearinghouse on Family Support
Children's Mental Health
Portland State University
P.O. Box 751
Portland, OR 97207

National Mental Health Association
1021 Prince St.
Alexandria, VA 22314
703-684-7722

National Resource Center on Special Needs Adoption
16250 Northland Dr., #120
Southfield, MI 48075
313-443-0300

National Organization on Fetal Alcohol Syndrome (NOFAS)
1815 H Street NW, Ste. 750
Washington D.C. 20006
800-66 NOFAS
This organization has local chapters as well.

North American Council on Adoptable Children (NACAC)
970 Raymond Ave., Ste. 106
St. Paul, MN 55114-1149
612-644-3036
http://www.nacac.org

PACT, an Adoption Alliance
3450 Sacramento Street, Ste. 239
San Francisco, CA 94118
425-221-6957
http://www.pactadopt.org
A placement and education service focused on placing children of color.

Spaulding for Children (SFC)
16250 Northland Dr, Ste. 120
248-443-7080
http://www.spaulding.org
Finds permanent homes for children who have been in the foster care system the longest.

Books for Parents or Professionals

Adopting the Hurt Child: Hope for Families with Special Needs Kids. 1995, 2009.
Gregory Keck and Regina Kupecky. NavPress.
Excellent resource for parents who have adopted traumatized children.

Adopting and Advocating for the Special Needs Child. 1997. L. Anne Babb and
Rita Laws. Bergin and Garvey.
A guide for adoptive parents of children with special needs.

After Adoption: The Needs of Adopted Youth. 2003. Jeanne A. Howard and Susan
L. Smith. Child Welfare League Press.
Overview of research into the needs and adjustment of children adopted from
the foster care system.

Being Adopted, The Lifelong Search for Self. 1993. David M. Brodzinsky, Marshall
D. Schecter and Robin Marantz Henig. Doubleday.
A book to help adoptive parents and adoptees understand the struggles and
stages of developing an identity when an individual experiences separation from
his birth family.

*Beyond Consequences, Logic, and Control: A Love-Based Approach to Helping
Children with Severe Behaviors.* 2008. Heather Forbes and Bryan Post. Beyond
Consequences Institute.
A book about providing emotional safety for traumatized children.

The Black Parenting Book. 1999. Ann C. Beal, Linda Villarosa and Allison
Abner. Random House.
A book that presents information on raising black children with healthy racial
identities.

*Brothers and Sisters in Adoption: Helping Children Navigate Relationships When
New Kids Join the Family.* 2009. Arleta James. Perspectives Press.

Children's Adjustment to Adoption: Developmental and Clinical Issues. 1998. Anne
B. Brodzinsky, Daniel W. Smith, David M. Brodzinsky. Sage Publications.
An excellent professional summary of pertinent adoption issues.

Child with Special Needs: Encouraging Intellectual and Emotional Growth. 1998. Stanley Greenspan and Serena Wieder. Addison Wesley.
A book about promoting and enhancing development.

A Child's Journey Through Placement. 1992. Vera Fahlberg. Perspectives Press.
An invaluable guide for professionals placing children or treating children who have experienced separation.

Connecting with Kids Through Stories. 2005. Denise Lacer, Todd Nichols, and Joanne May. Jessica Kingsley Publishers.
A guide for parents or therapists who want to help children understand adoption through storytelling.

Clinician's Guide to PTSD: A Cognitive Behavioral Approach. 2006. Stephen Taylor. Guilford Press.
Guide for improving therapist's competence in using Cognitive Behavioral Therapy.

The Family of Adoption. 2005. Joyce Pavao. Beacon Press.
A book of stories that provides insight into a variety of adoption issues.

Growing Up Again, Parenting Ourselves, Parenting Our Children. 1998. Jean Illsley Clarke and Connie Dawson. Hazeldon Book/Harper Collins.
Helps parents who did not have a good start themselves.

Helping Adolescents with ADHD & Learning Disabilities: Ready-to-Use Tips, Techniques, and Checklists for School Success. 2001. Judith Greenbaum and Geraldine Marke. Jossey-Bass.
Helpful for parents in dealing with school issues.

Inside Transracial Adoption. 2000. Gail Steinberg and Beth Hall. Perspectives Press.
Practical advice for parents who have adopted transracially or transculturally.

Journeys After Adoption. 2002. Jayne Schooler and Betsie Norris. Bergin and Garvey.

Drawing upon the experiences of dozens of triad members, the authors offer insight into the concerns, issues, joys, and pain experienced by those whose lives are framed by adoption.

The Martian Child. 2002. David Gerrold. Tom Doherty Associates.
This book is based on a true story of a single father adopting a son.

Nurturing Adoptions. 2007. Deborah Gray. Perspectives Press.
Outstanding, hopeful information for both parents and professionals.

Parenting Children Affected by Fetal Alcohol Syndrome—A Guide for Daily Living. 1998. Ministry for Children and Families, British Columbia. May download from snap@snap.bc.ca.
Practical guide with approaches for parenting children who are affected by prenatal exposure to drugs or alcohol.

Parenting from the Inside Out. 2003. Daniel Siegel and Mary Hartzell. Penguin/Putnam.
Explores family relationships through the lens of brain-based, attachment-focused work.

Parenting the Hurt Child: Helping Adoptive Families Heal and Grow. 2009. Gregory Keck and Regina Kupecky. NavPress.
Specific ideas for parents who have adopted traumatized children.

Promoting Successful Adoptions: Practice with Troubled Families. 1999. Susan Smith and Jeanne Howard. Sage Publications.
A comprehensive review of research on the well-being of adoptive families.

The Psychology of Adoption. 1993. David Brodzinsky and Marshall Schechter. Oxford University Press USA.
A clinical examination of a broad range of adoption issues.

Risk and Promise: A Handbook for Parents Adopting a Child from Overseas. 2006. Ira Chasnoff, Linda Schwartz, Cheryl Patt, and Gwendolyn Neuberger. National Training Institute.

A thorough description of issues for parents adopting internationally.

Skills Training for Children with Behavioral Problems—Revised Edition. 2006. Michael Bloomquist. Guilford Press.
A guide for parents and professionals who need practical suggestions for reducing anger and anxiety.

Supporting Brothers and Sisters: Creating a Family by Birth, Foster Care and Adoption. 2006. Arleta James. AJ Productions.
A curriculum with tips for helping siblings in a foster or adoptive home. An accompanying DVD is provided.

Telling the Truth to Your Adopted or Foster Child: Making Sense of the Past. 2000. Betsy Keefer and Jayne Schooler. Bergin and Garvey.
A book to help parents and professionals talk to children in a developmentally appropriate way about adoption.

Toddler Adoption: The Weaver's Craft. 1997. Mary Hopkins-Best. Perspectives Press.
A guide to attachment and learning issues for parents who adopt children between the ages of one and four.

Transracial Adoption and Foster Care: Practice Issues for Professionals. 1999. Joseph Crumbley. Child Welfare League of America.
Provides insight into ways adoptive and foster families can support positive racial and cultural identity formation.

Troubled Transplants: Unconventional Strategies for Helping Disturbed Foster and Adopted Children. 1993. Richard Delaney and Frank Kunstal. University of Southern Maine.
This book is easily understood and should prove useful to parents who are at the end of their ropes.

Questions Adoptees Are Asking. 2009. Sherrie Eldridge. NavPress.
A book for teen and adult adopted persons.

Twenty Things Adoptive Parents Need to Succeed. 2009. Sherrie Eldridge. Random House.
Encouragement for adoptive parents with insights into how their adopted child views the world. Written from the author's perspective as an adopted person.

Twenty Things Adopted Kids Wish Their Adoptive Parents Knew. 1999. Sherrie Eldridge. Dell Publishing.
A book written by an adult adopted person who provides insights into the feelings and concerns of adopted children.

What Every Adoptive Parent Needs to Know. 2008. Kate Cremer-Vogel and Dan and Cassie Richards. Mountain Ridge Publishing.
Offers insights into understanding adoption dynamics.

The Whole Life Adoption Book. 2008. Jayne Schooler and Thomas Atwood. NavPress.
Realistic advice for building a healthy adoptive family.

Books/Articles on Attachment
Attaching in Adoption: Practical Tools for Today's Parents. 2002. Deborah Gray. Perspectives Press.
A positive but realistic book for parents in any stage of adoption.

Becoming Attached: First Relationships and How They Shape Our Capacity to Love. 1994. Robert Karen. Oxford University Press.
Offers insight into the importance of early relationships.

Building the Bonds of Attachment: Awakening Love in Deeply Troubled Children. 2006. Daniel A. Hughes. Jason Aronson Publishing.
A highly acclaimed narrative case study that follows the developmental course of one maltreated child.

"Beyond Attachment Theory and Therapy: Toward Sensitive and Evidence-Based Interventions with Foster and Adoptive Families in Distress," *Child & Family Social Work* 10, no. 4 (November 2005). Richard Barth et al.

Creating Capacity for Attachment: Dyadic Developmental Psychotherapy in the Treatment of Trauma-Attachment Disorders. 2005. Arthur Becker-Weidman and Deborah Shell. Wood 'N' Barnes Publishing.
A comprehensive book for professionals and parents that describes the theory and practice behind Dyadic Developmental Psychotherapy.

Facilitating Developmental Attachment: Road to Emotional Recovery and Behavioral Change in Foster and Adopted Children. 2000. Daniel A. Hughes. Jason Aronson/Inghram Book Co.
Provides the foundations of emotional relationships and ways to enhance those relationships.

Fostering Changes: Myth, Meaning and Magic Bullets in Attachment Theory. 2006. Richard Delaney. Wood 'N' Barnes Publishing Co.
Good techniques to help older children in foster care.

Parenting from the Inside Out: How a Deeper Self-Understanding Can Help You Raise Children Who Thrive. 2003. Daniel Siegel. Jeremy P. Thatcher/Penguin Publishing.

"Report of The APSAC Task Force on Attachment Therapy, Reactive Attachment Disorder and Attachment Problems." Child Maltreatment, 11, (1). 2006. Mark Chaffin et al.

Theraplay: Helping Parents and Children Build Better Relationships Through Attachment-Based Play. 1999. Ann Jernberg and Phyllis Booth. Jossey-Bass.
Shows parents how to use play to communicate love and authority and to build trust.

Books/Articles on the Brain
Affect Regulation and the Origin of the Self: The Neurobiology of Emotional Development. 1994. Allan N. Schore. Lawrence Erlbaum Associates.

Affect Dysregulation and Disorders of the Self. 2003. Allan N. Schore. Norton Publishing.

"Brain Structure and Function II: Special Topics Informing Work with Maltreated Children." The Child Trauma Academy. 2002, 2-3. Bruce D. Perry. http:www.ChildTrauma.org.

The Developing Mind: How Relationships and the Brain Interact to Shape Who We Are 1999. Daniel J. Siegel. Guilford Press.

Books/Articles on Complex Trauma

"Complex Trauma in Children and Adolescents," *The National Child Traumatic Stress Network,* 2003, 8. Alexandra Cook et al. eds. http://www.nctsnet.org/nctsn_assets/pdfs/edu_materials/ComplexTrauma_All.pdf.

Creative Interventions with Traumatized Children. 2008. Cathy Malchiodi. Guilford Press.
Use of music, art, and play to enhance the development of traumatized children.

Healing Trauma: Attachment, Mind, Body, and Brain. 2003. Marion F. Solomon and Daniel Siegel. W. W. Norton and Co.
Research and theory on attachment and trauma.

The Trauma Spectrum: Hidden Wounds and Human Resiliency. 2005. Robert Scacr. W. W. Norton and Co.
A book written by a neurologist about the impact of trauma on the brain-mind-body continuum.

Trauma and Recovery: The Aftermath of Violence — From Domestic Abuse to Political Terror. 1992. Judith Herman. Basic Books.

Traumatic Stress: The Effects of Overwhelming Experience on Mind, Body, and Society. 2007. Bessel van der Kolk, Alexander McFarlane and Lars Weisaeth. Guilford Press.
Presents the current state of research and clinical knowledge about traumatic stress and its treatment.

Books/Articles on Education

Attachment in the Classroom: The Links Between Children's Early Experience, Emotional Well-Being and Performance in School. 2006. Heather Geddes. Worth Publishing Ltd.

Shouting Won't Grow Dendrites: 20 Techniques for Managing a Brain-Compatible Classroom. 2007. Marcia L. Tate. Corwin Press.

"Reactive Attachment Disorder: Implications for School Readiness and School Functioning," *Psychology in the Schools* 43, no. 4. 2006. Eric Schwartz and Andrew Davis.

Books for Children or Young Adults

The Adopted One. 1979. Sara Bonnet Stein. Walker & Co.
Unusually insightful book for preschool and early elementary age children. Outstanding text is provided for adoptive parents and older children about normal feelings of adoptees.

All About Adoption. 2004. Marc Nemiroll and Jane Annunziata. Magination Press.
A children's book for ages six through eleven, with good information about children's feelings, adoptive families, and birth parents.

A Place in My Heart. 2004. Mary Grossnickle. The Guest Cottage. http://www.speakingofadoption.com.
A beautifully crafted, insightful story for preschool or early school age children about a chipmunk adopted by a family of squirrels and his feelings about his birth family.

Being Adopted. 1984. Maxine Rosenberg and George Ancona. Harper Collins.
Helpful for children, ages five through ten, when they first have questions about adoption. Three children relate their adoption stories.

The Best Single Mom in the World: How I Was Adopted. 2001. Mary Zisk. Albert Whitman and Co.

A good book for children adopted by a single parent.

Borya and the Burps. An Eastern European Adoption Story. 2005. Joan McNamara. Perspectives Press.
A book that is fun to read and helpful for young children in understanding their adoption history.

Filling In the Blanks: A Guided Look at Growing Up Adopted. 1988. Susan Gabel. Perspectives Press.
A book for pre-teens and early teens working on identity formation.

Forever Fingerprints—An Amazing Discovery for Adopted Children. 2007. Sherrie Eldridge. EMK Press.
When Lucie's pregnant aunt visits, it opens the door for Lucie to talk about babies and the bittersweet feelings she has about her adoption. The story concludes with Lucie's discovery that her uniquely created fingerprints connect her to her whole family. A great tool for parents to talk with young children about adoption.

How I Was Adopted. 1999. Joanna Cole and Maxie Chambliss. William Morrow and Company.
A story of what makes people different and what makes them the same.

Is That Your Sister? A True Story of Adoption. 1992. Catherine and Sherry Bunin. Our Child Press.
Six-year-old tells what is like to be adopted in a multiracial family. For children ages four through eight.

The Mulberry Bird. 1996. Anne Braff Brodzinsky. Perspectives Press.
A book for elementary school-age children.

Sam's Sister. 2004. Juliet Bond and Dawn Majewski. Perspectives Press.
A read-aloud book for children who have birth siblings living in another family.

Teenagers Talk About Adoption. 1989. Marion Crook. Seven Hills Books.
Based on interviews with more than forty adopted teens in Canada, this book

conveys the feelings they have about their birthparents, being adopted, and the attitudes of others toward adoption.

Tell Me Again About the Night I Was Born. 1996. Jamie Lee Curtis. Harper Collins.
Helps children understand the excitement of adoptive parents awaiting a child.

Tell Me a Real Adoption Story. 1993. Betty Lifton and Claire Nivola. Alfred Knopf Publishing Co.
A book for children ages six through twelve regarding identity formation.

Questions Adoptees Are Asking. 2009. Sherrie Eldridge. NavPress.
Book for older teens and young adults. Reads like a novel while addressing adoption issues.

We See the Moon. 2003. Carrie A. Kitze. EMK Press.
A book for young school-age children adopted from China.

When You Were Born in China. 1997. Sara Dorow. Yeong and Yeong.
A book to help children adopted from China understand their histories in a realistic way.

Who Is David? 1985. Evelyn Nerlove. Child Welfare League of America.
An excellent novel about an adolescent adoptee struggling with identity who participates in a support group for adopted adolescents.

You Be Me, I'll Be You. Pili Mandlebaum. 1990. Kane/Miller Book Publishing.
A bi-cultural child decides she dislikes her brown skin. Her father devises a creative alternative.

Zachary's New Home. 2001. Geraldine Bloomquist and Paul Bloomquist. Magination Press.
A book to help children learn to trust after abuse.

Notes

CHAPTER ONE: EMBRACING A LOVE LIKE NO OTHER:
A STORY OF HOPE

1. G.M. Bloomquist and P.B. Bloomquist, *Zachary's New Home: A Story for Foster and Adoptive Children* (Washington, D.C.: Magination Press, 1990).

CHAPTER TWO: THE POWER OF UNMET EXPECTATIONS

1. http://www.adoptionsupport.org/pub/docs/harvard08copyright2.pdf.
2. D. Linville and Anne Lyness, "Twenty American Families' Stories of Adaptation: Adoption of Children from Russian and Romanian Institutions," Journal of Marital and Family Therapy 33 (January 2007):78.
3. Linville and Lyness, 78.
4. Jayne Schooler and Thomas Atwood, *The Whole Life Adoption Book* (Colorado Springs: NavPress, 2008), 80.
5. Marie Adams, *Our Son a Stranger: Adoption Breakdown and Its Effects on the Parents* (Montreal: McGill-Queens University Press, 2002), 19.
6. Adams, 19.
7. Adams, 19.
8. From personal interview with Debbie Riley, April 2008.
9. Megan Hirst, *Loving and Living with the Traumatised Child* (London: BAAF, 2005), 42.
10. Schooler, 89.
11. K. Foli and J. Thompson, *The Post Adoption Blues: Overcoming the Unforeseen Challenges of Adoption* (New York: Rodale Publishers, 2004), 197.
12. Foli and Thompson, 198.
13. Foli and Thompson, 20.

14. From the course writing of Dr. David Schooler.

15. J. Rycus and R. Hughes, *Field Guide to Child Welfare*, Volume IV (Washington, DC: CWLA Press, 1998), 894.

16. Rycus and Hughes, 894.

Chapter Three: Adoptive Parents and the Impact of Their Own Personal Trauma History

1. Bruce D. Perry and Maia Szalavitz, *The Boy Who Was Raised As A Dog: What Traumatized Children Can Teach Us About Loss, Love, and Healing* (New York: Basic Books, 2006), 5.

2. Deborah Gray, *Nurturing Adoptions: Creating Resilience After Neglect and Trauma* (Indianapolis: Perspectives Press, 2007), 34.

3. Daniel J. Siegel and Mary Hartzell, *Parenting from the Inside Out: How a Deeper Self-Understanding Can Help You Raise Children Who Thrive* (New York: Penguin Group, Inc., 2003), 19.

4. Heather T. Forbes and Bryan B. Post, *Beyond Consequences, Logic and Control: A Love-Based Approach to Helping Children with Severe Behaviors*, Vol. 1 (Redington Shores, FL: PPC Books, 2006), 36–37.

5. David J. Wallin, *Attachment in Psychotherapy* (New York: The Guilford Press, 2007), 253.

6. Siegel and Hartzell, 21.

7. Daniel A. Hughes, *Attachment-Focused Family Therapy* (New York: W.W. Norton & Company, Inc., 2007), 252.

8. Hughes, 236.

9. Personal interview with Daniel A. Hughes, December 9, 2008.

10. Gray, 137.

11. Gray, 13.

12. Siegel and Hartzell, 103.

13. Gray, 129.

14. *Understanding and Building Attachment* training curriculum (Institute of Human Services, Columbus, OH, 2006), 73.

15. Gray, 131.

16. Gray, 132.

17. Siegel and Hartzell, 102–103.

18. Personal phone interview with Kate Cleary, June 2008.

19. Personal phone interview with Cleary, June 2008.

20. Personal interview with Linda Sanford, 2008.

Chapter Four: Attachment, Development, and the Impact of Trauma

1. Daniel A. Hughes, *Building the Bonds of Attachment: Awakening Love in Deeply Troubled Children* (Lanham, MD: Jason Aronson, 2006), 2.

2. Harry W. Gardiner, Jay D. Mutter, Connie Kosmitzki, *Lives Across Cultures: Cross-Cultural Human Development* (Needham Heights, MA: Allyn and Bacon, 1998), 164.

3. Daniel J. Siegal, *The Developing Mind: How Relationships and the Brain Interact to Shape Who We Are* (New York: Guilford Press, 1999), 18.

4. Siegal, 19.

5. Bruce D. Perry et al., "Childhood Trauma, the Neurobiology of Adaptation and 'Use Dependent' Development of the Brain: How 'States' Become 'Traits'," *Infant Mental Health Journal* 16, (4) (1995): 272.

6. Siegal, 13.

7. Allan N. Schore, *Affect Regulation and the Origin of the Self: The Neurobiology of Emotional Development* (Hillsdale, NJ: Lawrence Erlbaum, 1994), 305.

8. Allan N. Schore, *Affect Dysregulation and Disorders of the Self* (New York: Norton, 2003), 44.

9. Schore, *Affect Dysregulation and Disorders of the Self*, 38.

10. Schore, *Affect Dysregulation and Disorders of the Self*, 38.

11. Schore, *Affect Regulation and the Origin of the Self*, 31–33.

12. Schore, *Affect Dysregulation and Disorders of the Self*, 38.

13. Robert V. Kail, John C. Cavanaugh, *Human Development: A Life-Span View* (Belmont, CA: Wadsworth/Thompson: 2004), 175.

14. Daniel Hughes, *Facilitating Developmental Attachment: Road to Emotional Recovery and Behavioral Change in Foster and Adopted Children* (Northvale, NJ: Jason Aronson, 1997), 28.

15. Schore, *Affect Regulation and the Origin of the Self*, 80–91.

16. Schore, *Affect Regulation and the Origin of the Self*, 328, 383.

17. Arthur Becker-Weidman and Deborah Shell, *Creating Capacity for Attachment: Dyadic Developmental Psychotherapy in the Treatment of Trauma-Attachment Disorders* (Oklahoma City: Wood 'N' Barnes, 2005), 13.

18. Schore, *Affect Regulation and the Origin of the Self*, 31.

19. Schore, *Affect Regulation and the Origin of the Self*, 360–364

20. Daniel Stern, *Interpersonal World of the Infant* (New York: Basic Books, 1985), 70.

21. Siegal, 150.

22. Schore, *Affect Regulation and the Origin of the Self,* 479–482.

23. Kail and Cavanaugh, 102-103.

24. Mark Chaffin et al. "Report of the APSAC Task Force on Attachment Therapy, Reactive Attachment Disorder and Attachment Problems," *Child Maltreatment* 11, (1), (2006): 81.

25. *American Psychiatric Association, Diagnostic and Statistical Manual of Mental Disorders*, 4th edition text revision (Washington, D.C.: American Psychiatric Association, 2000), 463–468.

26. Bessel van der Kolk and Christine A. Courtois, "Editorial Comments: Complex Developmental Trauma," *Journal of Traumatic Stress* 18, no. 5 (October 2005): 385-388.

27. Judith Herman, *Trauma and Recovery: The Aftermath of Violence–From Domestic Abuse to Political Terror* (New York: Basic Books, 1992), 119–120.

28. Alexandra Cook et al. eds., "Complex Trauma in Children and Adolescents," *The National Child Traumatic Stress Network* (2003):8, http://www.nctsnet.org/nctsn_assets/pdfs/edu_materials/ComplexTrauma_All.pdf.

29. Cook et al., 8.

30. U.S Department of Health and Human Services, Administration on Children, Youth and Families, Child Maltreatment 2005 (Washington, D.C.: U.S. Government Printing Office, 2007), 26.

31. Cook et al., 7.

32. A. Cook, J. Spinazzola, J. Ford, et al., "Complex Trauma in Children and Adolescents," *Psychiatric Annals* 35, no.5 (May 2005): 390–398.

33. Marie Kanne Poulsen, "Defining Early Childhood/Family Mental Health," *CWTAC Updates: Series on Infant and Early Childhood/Family Mental Health* 5, no.3 (July/August 2002): 4–5, http://www.cimh.org/downloads/CWTACJuly-Aug02.pdf.

34. Herman, 116–119.

35. B.D. Perry et al., 275.

Chapter Five: Living with Traumatized Children: The Impact on Parents

1. http://www.cavalcadeproductions.com/traumatized-children.html.
2. Adapted from a story by Bruce Perry in "Traumatized Children: How Childhood Trauma Influences Brain Development," http://www.childtrauma.org/ctamaterials/trau_CAMI.asp.
3. http://www.allaboutfrogs.org/stories/boiled.html.
4. Megan Hirst, *Loving and Living with the Traumatised Child* (London: British Adoption and Fostering, 2005), 7.
5. Hirst, 8
6. Hirst, 8.
7. A. Cook, J. Spinazzola, J. Ford, et al., "Complex Trauma in Children and Adolescents," *Psychiatric Annals*, 35.5 (May 2005). 390–398.
8. Richard Delaney and Frank Kunstal, *Troubled Transplants* (Washington, D.C.: National Child Welfare Resource Center for Management and Administration, 1993).
9. Delaney and Kunstal, 36.
10. Delaney and Kunstal, 33, 54.
11. Delaney and Kunstal, 33.
12. Delaney and Kunstal, 34.
13. http://www.cavalcadeproductions.com/traumatized-children.html.
14. "The High Cost of Caregiving," Childtrauma.org, http://www.childtraumaacademy.com/cost_of_caring/lesson02/page03.html.
15. "The High Cost of Caregiving," Childtrauma.org, http://www.childtraumaacademy.com/cost_of_caring/lesson02/page03.html.
16. "The High Cost of Caregiving," Childtrauma.org, http://www.childtraumaacademy.com/cost_of_caring/lesson02/page03.html.
17. Quotations from 2007 and 2008 workshops by Timothy J. Callahan, and/or Jayne Schooler on this subject across the country.
18. Hirst, 32.
19. Michael Orlans and Teri Levy, *Healing Parent: Helping Wounded Children to Trust and Heal*, (Washington, DC: CWLA, 2007), 109.
20. Hirst, 54–56.

Chapter Six: Living with Traumatized Children: The Impact on Birth and Other Adopted Siblings

1. D. A. Wozny and S. J. Crase, "Adoption-Specific Family Challenges of Special-Needs Adoptive Placements," *Vistas* (American Counseling Association Monograph), 1, (2004): 91-98.

2. C. Kaplan. "The Reactions of Foster Parents' Biological Children to the Fostering Experience," (February 1986), PsycINFO database.

3. E. S. Mullin and L. Johnson, "The Role of Birth/Previously Adopted Children in Families Choosing to Adopt Children with Special Needs," *Child Welfare*, 78(5), (1999): 579–591.

4. J. Safer, *The Normal One: Life with a Difficult or Damaged Sibling* (New York: Bantam Dell, 2002), 19.

5. Safer, 25.

6. K. Strohm, *Being the Other One: Growing Up with a Brother or Sister Who Has Special Needs* (Boston: Shambhala, 2005), 25.

Chapter Seven: Confronting the Crisis of Adoption Breakdown

1. "Post-Legal Adoption Services for Children with Special Needs and Their Families. Challenges and Lessons Learned." Child Welfare Information Gateway, Children's Bureau/ACYF. U.S. Department of Health and Human Services, (June 2005): 1.

2. Deborah Gray, *Nurturing Adoptions: Creating Resilience After Neglect and Trauma* (Indianapolis: Perspectives Press, 2007), 22.

3. S. L. Smith, J. A. Howard, P. Garnier and S. Ryan, "Where Are We Now?: A Post-ASFA Examination of Adoption Disruption," *Adoption Quarterly*, Vol. 9, 4, 2006, http://www.haworthpress.com.

4. Jennifer Coakley and Jill Berrick, "Research Review: In a Rush to Permanency: Preventing Adoption Disruption." *Child and Family Social Work*, 13, (2008): 101–112.

5. M. Freundlich and L. Wright, *Post Permanency Services* (Seattle: Casey Family Programs, 2003), 23.

6. Ann Atkinson and Patricia Gonet, "Strengthening Adoption Practice, Listening to Adoptive Families." *Child Welfare*, Volume 86, #2, (March/April 2007): 94.

7. Denise Goodman, 2000. *Here Today, Gone Tomorrow: An Investigation of the Factors that Impact Adoption Disruption*, PhD diss., The Ohio State University, 1995.

8. Judith Rycus and R. Hughes, *The Field Guide to Child Welfare* (Arlington, VA: Child Welfare League of America, 1998), 703–704.

9. Melissa Greene, "A Love Like No Other: Post-Adoption Panic When There Is No Love at First Sight," *Redbook*, December 2005, 141.

10. Marie Adams, *Our Son, A Stranger: The Impact of Adoption Breakdown on the Parents* (Montreal: McGill-Queens University Press, 2002), 107.

11. Adams, 109.

12. Adams, 110.

13. Gregory Keck and Regina Kupecky, *Adopting the Hurt Child* (Colorado Springs: NavPress, 1995, 2009), 175.

14. Adams, 120.

15. S. Partridge, H. Hornby and T. McDonald, *Learning from Adoption Disruption: Insights for Practice* (Portland: University of Southern Maine, 1986); D. Goodman, *Here Today, Gone Tomorrow: An Investigation of the Factors that Impact Adoption Disruption*, 54,4259A, Dissertation Abstracts International (University Microfilms No. 94-11-949); as cited in Rycus and Hughes, *Field Guide to Child Welfare* (Washington, D.C.: CWLA Press, 1998) and (Columbus, OH: Institute for Human Services). The steps toward adoption disillusionment were adapted with permission from Vol. IV of the *Field Guide Post-Placement Services to Adoptive Parents*; Gregory Keck and Regina Kupecky, *Adopting the Hurt Child* (Colorado Springs: NavPress, 1995, 2009), 171.

Chapter Nine: The Maltreated Child in School

1. Alexandra Cook et al., eds., "Complex Trauma in Children and Adolescents," *The National Child Traumatic Stress Network*, 2003, 7-16, http://www.nctsnet.org/nctsn_assets/pdfs/edu_materials/ComplexTrauma_All.pdf.

2. Heather Geddes, *Attachment in the Classroom: The Links Between Children's Early Experience, Emotional Well-Being and Performance in School* (London: Worth Publishing Ltd., 2006), 53–54, 56.

3. Geddes, 56–57; Eric Schwartz and Andrew Davis, "Reactive Attachment Disorder: Implications for School Readiness and School Functioning," *Psychology in the Schools* 43, no. 4 (2006): 473.

4. Geddes, 53–64.

5. Cook et al., 11–13.

6. Lyn Meltzer, ed., *Executive Function in Education: From Theory to Practice* (New York: Guilford Press, 2007), 1–2.

7. Cook et al., 14–15.

8. Gerard A. Giogia et al., "Behavioral Rating Inventory of Executive Function–Professional Manual" (Lutz, FL: Psychological Assessment Resources, Inc., 2000), 17–20; Martha Bridge Denckla, "Executive Function: Binding Together the Definitions of Attention Deficit/Hyperactivity Disorder and Learning Disabilities," *Executive Function in Education: From Theory to Practice* (New York: Guilford Press, 2007), 5–6.

9. Giogia et al., 17–18.

10. Bruce F. Pennington et al., "Executive Functions and Working Memory: Theoretical and Measurement Issues," in G.R. Lyon and N.A. Krasnegor, eds., *Attention, Memory and Executive Function* (Baltimore: Paul H. Brooks, 1996), 327–348.

11. Giogia et al., 20.

12. Cook et al., 7, 11.

13. Cook et al., 11.

14. Cook et al., 14–16.

15. Allan N. Schore, *Affect Dysregulation and Disorders of the Self* (New York: Norton, 2003), 178–187; Schwartz and Davis, 473.

16. Geddes, 21.

17. Schwartz and Davis, 473–475; Cook et al., 14.

18. Schwartz and Davis, 475–476.

19. Geddes, 108–109; Arthur Becker-Weidman and Deborah Shell, *Creating Capacity for Attachment: Dyadic Developmental Psychotherapy in the Treatment of Trauma-Attachment Disorders* (Oklahoma City: Wood 'N Barnes, 2005), 210.

20. Cook et al., 14.

21. Bruce D. Perry et al., "Childhood Trauma, the Neurobiology of Adaptation and 'Use Dependent' Development of the Brain: How 'States' Become 'Traits'," *Infant Mental Health Journal*, 16, (4), 1995: 275.

22. Cook et al., 7–10.

23. Geddes, 57–59.

24. Schwarz and Davis, 275–276.

25. Schore, 184–187.
26. Robert V. Kail and John C. Cavanaugh, *Human Development: A Life-Span View* (Belmont, CA: Wadsworth/Thompson, 2004), 336–345.
27. Cook et al., 7, 14–15.

Chapter Ten: School Interventions for the Maltreated Child

1. http://www.quoteworld.org/categories/school/7/.
2. Alexandra Cook et al., eds., "Complex Trauma in Children and Adolescents," *The National Child Traumatic Stress Network*, 2003, 7–21, http://www.nctsnet.org/nctsn_assets/pdfs/edu_materials/ Complex Trauma All.pdf.
3. Eric Schwartz and Andrew Davis, "Reactive Attachment Disorder: Implications for School Readiness and School Functioning," *Psychology in the Schools* 43, no. 4 (2006): 471–477.
4. Bruce D. Perry, "Brain Structure and Function II: Special Topics Informing Work with Maltreated Children," *The Child Trauma Academy*, 2002, 2-3, http://www.ChildTrauma.org.
5. Arthur Becker-Weidman and Deborah Shell, *Creating Capacity for Attachment: Dyadic Developmental Psychotherapy in the Treatment of Trauma-Attachment Disorders* (Oklahoma City: Wood 'N' Barnes, 2005), 14.
6. Becker-Weidman and Shell, 14.
7. Heather Geddes, *Attachment in the Classroom: The Links Between Children's Early Experience, Emotional Well-Being and Performance in School* (London: Worth Publishing Ltd, 2006), 49.
8. Schwartz and Davis, 276.
9. Allan N. Schore, *Affect Dysregulation and Disorders of the Self* (New York: Norton, 2003), 38.
10. Geddes, 54.
11. Geddes, 55.
12. Schore, 36-37.
13. Schwartz and Davis, 474.
14. Schwartz and Davis, 474–475.
15. Perry, (2002), 2.
16. Becker-Weidman and Shell, 207-208.
17. Bruce D. Perry, "Bonding and Attachment in Maltreated Children:

How Abuse and Neglect in Childhood Impact Social and Emotional Development," *Child Trauma Academy: Parent and Caregiver Education Series*, Vol. 1, no. 5 (1998): 6, http://www.childtrauma.org/ctamaterials/bonding.asp.

18. Perry, (1998), 6.
19. Becker-Weidman and Shell, 213.
20. Becker-Weidman and Shell, 212.
21. Perry, (1998), 6.
22. U.S. Department of Education—Office of Special Education Programs, "School-Wide Positive Behavioral Support," *OSEP Technical Assistance Center on Positive Behavioral Interventions & Supports*, 2007, http://www.pbis.org/schoolwide.htm.
23. Marcia L. Tate, *Shouting Won't Grow Dendrites: 20 Techniques for Managing a Brain-Compatible Classroom*, (Thousand Oaks, CA: Corwin Press, 2007), 115.
24. Cook et al., 14–15.
25. Tate, 49–54.
26. Tate, 116.
27. Daniel J. Siegel, *The Developing Mind: How Relationships and the Brain Interact to Shape Who We Are* (New York: Guilford Press, 1999), 50–66.
28. *Webster's New World Dictionary and Thesaurus*, 2nd Edition, (Cleveland: Wiley Publishing, Inc., 2002), 408.
29. Becker-Weidman and Shell, 212.
30. Becker-Weidman and Shell, 205, 212.
31. Becker-Weidman and Shell, 212.
32. U.S. Department of Education—Office of Special Education Programs, "Individualized Educational Program," IDEA Regulations: 34 CFR 300.320-300.324, 2006, http://www. idea.ed.gov/explore/view/p/%2Croot%2Cdynamic%2CTopicalBrief%2C10%2C.

CHAPTER ELEVEN: LIVING WITH CHILDREN WITH ATTACHMENT TRAUMA: UNDERSTANDING THE TERMINOLOGY, DIAGNOSIS, AND PARENTING STRATEGIES

1. Daniel Siegel, *Parenting from the Inside Out: How a Deeper Self-Understanding Can Help You Raise Children Who Thrive* (New York: Jeremy P. Thatcher/Penguin, 2003), 10.
2. Daniel Hughes, *Facilitating Developmental Attachment: Road to*

Emotional Recovery and Behavioral Change in Foster and Adopted Children (Northvale, NJ: Jason Aronson, 1997), 1–2.

3. Mark Chaffin et al., "Report of the APSAC Task Force on Attachment Therapy, Reactive Attachment Disorder and Attachment Problems," *Child Maltreatment*, 11, no. 1 (2006): 76.

4. American Psychiatric Association, *Diagnostic and Statistical Manual of Mental Disorders*, 4th ed. (Washington, D.C.: American Psychiatric Association, 2000), 128.

5. *American Psychiatric Association*, 127–130.

6. Chaffin et al., 82.

7. U.M. Walter and C. Petr, "Reactive Attachment Disorder: Concepts, Treatment and Research," State of Kansas Department of Social and Rehabilitation Services–Best Practices in Children's Mental Health, 2004 report #11, 3.

8. T. G. O'Conner and C.H. Zeanah, "Attachment Disorders: Assessment Strategies and Treatment Approaches," *Attachment and Human Development*, 5 no. 3, (2003): 223–224.

9. Hughes, 30–31; Arthur Becker-Weidman, Deborah Shell, eds., *Creating Capacity for Attachment: Dyadic Developmental Psychotherapy in the Treatment of Trauma-Attachment Disorders* (Oklahoma City, OK: Wood 'N' Barnes, 2005), 15–16.

10. *U.S. Department of Health and Human Services, Administration on Children, Youth and Families, Child Maltreatment 2005* (Washington, D.C.: U.S. Government Printing Office, 2007), 26.

11. American Psychiatric Association, 129.

12. Chaffin et al., 81.

13. Richard Barth, et al., "Beyond Attachment Theory and Therapy: Toward Sensitive and Evidence-Based Interventions with Foster and Adoptive Families in Distress," *Child & Family Social Work* 10, no. 4, (November 2005): 260.

14. Walter and Petr, 6.

15. Chaffin et al., 81.

16. Chaffin et al., 83.

17. Chaffin et al., 77.

18. Chaffin et al., 86–87.

19. Chaffin et al., 87.

20. Chaffin et al., 87.

21. Chaffin et al., 86–87.

22. Hughes, 193–214.

23. Becker-Weidman and Shell, 221–224.

Chapter Twelve: Taking Care of Yourself: The Parent's Neglected Task

1. Daniel Hughes, *Facilitating Developmental Attachment: The Road to Emotional Recovery and Behavioral Change in Foster and Adopted Children* (Lanham, MD: Jason Aronson, Inc., 1997), 212.

2. Interview with Heather Forbes, June 4, 2008, http://www.beyondconsequences.com.

3. Robert Wicks, *Riding the Dragon: 10 Lessons for Inner Strength in Challenging Times* (Notre Dame: Sorin Books, 2003), 35.

4. Debra McMahon, "Self-Care: Barriers and Basics for Foster/Adoptive Parents," *Adoptalk*, Fall 2005, http://www.nacac.org/adoptalk.selfcare.html.

5. "Selecting and Working with an Adoption Therapist: A Factsheet for Families," *Child Welfare Information Gateway*, 2005, http://www.childwelfare.gov/pubs/f_therapist.cfm.

6. "Selecting and Working with an Adoption Therapist: A Factsheet for Families," *Child Welfare Information Gateway*, 2005, http://www.childwelfare.gov/pubs/f_therapist.cfm.

7. Heather Forbes, personal interview, June 4, 2008, http://www.beyondconsequences.com.

8. Juli Alvarado, personal interview, June 19, 2008, http://www.coaching-forlife.com.

9. Wicks, 46.

10. McMahon, "Self-Care: Barriers and Basics for Foster/Adoptive Parents," *Adoptalk*, Fall 2005, http://www.nacac.org/adoptalk.selfcare.html.

11. Jayne Schooler and Thomas Atwood, *The Whole Life Adoption Book: Realistic Advice for Building a Healthy Adoptive Family* (Colorado Springs: NavPress, 2008), 162.

12. Alvarado, personal interview, http://www.coaching-forlife.com.

13. N. Ginther; L. Wilkins, J. Schooler, B. Keefer Smalley, *Discipline in Foster Care: Managing Our Behaviors to Manage Theirs* (The Institute for Human Services for the Ohio Child Welfare Training Program, 2006), 44–45.

14. Deborah Gray, *Nurturing Adoptions* (Indianapolis: Perspectives Press, 2007), 431.
15. Gregory Keck and Regina Kupecky, *Adopting the Hurt Child* (Colorado Springs: NavPress, 1995, 2009), 184–185.
16. Ginther, Wilkins, Schooler, Keefer Smalley, 46–48.
17. C. Barr, P. Severs, B. Keefer, *Play with a Purpose* (The Institute for Human Services for the Ohio Child Welfare Training Program, 2005), 18–19.
18. Gray, 430.
19. Wicks, 68.
20. Gray, 440.

CHAPTER THIRTEEN: HOPE: THE REST OF THE STORY

1. Daniel Hughes, *Building the Bonds of Attachment: Awakening Love in Deeply Troubled Children* (Lanham, MD: Jason Aronson Books, 2006).
2. Hughes, 2.

Authors

JAYNE E. SCHOOLER'S passion for more than twenty years has been the training and education of adoption and foster care professionals and families. She has been been a featured speaker at numerous state and national conferences and trains regularly for the Ohio Child Welfare Training Program. She is the author or coauthor of five books related to adoption

BETSY KEEFER SMALLEY, LSW, coauthor of the award-winning *Telling the Truth to Your Adopted or Foster Child: Making Sense of the Past*, has thirty-six years of experience in child welfare, adoption placement, post-adoption services, and training.

TIMOTHY J. CALLAHAN, PsyD, is a clinical psychologist who received his doctorate from Wright State University in Dayton, Ohio. Dr. Callahan has twenty years of experience working with children and families as well as adults and teens.

NavPress has the resources you need to help you with your adoption!

Adopting the Hurt Child
Gregory C. Keck, PhD, and Regina M. Kupecky, LSW
978-1-60006-289-6

In this revised and updated guide to healing the emotional trauma of the child in your life, authors Gregory C. Keck and Regina M. Kupecky provide a clear picture of what it's like to hurt and what it means to heal. With advice, tips, and success stories from adoptive children, you'll get valuable insight and hope. Now with new information on foreign adoption.

Parenting the Hurt Child
Gregory C. Keck, PhD, and Regina M. Kupecky, LSW
978-1-60006-290-2

In this updated and revised sequel to *Adopting the Hurt Child*, authors Gregory C. Keck and Regina M. Kupecky share valuable suggestions to help your hurt child heal, grow, and develop. You'll learn what works and what doesn't work as well as read stories from adoptees who have experienced it all.

Parenting Adopted Adolescents
Gregory C. Keck, PhD
978-1-60006-281-0

Dr. Gregory Keck offers new insights and suggestions to the parents of adopted adolescents. You'll find humor and relief in what once might have been painful and begin to understand and appreciate your adolescent.

Questions Adoptees Are Asking
Sherrie Eldridge
978-1-60006-595-8

As an adopted person, you have questions and difficult choices. In this book, more than seventy other adoptees share their stories, questions, and challenges, giving you encouragement from the answers they've discovered. Written for adoptees and the parents of adoptees.

The Whole Life Adoption Book
Jayne E. Schooler and Thomas C. Atwood
978-1-60006-165-3

Recommended by the National Council for Adoption, *The Whole Life Adoption Book* has long been an indispensable guide for prospective parents of adopted children and blended families. This revised and updated edition addresses the needs and concerns adoptive parents face, providing encouragement for the journey ahead.

Available wherever books are sold.